A STRANGER IN PARADISE

A Stranger in Paradise
Julie Chimes

BLOOMSBURY

First published 1995

This paperback edition published 1996

Copyright © 1995 by Julie Chimes

The moral right of the author has been asserted

Bloomsbury Publishing Plc, 2 Soho Square, London W1V 6HB

A CIP catalogue record for this book is available from the
British Library

10 9 8 7 6 5 4 3 2 1

ISBN 0 7475 26443

Typeset by Hewer Text Composition Services, Edinburgh
Printed in Great Britain by Cox & Wyman, Reading, Berkshire

Acknowledgements

My thanks to my family and friends for their love and support and to everyone who read, commented on, questioned, corrected, criticised and discussed the many stages of the manuscript; to all at Bloomsbury for their encouragement and sensitivity; to the trustees of the estate of Max Wall for permission to publish 'Ode to an Odd Soul'; to Bartholomew for all the laughter, insights and inspiration; to those who devote their lives to the awakening of human consciousness; and finally to Richard – for all those cups of tea.

TO
MY MOTHER'S TREASURED MEMORY
MY BELOVED HUSBAND
AND
THE LIGHT WITHIN US
(THAT SHOULD COVER EVERYONE)

Contents

Preface

This is an autobiographical work based on a kaleidoscope of events and experiences that happened to me, a working, fun-loving woman, whose life almost ended as a result of an 'out of the blue' vicious and frenzied stabbing. It is an extraordinary story, told from the unusual perspective of the one who was supposed to be dead.

It is a multi-faceted real life drama; a story of crime due to mental illness; a story about survival; the battle to regain physical and mental well-being; a woman's quest for truth; an account of false accusation and injustice; an adventure far beyond the confines of a physical body; a humorous narrative of a voyage through our supposedly caring and free-speaking society – a society where justice is very often directly proportional to the amount you can afford to pay your lawyer; it is, ultimately, the story of a spiritual awakening.

Other than the obligatory police statement, taken whilst I was reeling from the pain and disbelief that constitute deep shock, nobody in the system, which was supposed to support me, asked me what I experienced. Most people were so busy piecing the crime together, or covering their rears, they seemed to overlook the fact that I had survived. I was not a corpse on the marble slab of the mortuary, whose body and life could be dissected and judged by a group of strangers, but a very alive and questioning woman, with ideas and opinions that contradicted much of the official storyline. I was also a woman with a willingness to look beyond the mundane for answers. All that I experienced leading up to the attempted murder, during the attack and my recovery, provides a bizarre and humorous insight into life, death, and the western way of dealing with it.

It was not something I had ever anticipated – to find the only thing between myself and a paranoid schizophrenic woman intent on saving the world to be a fourteen-inch carving knife buried in my chest. Nothing in my life had prepared me – being 'murdered' was nothing like I would have imagined it to be. It was considered something of a miracle for the victim of such mindless savagery to stick around after the event, and even more unusual was the fact I could remember all that happened during the assault.

It has not been easy to relive the 'incident' and the subsequent events. Many times I have given up, filled with despondency and hopelessness, experiencing a mental paralysis that led to deep depression. Other than my beloved husband no one could have guessed the depth of my despair and no one could have given me such constant support, patience and love and convinced me that I had to continue. In the darkness of my human confusion he reminded me constantly that I also had the memory of something incredible. For in the midst of attempted murder, I had discovered a place filled with love, light, compassion, laughter and excitement, a place so vast it contained all of creation in its arms. I had found that not only does God exist but He also has a wonderful sense of humour, and although I could not change what had happened to me, I could change my attitude. Within that memory lay the miracle of my recovery. I am now convinced that the moment we stop blaming whatever is out there for the state of our lives, we fling open the doors of our hearts and discover a far greater canvas on which to paint our future.

Having spent several years leading the self-inquiry into my attempted murder, and my subsequent experiences, I realise that to isolate and lay the blame for what happened that day on any one of the many incidents or persons is perhaps the biggest crime of all. *A Stranger in Paradise* is not a witch-hunt. For this reason, I have changed many of the names. Everyone involved in this story is responsible. We will all have to face ourselves one day, and stand accountable to our highest Self for all we have ever done. Divine justice prevails. No one gets away with anything, for as we sow, we do indeed reap. The fruits of our thoughts and actions are manifest every moment of our lives. If we learn to read the signs, we can learn so much about ourselves, and the purpose of our life.

At the time, fighting for my physical life, I cried out to God to help me. I believed I was alone, life was totally unfair, and God was a myth marketed by religious zealots. Thanks to my many experiences, including writing this book, I have discovered that He was in fact with me all the way.

'How will you tell the story,' they asked.
'I will tell the truth.'
'Don't be ridiculous,' they chorused.

THIS
IS
A
TRUE
STORY ...
WELL,
AS
TRUE
AS
MY
UNDERSTANDING
CAN
BE
WITHIN
THIS
MOMENT
OF
INFINITY.

THE BACKGROUND

I should have realised my life was going to be different from most. To be born to a mother who was to be chosen as one of the most beautiful women in the world before I had reached my first birthday was a good start. Less than a year later she left my father to live with and then marry one of Britain's stranger entertainers. She was innocent and passionate enough to announce to the British press that she could not believe that God intended people to remain together if they could not love each other. This provided a fertile bed in which to grow a nonconformist child.

My early memories were a kaleidoscope of images: Max Wall, comedian, musician, dancer, writer, manic-depressive, estranged father of five, and target for Fleet Street's venom. A man in black tights, black centre-parted wig, shoes a foot longer than his feet, shuffling up and down by my cot, his bum sticking out at right angles. The expression on his face closely resembling London zoo's Guy the gorilla, a creature we visited regularly, Max and Guy fascinated by each other – the human personification of this magnificent beast humming the St Louis Blues for all he was worth as he attempted to lull me to sleep. The same man stripped of his stage persona, on his knees, like a child, side by side with my mother, praying that all those they knew be blessed and protected in God's Grace, followed by readings of Shakespearean plays and sonnets, extracts from Gibbon's *Decline and Fall of the Roman Empire*, interspersed with songs from shows and his own repertoire – no ordinary bedtime stories, and no ordinary voice. The click-clack of his typewriter into the early hours, writing yet another play, poem or piece no publisher would understand. Senior Service cigarettes.

Guinness. A passion for good diction, all things Italian, pathos, musical instruments, carpentry, expensive shoes, and Jennifer, my mother. A mother with a face like an angel, singing to my autistic brother and me haunting exquisite sounds stirring memories of a paradise I had somehow left behind. Her patience and serenity as she dealt with us all, baking her bread, creating beautiful clothes, weaving the strands of eccentricity and madness into homes filled with love.

The screams and torrents of gibberish from my brother, which I intuitively understood. His face red with the frustration of trying to articulate wild sounds into something intelligible. His first speech delivered, during a mealtime, five years after being labelled a medical write-off and classified as a vegetable. No practice words, no baby-speak, no warning, a simple statement: 'God doesn't want you to eat meat. It's against his will.' The shock in my mother's face, the reward for her unshakeable belief in God and Martin arriving in such a profound way.

Men with large cameras who lived in our garden, up trees, behind doors and outside any shops or restaurants we visited. Men who could run backwards on their haunches and explode flash bulbs in our faces whilst asking questions of my mother and stepfather; intrusive, sarcastic, judgemental voices loosely disguised with a thin coating of respect.

Walks in Richmond Park, peanut butter and marmite sandwiches of freshly baked bread accompanying long discussions about other kingdoms, fairies, gnomes, magic, and God. 'This body is the temple of your soul, always remember that, and respect it for it will serve you well in this lifetime,' my wise mother would tell me often during these conversations.

Violent earth-shattering rows long into the night, screams . . . tears . . . watching Max, possessed with a demonic rage, smash with ruthless precision every thing we owned. Leaving until last a stool to stand upon so he could rip all the lights from their sockets. The stool demolished finally in the darkness. My mother lying unconscious somewhere in the trail of debris. He often used a piano-stool in his act, extracting many laughs; an act I would never find very funny. Hiding in the black of fear until the police Jaguar arrived. The distinctive smell of leather seats – sitting in the front with kind men in uniforms taking us for a ride into the London night. My mother applying Max Factor pancake make-up to cover the bruises, her loyalty to Max respected by the men in blue. A tacit understanding between us all that he would be returned when he was 'feeling better'.

Frantic, frequent and often grief-filled journeys to and from our beautiful, ever-loving Nan. Martin and I given to her by mother for our safe-keeping until Max would agree to allow us back, or during extensive periods of their travelling. Nan's three sons, mother's brothers, my uncles and best friends in all the world, providing comparatively ordinary family life. Short bursts of new friends, schools and experiences. Relatives, blood, step and distant, forming the cocoon, my happiness marred only by nightmarish struggles with a man who should have known better. A man who would burn my wrists with the force of his rough hands as he tried to force me to grasp his erect penis wobbling around like an out of control joy-stick whilst he sat in his chair watching *Wagon Train*, ostensibly 'baby-sitting'. My decision to stay silent, having the strong feeling that no one would believe me, but never holding it against him, so to speak. The excruciating shyness that developed as a result of being looked at in 'that way', which was to haunt me for thirty years.

The dreadful moments when the tragic comedian with his physically and mentally bruised wife, my mother, would come to take us back, often amidst tears, rows, or stony silence. The wrench of my heart for loving both my grandmother and mother, the former wishing to keep us and protect us, the latter heartbroken without us. Their love for us nearly always clashing. Max's eyes filled with remorse, rooms crowded with red roses and champagne, trips to the Savoy or Harrods for tea, Soho for dinner, drives in the country. Always watching him for some sign of the next onslaught of madness, never truly relaxed. I knew the monster created out of his jealousy was not really him, but he still terrified me. Miraculously, the monster in him never laid a finger on Martin or me.

Sackfuls of mail containing letters of support, far outweighed by letters of hatred. The illiterate resorting to sheets of used toilet paper to express their opinions of mother and Max's 'public-property' relationship. Strict instructions never to discuss 'anything' at school taken literally. Early teachers wondering if I was mentally defective as I stoically refused to answer ANY questions in class. Yogic postures and acrobatics, walks with the cats, all the kids in the neighbourhood in love with my mother, theatres, show-business characters, audiences, joke-telling long into the night, spiritualist meetings, prayers, hysterical laughter and conversations with the angels who stood over my brother each night, stroking his head as they talked with him.

Max and mother's professional, social and financial exile in the Channel Islands with Martin, a pet goat called Jane, a dog, two cats and me. Courtesy of the British press Max had no offers of work, and thus no income. The alimony payments to his ex-wife were based on his highest earnings, the net result of which left us very hard up. He had no contact with his beloved children. He would tell me all about them and I got to know all the shining little faces that peeped out at me from the photographs which accompanied us everywhere. In my innocence I couldn't understand why we didn't all live together. Max cried whenever he spoke about them, yet right under his nose were two children, Martin and me, not allowed to mention or see our own father because of Max's disapproval of anyone else my mother had loved. Thanks to his and my mother's great humour, creativity and resourcefulness, in spite of everything for a short while we had a wonderful home life, with many soirées of singing, dancing, mime, and laughter. Max would teach me songs and dance routines from all the musicals. He was a very accomplished guitarist and one of my favourite times was when he would play for us. He also taught me jokes that no seven-year-old should have understood. Tap dancing in the garden with Max, Mum, Jane the goat and me. Me, after several interviews, attending a catholic convent. Me, the child of two twice-married adults, with not one shred of Catholicism between them. Me, a little girl with a passion for Enid Blyton, angels and ponies. An innocent child, who, unbeknown to the nuns, had never even been christened.

All this and not even eight. I should have realised my life was going to be different.

After ten tempestuous years my mother left Max. As his self-confidence diminished, his drinking, smoking, gambling and resulting manic depression increased. She had endured the extremes of human love and hatred with dignity and grace, but her last shred of hope shattered when he vented his insane rage on her because she was invited to work in the wonderfully pioneering school which my brother Martin attended.

It was her dream to work with mentally handicapped children, but instead of starting her new job, she woke up in hospital. For Max to be so cruel because of his jealousy of such lost little souls, and thus deprive them of having her love for several days a week, was the end. A new-found strength arose within her, the phoenix from the ashes, and clutching Martin and myself under each arm, hearts pounding in terror in case we were caught, we left the island of Jersey forever. I cried all the way to England, thinking of my little dog, the cats and goat, not to mention the secret stash of childhood treasure hidden in the centre of the revolving blue globe on my desk. We had one suitcase and no money, everything we had in the world was left behind. England was grey and it was raining. We were all silent. We each knew that no matter how painful, it had to be done. In the ensuing years, the only thing my mother ever asked of Max was to send the photographs of Martin and me, virtually the only memento of our childhood we had. Contrary to all the press reports, she never asked Max for one penny, although he loved to blame women for his downfall. His grief, anger and hurt remained so great he refused to give us any of our things back and told my mother he'd burnt everything. He did however send poems.

Ode to an Odd Soul

For Jennifer

How oft are we condemned and cast aside
Because our train of thought runs only on its private track
And does not stop for alien minds to climb aboard . . .
Because a liquid soul into an odd-shaped mould is poured
And so retains its shape for evermore
Such individuals are placed upon the rack
This could perhaps be you – do you agree
And by the selfsame token it could well be me
And yet within the scheme of things this odd-shaped soul
Inexorably will reach its final goal
And having thus arrived at journey's end
By tortuous route of Earth life's ruthless hill . . .
Shall humbly wait upon the master's will
T'will be the end of all uncertainty for thee
And also dearest Jennifer – for me . . .
It will eventually be known in some far distant sphere
When all that now exists is lost in limbo of forgotten past
That all our souls pursued pre-destined course
And finally by grace of God are come to rest at last . . .
And there no rack or pulley will distort with pain
For understanding shall prevail and opportunities perchance –
    to start again
So live your life and climb your tortuous hill
Remembering that this odd-shaped soul doth love thee still . . .

Max

After four wonderful, crazy, hair-raising years my mother eventually remarried a local solicitor. I was fourteen. I had to ask for a day off school to attend the wedding. My spinster headmistress peered at me over her half-moon glasses, cleared her throat and informed me that my request was most irregular, and did I not know that second marriages were a sin in the eyes of God. I did not have the heart to tell her it was in fact a third. She sighed a long weary sigh as she signed my exeat, and muttered that as it was my mother she had no option but to concede. I was dismissed from her study, and I believe from her thoughts for my remaining years in her scholastic care.

On reflection, my headmistress was right. My life was most irregular. I felt I did not belong in the evolving middle-class world of a nine-to-five business community. A world of expensive village homes, Saturday-night dinner parties, Sunday-morning cocktails, Casa Pupo ashtrays and an account with a posh frock shop. I found life in the conventional lane excruciatingly painful. I gradually withdrew and buried my secret dreams of a life in art, music, literature and philosophy in a body that gained three stone in weight in under a year. The extra flesh had little to do with my food intake.

Learning was so easy for me, I was totally lazy in most subjects, always doing the absolute minimum. The majority of my teachers, with their dowdy appearance and dull delivery, did little to inspire me, and in turn, being plump, blonde, made-up and indolent, I did little for them.

I talked to God most nights, but considered it prudent not to mention it to anyone. My dreams were frequent, vivid, some-times prophetic, most often disturbing, swirling, nightmarish experiences. The main theme was watching my own funeral, yet at the same time knowing I was still alive within the coffin. Each time the dream occurred the coffin was a little nearer the gaping hole of the grave, and suddenly I would be suffocating, screaming, stuffed and wired for death, unable to move, or to be heard by the mourners. Waking up, bolt upright, dripping with the juices of terror, my vocal chords reconnected and calling into the silence of my purple bedroom: 'I AM NOT DEAD! FOR GOD'S SAKE . . . I AM NOT DEAD.' The stark clarity which always followed the terror, knowing the dream was somehow a reflection of my outer life. There was no one to talk to. My mother and stepfather Mk 2 were caught up in their passion and new life to the point of obsession, totally unaware of my loneliness and confusion. Who was it that watched my dreams, nightmares and waking state without emotion, yet knowing everything? What was inside me that seemed to know my thoughts, and everyone else's? I would stare for hours into mirrors, in the hope that some clue would emerge, but my reflection would blur and break into a mosaic that gradually disappeared. Once I drew this fractured image as a self-portrait for art homework. It was returned to me with a low mark and the comment 'This doesn't make sense'. I agreed with my art-master, but not for the same reasons.

I started to read books about the paranormal, in the hope they would lead to some clues about the purpose of life, the nature of good and evil, not to mention God. I found little to help, and conversations with my all-girl contemporaries revealed only a stunning knowledge of Dennis Wheatley, ouija boards, and John Lennon's inside-leg measurement. Whilst their world consisted of the ever-exploding sixties, with long-haired, baby-faced pin-ups inside the desk lids, I was intrigued by Gandhi and had a secret picture of Jesus in my school bible. I was smart enough to know that this had to change if I was to survive the remainder of my days as a dependent teenager. I consciously closed my mind, and hid my questions under a Mary Quant duvet, mini-skirt and white lacy tights. I entered most reluctantly into the game of being what everyone else expected of me. The nightmares and dreams stopped abruptly.

I drifted out of school and into college without a clue about what I really wanted to do, all my early passions and dreams silted over with the belief that life was hard, and the only way to be respected was to take it all very seriously. I therefore worked hard, passed all the necessary exams and was placed straight into a management job with a local branch of a national department store. Within one year I was transferred to London. My career became action-packed, leading me into the world of hotels, catering, managing restaurants, racing saloon cars for relaxation, then moving into advertising and marketing based in the very heart of the Fleet Street which had figured so largely in my early childhood. I even worked with some of the newspapers responsible for the propaganda which had sought to destroy the reputations of my mother and Max. Redundancies, freelance work, company directorships, and finally, in my early thirties, running my own business consultancy on advertising. All appeared to be going well until, that is, something decided it was time for me to wake up.

A TELLING TALE

Once upon a moment in eternity there was a small, once pretty, woman walking along a dirty street in central London. The rain bounced off the uneven pavement. Her worn shoes absorbed the murky puddles, and her feet were soaked. Trickles of water formed icy rivulets down her spine. Shivering, she angrily pushed back a crop of matted hair from her face; her sodden lashes doing nothing to improve her dark countenance.

'ALRIGHT, GOD, WHAT THE HELL DID I DO TO UPSET YOU?' she cried, looking up into the infinite grey. She walked on, half in the gutter, muttering to herself in bewilderment.

'MY HUSBAND TELLS ME HE DOESN'T LOVE ME, AND NEVER REALLY HAS, AND HOPES I UNDERSTAND WHY HE'S MOVING IN WITH MY ONCE BEST FRIEND . . . MY KIDS RAN AWAY BECAUSE THEY THOUGHT WE DIDN'T UNDERSTAND THEM . . . I HAVE JUST FOUND OUT THE EXTENT OF THE ARREARS IN RENT AS THE BAILIFFS REMOVED ME AND MY FEW PATHETIC BLOODY POSSESSIONS FROM MY HOME . . . SO HERE I AM, GOD, ON THE STREET. PERHAPS YOU COULD TAKE A MOMENT OUT OF YOUR BUSY SCHEDULE AND EXPLAIN . . . WHY ME?'

She kicked a pile of soggy rubbish out of her path, and continued her imaginary conversation with God.

'THE COMPANY I WORKED FOR HAS FOLDED . . . AND REGRETS TO INFORM ME THAT MY PENSION SCHEME MONEY WAS GAMBLED AWAY BY CORRUPT MANAGEMENT, AND THERE IS NO MONEY FOR REDUNDANCIES. I AM HOMELESS, JOBLESS, HUSBANDLESS, CHILDLESS, AND NOW BLOODY PENNILESS . . . GOD, WHY ME?'

She shook her fist at the sky.

'I'VE QUEUED ALL BLEEDIN' DAY IN THAT HELL-HOLE THAT IS SUPPOSED TO BE FOR MY BENEFIT ... AND WHEN THEY GET TO MY TURN WHAT HAPPENS? OF COURSE ... THEY RUN OUT OF FORMS DON'T THEY? "COME BACK TOMORROW, DEAR" THEY TELL ME! THE HOMELESS HOSTELS ARE ALL FULL, SO I GO TO A LITTLE WARM SPOT IN THE UNDERGROUND. THAT IS UNTIL A DRUNK PEES ON ME. IT'S COLD, IT'S RAINING, I AM UNBELIEVABLY PISSED-OFF AND JUST WONDER WHAT THE HELL IT IS ALL ABOUT ... SO CAN YOU HEAR ME UP THERE?'

She is now screaming with rage.

'WHY ME?'

A bolt of lightning forks to the road in front of her. The heavens open, and in a shimmer of golden light, a large thumb descends and slowly squashes her into the damp tarmac. A voice is heard.

'BECAUSE ...
I DON'T BLOODY LIKE YOU!'

This was one of my favourite stories.

THE SET-UP . . .

London

January

I was not in the habit of visiting clairvoyants, but walking past the Spiritualist Association in London's beautiful Belgrave Square I was tempted to enter. My business appointment was postponed so I had some time to kill, and besides, my mother had taken me there in the late fifties so I was curious to see the inside from an adult perspective.

'You must be the three o'clocker,' said the small neat woman who looked up from behind the reception desk.

'Oh, no! I don't have an appointment, I just wanted to have a look.'

She gave me a knowing smile.

'Well, you are the three o'clocker now if you want, so why don't you take the reservation?'

I looked around the rather seedy entrance hall, which had only a few traces left of the splendour of my childhood memories. I was aware of her steady gaze, waiting for my reply.

'First time is it, dear?' she added gently.

I had the feeling that I was entering a brothel and I hoped she couldn't read minds.

'No, I've been here before,' I smiled. I didn't add I was only five at the time as I did not think it would impress her.

'Yes, I will take the appointment. Where do I have to go?' The words were a surprise to me. I wondered where they came from.

'Follow the main staircase up to the top, and knock on the third door on the left.'

' I climbed the once magnificent staircase. The place seemed very shabby, probably only held together by good intent and donations. I entered a small dark room, and was welcomed warmly by a charming softly spoken man. We sat down. He had the sort of eyes that left me in no doubt he was psychic. He closed them for a few moments, took a deep breath, and proceeded to describe my paternal great-grandfather. Drawing his fingers across his chest he described the chain of office this man had been so proud to wear. I was shocked at such accuracy, because great-grandad had been a mayor, and the only photograph I possessed of him showed him wearing his chain. I sat forward and listened with a new interest, certain the image he saw was in some way real. Suddenly he opened his eyes wide and banged his fist down on the small table beside him with such force I almost jumped into his lap.

'You MUST change your front door, do you understand what I am saying? Change the door, change the door, change the door. You MUST change the door.'

He was swaying with the force of the words, and was obviously troubled deeply. He stopped this chanting message as abruptly as he had started, and told me all sorts of other things in a normal voice, some of which made sense, others did not.

I did not really take too much in for I could still hear the ringing in my ears about changing the door. My thoughts wandered to the garage of my cottage home, which I shared with TC, my doctor boyfriend. A new front door had been standing in there for months. We had not bothered to have it fitted, because it opened in the opposite way to the existing door and changing the hinges over required professional help. I knew it would make sense to have it done, for the present door trapped us in the tiny entrance hall and saying goodbye to anyone left us plastered, cartoon-like, against the wall.

'Well, that's about it, dear, I hope you have found it helpful.'

Shaking myself out of my thoughts I thanked him and left the room. He followed me.

'Don't forget the door.' His words tumbled down the stairs after me.

How could I, I thought, after all that fist banging. I felt slightly irritated, and disappointed I had not received some deep and meaningful message; only a chide from the other side about outstanding home improvements.

'Was that helpful, dear?' the receptionist enquired as I paid the fee.

'Yes, most interesting,' I lied, vowing silently not to waste any future money on predictions.

Walking into the cold air I felt relieved to be outside. I looked up into the pale blue January sky.

'OK, OK . . . I'll change the door!' I shouted at the mental image of my great-grandfather's stern face, which seemed to fill the air. Running towards a free taxi, I had absolutely no idea that I had just received one of the most profound communications of my life.

The Cottage

It was a gorgeous day for late January. The sun was streaming into the new breakfast-room extension, reminding us all that spring was not too far away. This was probably why we were in such high spirits.

TC had decided to enrol for a course on Self-Awareness to be held locally. A delightful patient kept leaving literature about it in the surgery, and TC, ever-curious about alternative therapies for the human mind and body, had decided to give it a go. Although we had no idea what the course was about, his sister and I were teasing him.

'I've read about this sort of thing,' I said. 'It's all very American, and they make you do really embarrassing things to break down your personality.' I winked at his sister.

She looked at TC, her face full of mischief. 'You will probably have to pretend to be a dog or something, and they'll take you back to childhood and you'll have to be a baby in front of everyone.'

'Your patients will love that,' I giggled.

'Oh God, no,' he groaned, laughing nervously. 'I think I'll phone the organisers, and get them to confirm that, if any of my patients are on the same course, I won't have to do group work with them.'

He telephoned there and then and was told by a member of the course management not to worry. She pointed out that he was doing the course for himself, a private individual, not as a duty doctor. He was reassured and, understandably, rather nervous.

The course started the following Thursday. TC left the cottage in the early evening for the first-night venue, a hotel in the nearby town of Guildford. He clutched his file to his chest as though it were the shield of a warrior about to go into battle.

'Have fun, TC,' I called after him, blowing him a good-bye kiss.

'Oh, God, what have I let myself in for?'

'You are about to find out, my friend. I'm glad it's you first. I'll wait up. I have a funny feeling you will be late back!'

His car jerked and stuttered out of the drive, perhaps reflecting his nervousness.

At 2:30 a.m. I had just about given up the idea of waiting up and was getting ready for bed when I heard the car roar up to the garage.

'Tell me, tell me?' I demanded impatiently of a rather dazed looking TC as he came into the bedroom.

'You won't believe what happened, you just won't believe it,' he said, laughing to himself while getting undressed.

'What? Come on, TC, tell me?'

As his head hit the pillow he let out a soft sigh.

'TC?'

I discovered nothing that night. He was asleep.

Early February

Even though I felt nervous I was looking forward to going to the open-evening of the Self-Awareness organisation. TC was more than halfway through the basic course and was totally taken with the whole thing. I persuaded JR, my friend and business associate, to come with me as I was apprehensive about going alone. We arrived in the brightly lit hired Salvation Army hall, feeling that delighful mixture of giggles and nerves which always heralds a journey into the unknown.

We were welcomed by helpers, people who had done one or

more courses and had volunteered to work with the potential new recruits. They were being so sincere and nice whilst sticking name-tags onto us, beaming with a shiny-faced innocence that always makes me want to shout loudly phrases that involve sex and travel. I considered what a dreadful strain it is maintaining that degree of niceness, and wondered why, the moment human beings get themselves involved with anything that smacks of a spiritual/do-gooder path, they wear such a beatific mask? Some English priests and American evangelists are particularly good at it, although one suspects they may be doing unspeakable things with choirboys and selected members of their congregations.

I found the talk during the first half of the evening fascinating. It was explained there were a number of courses available offering a progressive understanding of life. The first course was about how to learn to develop the ability to manage one's personality and relationships and how to discover the strength and inner resources to bring out one's full potential as a human being. I felt it could be a tall order for one weekend and a few evenings! The concept was not just intellectual, but experiential down to the fibre of one's being. The organisation was not religious and there was no mention of God, but there was talk of our spiritual nature. As the lecture went on, it was explained that there were various levels of awareness, or consciousness, and the courses were designed to work through these stages helping participants to reveal their inner truths and beliefs and, therefore, ultimately to gain a conscious mastery over their lives. A flip chart was used, and humans were depicted as triangles full of nasty little repressed squiggles which represented locked-away emotions and unconscious thoughts and memories. These squiggles were responsible for what we were attracting into our lives without even knowing it. They had to be released and the courses, it was mooted, were the way to do it. The speaker suggested we were all walking icebergs only revealing the smallest tip of who we really were. The illustrative talk demonstrated that these icebergs were all connected underneath the surface, and that there was nothing 'out there' going to get us – our lives were about becoming masters and not victims. The presentation was a heady mixture of philosophy, metaphysics and humour. I knew there must be something more to life than the carry-water-chop-logs syndrome, and this was the first time I had seen and heard things that seemed to make sense. The teacher, Cosmo Greene, was dynamic and fun – nothing like the beatific brigade working with him. He bounced up and down the hall, full of energy and a razor-sharp awareness of everyone in the place. I didn't want to catch his eye, feeling sure he would pick on me. I could see why TC was having such an amazing time, and understood why he could not explain easily what went on in the sessions. Taken out of context, any description would seem rather odd.

And what a lively second half. Several people decided to share some of their varied life experiences. They were all very sincere and I had no doubt that, as a result of the course, something fundamental had shifted in their perspectives. There was an openness about them which was strange to watch and hear. It was so un-British. They kept applauding each other and grinning a lot. I felt slightly hot and embarrassed by it all.

Events then took an even more interesting twist. Some participants had stirred up painful realisations about their lives, and wanted Cosmo to help them deal with these immediately, rather than wait until we visitors had adjourned to another part of the building. Suddenly I was seeing some of the things TC had tried to describe to me: individuals being guided skilfully through extraordinary revelations about themselves, leading to new, and from what I could see, greater understanding of their lives. I wondered whether this would be enough to sustain happier lives after the euphoria of the group experience disappeared. It was fascinating to be a fly on the wall.

'This has never happened before,' said an amused and slightly wary-looking Cosmo. 'So we'll just see where it leads.' Taking the hand of one of his distressed pupils he led her out to the front. She wanted to talk about her rather strange sex life. As she went into some detail about the odd demands of her partner I began to giggle with embarrassment. Cosmo was encouraging her to stand up for herself, by acting out the ways she could refuse the demands. She followed his instructions with her eyes closed, hands over her ears, and stamping her feet. I heard JR spluttering next to me. I couldn't believe it when a large man stood up and told us in a well-educated booming voice that he was the husband. After what his wife had just revealed about his requirements, which involved full moons, ropes and lots of plant life, I thought he might have been too embarrassed to speak – particularly on an open evening. I cracked finally at the point he was explaining that his actions were caused by what his childhood nanny made him do. Those pram-pushers have a lot to answer for. By now JR was almost on the floor doubled up, shaking uncontrollably, and in danger of needing an underwear change. We were hysterical. I stared into the air directly in front of me and as other participants related their various experiences I managed to calm myself down.

As I looked around the hall, most of the people on the course appeared normal to me; in fact, they seemed to be very respectable and well-dressed types, nothing like I had imagined. It was comforting to see everyday people, and not some bunch of cosmic weirdos. The only oddball that I noticed was a woman sitting next to TC. She was tall and rather lanky, probably only in her thirties, but with a dishevelled look of self-neglect and shabby clothes. She kept turning round and staring at me with such intent I wondered if I should have known who she was. I smiled, but her expression never changed; her strange eyes remaining fixed on me made me feel very uncomfortable. During the break she was hanging around TC rather possessively. I could see he was feeling such love for everyone and such interest in the proceedings, chatting animatedly amidst his new friends, who included a fellow doctor, that I wondered if he had noticed her. I could see the harmonious possibilities of a group of people getting together and removing some of their inhibitions in order to experience their oneness, but my cynicism questioned the interpretation of this universal love. From the glint in some of the helpers' and participants' eyes, the message was being received and translated from the waist down.

After something tasteless and healthy to drink JR and I were ushered into the newcomers' discussion group. It was a gas. Our hostess was rather like an overgrown girl-guide leader. She was obviously very nervous, and easy meat for the earth-mother course junky who had done everything available in the human potential repertoire and therefore felt it her divine right to take over the entire meeting. JR and I felt so sorry for her that we fielded most of earth-mamma's questions between us. It came to me during the ensuing three tedious hours why I needed to do an awareness course. I wanted to be cured of the polite paralysis that locks me in my chair during all sorts of boring occasions, too scared to get up and walk out.

In spite of all the hilarity – and the boredom – I decided to have a go at the course. What the hell, I figured that there must be a meaning to this kaleidoscope of experiences called life, and was determined to keep searching until I found it . . . especially if it looked like fun. Hearing all those people sharing their life experiences with such honesty and openness made me feel great love for them. I knew I would like to have that feeling more often. My name was on the list for the next course. There was nothing to lose in giving it a try.

The Cottage

Mid-February

'You are very honoured, you know,' said TC, looking up from behind an assortment of patients' notes and cricket fixtures that seemed to be permanently piled on the kitchen table.

'And why is that?' I enquired.

'Well, you're probably the only non-course participant who has been invited tonight.'

'I'm not that certain I want to go. I feel very much like an outsider, and I won't understand that course-speak you have all adopted.'

'Honestly, Jules, they are a lovely group of people. You'll really like them, and anyway, it's only an informal supper.'

I was looking forward to my own experience of doing the SA course and, even though I was curious, I did not want to know too much in advance. I felt not only shy but also reluctant about meeting a group of strangers who all belonged to something that, as yet, I did not understand.

TC was enthralled from that very first night. We had spent some hilarious and soul-searching moments discussing what the course was about. As the three weeks of his involvement passed, it was apparent that he was having a very stimulating, if somewhat exhausting time. I was used to him returning from workshop evenings at all sorts of late hours, in varying states of highs and lows – he was obviously releasing lots of squiggles. It was very moving to see how open and excited he was by the whole experience, even though I could not grasp much of what it was all about. There was an agreement by course participants not to discuss with outsiders what happened during the sessions, so the questions I asked TC received some obscure answers after much teasing and copious cups of late-night tea.

TC had decided to go straight from the basic course onto a second-level one, which was being held in London. Although he was on a high and more alive and energetic than I had seen for a long time, something about his state did not feel right. It was too driven.

I was also getting used to the extra phonecalls. All thirty-five participants from the first course, plus the new lot, were encouraged to phone each other and 'share' their experiences and gain support from each other if they were feeling low. Sometimes it seemed they all phoned on the same night. Raking around in their subconscious often stirred up deep feelings and emotions, together with wonder-filled insights into why life experiences manifest in so many different ways. These revelations were exchanged with great enthusiasm as inter-course friendship was much encouraged. Even I was beginning to recognize all the different voices, but I was very fed up with the daily caller who hung up without speaking every time I answered the phone.

'Well, I'd better go and get ready to meet this crowd.'

The phone rang at that precise moment.

'Can you give me a lift to the party, TC?' I heard a woman's voice enquire.

'We are just finishing off some paperwork, and will probably be arriving a little bit late, so I think it would be better for you to get a lift from someone else, Helen,' he replied, balancing the phone between his shoulder and ear, still writing up notes.

'We?' questioned the voice sarcastically.

'Yes, Jules and I will be down later, so can you get a lift . . .?'

The line went dead – she had hung up. TC stared at the phone with a puzzled look.

'What's eating at her?' I said.

'Oh, I don't know. She's very lonely and needs a lot of support from the group,' TC replied wearily.

'Especially you?' I went to change. This was the woman who had been on the phone to him earlier in the week for over an hour, expressing her sexual frustrations and desperation to find a partner. He had been taken aback somewhat by her remarks, but felt it was part of the course to deal with her kindly, and so listened to her with compassion, not wishing to hurt her feelings, even though it concerned him that she was his patient. After the call we had laughed at how certain women projected their lust-filled desires in his direction, and, equally, how certain men fell in love with me, when nothing whatsoever had been done to invite their attentions. They were always people we did not find remotely attractive. It baffled us both, and we dismissed the subject, none the wiser. She had sent him a bouquet of flowers the following day, with a card containing a cryptic message. He was so busy he hadn't noticed them. In fact TC rarely appeared to notice when women made advances. Ironically it was that innocent quality that often made them even more tenacious. He already had several other female patients who were obsessed with him and telephoned regularly.

'Tell him to keep out of my dreams,' one had screamed down the phone a few weeks before. 'I know he's interfering with my brain waves.'

'What does one say to them?' I pondered, getting into my glad-rags. The gentle approach that we both used did nothing to discourage them – sad lonely people who latched on to kindness like black widow spiders onto their prey. 'They'll eat us all in the end,' I warned my reflection as I put the finishing touches to my make-up.

'TC?' I called from the bedroom. 'Come on, or we'll be late.'

We were.

We parked the car on a grass verge in front of Annie's small neat cottage. I stubbed my cigarette out, inhaling the smoke deeply, suspecting that it would be my last for a few hours. It did not help my feelings of shyness. Meeting new people was not one of my favourite pastimes, although it was necessary in my work.

We entered a cosy lounge filled with the sounds of animated chatter. TC was immediately in the middle of it all, laughing and affectionately greeting people. I stood on the edge of the group, hoping not to be noticed. No such luck. An exceptionally tall slim man wearing glasses scooped me up into his arms and hugged me. I felt the blood rush to my cheeks with embarrassment, my feet dangling helplessly in the air. He lowered me gently to the ground, and proceeded to explain how he too had been unable to feel anything other than rigidity when being embraced, but was loving the new experience of receiving affection. He went on about the importance of the spine in relation to physical experience, but he lost me somewhere on the way. A petite woman at his side smiled knowingly. I longed for a cigarette already.

We were called into the large kitchen fairly soon after our arrival, and seated ourselves around a scrubbed wooden table. The array of food was magnificent, and we all dived in, chattering and teasing on the way. I felt part of a big and boisterous family. Diagonally opposite me was a pale-faced woman I recognised from the introductory evening. She was staring at me. I smiled, but she continued to stare, miles away. I asked TC who she was. 'That's Helen Black,' he whispered. I suppose I could have guessed as much. Sensing my discomfort he put his arm protectively around my shoulder, joking about how well I was taking all this mind-blowing conversation. It was not like him to be demonstrative, but I was grateful for his attention. In that moment I was convinced she was the caller who kept hanging up when I answered the phone – I reasoned that if she was projecting some sort of relationship onto TC, she would not be overly keen to leave a message with me. As I held her gaze, once again, something in her eyes troubled me deeply. Occasionally my intuitive understandings disturbed me, so for the most part I used to ignore them. If what someone said did not equate with their energy field, I could always sense the discrepancy. More often than not I viewed this as a curse, for the other person would know that I knew he or she was lying or hiding something and quite frequently this produced varying degrees of anger in those involved.

After supper we all adjourned to the lounge, and I became involved in a heated debate about the squiggles – whether individuals should be allowed to peek into their subconscious, or are those hidden fears and memories best left buried, or should they be allowed to work themselves into our awareness at their own pace. We questioned whether these awareness courses were helpful or harmful. Did they force participants to open old wounds before they were ready? Was the euphoria felt after the courses an adrenalin-driven high enforced by late nights, little sleep, and a lot of emotions dragged from the subconscious? Was it true that some people experienced terrible depression afterwards, missing all the attention from Cosmo and all the hugs from fellow participants? It was frustrating not knowing what experiences they had all shared together, so for much of the time I stayed on the edge of the conversations. The consensus of the group was that they were in favour of the courses, with the exception of one beautiful woman's husband, who was so vehemently against them and any related discussion that he left rather abruptly. It did not dent the boisterous atmosphere and the conversations continued. They were able to be much cheekier with one another than the usual supper party gatherings – it was evident rank and title held no sway.

I knew I was still being stared at, even though Helen was sitting on the edge of my field of vision. She did not join in the banter. For a long time I deliberately avoided looking her way, then, for no explicable reason, I suddenly felt very sad. Who was I to turn my back on this lost lanky woman? I looked her way and smiled. She seemed glad of the recognition, and held out a shaking hand offering me a herbal cigarette. Desperate though I was for a Marlboro, I could not bring myself to accept it. Those supposedly healthy alternatives always reminded me of autumnal bonfires. She explained she was giving up smoking, and that these foul-smelling things were helping her. I thanked her and replied laughingly that I would stick to the real thing. I wondered if her shakes and far-awayness were due to nicotine withdrawal.

When the evening drew to a close, I felt compelled to give everyone a goodbye hug – something very out of character. It was really rather a lovely feeling. This wonderful assortment of people were brave enough to take a long hard look at themselves and their lives, and openly talk about their fears and beliefs. I admired their courage, and had enjoyed their company enormously. I felt I had completed a mini-course myself by the time we walked out of the door.

Curling up to go to sleep that night I felt a deep excitement. Something was happening to me: I had an overwhelming feeling that my life was going to change for the better. How or when did not come to me, just an excitement that seemed to spread throughout my being.

The Cottage

March 1st

We sat at the long pine table in the breakfast room, drinking hot chocolate with far too much whipped cream on the top.

'I am feeling very discombobulated,' I said, using one of TC's favourite words.

'It's a good sign,' he said smiling.

'Why?' I asked, scooping up the last bit of cream with my finger.

'Well, they say that before a course things start to churn up a bit.'

I walked around the table into the kitchen and in silence washed the mugs. When I had finished I leant across the central work unit, my chin on my hands.

'What sort of things churn-up, then?'

'Everything, Jules ... just about everything!' he replied confidently, giving me a gentle reassuring grin.

'TC, I'm going to spend a few days in Spain with Mum and Herbert.'

'Probably a good idea,' he replied, continuing to hum a tuneless little hum, which he always did when his thoughts were elsewhere.

'I feel tired, and need a break from work.'

He stopped humming. 'I wish I could come too, I'm pretty exhausted.'

He looked drawn. The combination of a heavy workload, nights on duty and the intensity of the second SA course was beginning to tell.

'Perhaps it's too much, doing a second course so quickly after the first,' I suggested.

'No, it's not really. I could just do without being on call for a couple of weeks.'

I wondered if the medical profession would ever change. The hours seemed horrendous. I thought of my own profession in advertising, marketing and publishing and of how the unions would react if they were asked to be on duty for such unpredictable and long hours. The comparison was laughable.

As I climbed the stairs to bed that night my head was swimming with unanswered questions, and huge doubts about my entire life. The excitement of the other evening had disappeared, something seemed to be wrong. I felt curdled.

Costa del Sol – Spain

Early March

The plane touched down with remarkable smoothness for such a huge lump of metal. Flying always filled me with a childish wonder. When the doors opened a wave of Spanish heat rolled into the plane. I climbed down the aircraft stairs relishing the fabulous blue of the sky and the intense warm yellow of the sun, too bright to look at even in March.

I picked up my hire car with surprising ease and speed, and was soon on the notoriously dangerous *auto-via* heading towards Marbella. The light on the Mediterranean sparkled and danced and, spotting my first burst of scarlet geraniums against a white building, my heart leapt with joy. I hated the grey of the British winter. The vibrance of the colours of southern Europe always managed to intoxicate me.

I negotiated my way off the motorway, thanks to my step-father's detailed instructions. He was very good at meticulous directions. I supposed it came from the discipline of being a solicitor. 'Get it wrong and you're a dead 'un,' he had told me grimly over the phone, when explaining how to find the new turn into their urbanisation. 'They drive like madmen here.'

The urbanisation had grown considerably since my last visit. The number of new villas and apartments was incredible. I wondered who was supposed to buy all these expensive homes, which appeared to be mainly empty and neglected. This was not the Spain I loved. It was like a Milton Keynes housing estate painted white.

I drove up to the villa, which belonged to clients of my stepfather. It was one of the first, beautifully built in the traditional style, but it looked rather sad hemmed in by cheap apartments and new villas squeezed in on small *parcelas*. The bougainvillaea draped itself in abundance along the outer wall, and several cats lazed in the porch, having discovered my mother's generosity and excellent cooking. Mum and Herbert were waiting for me like a couple of excited kids. It was to be one of the best times we had ever spent together.

I was able to unwind very quickly, the terracotta warmth with its primary coloured landscape bringing out my childish delight and playfulness. The days were long and leisurely. For the first time in years mother and I talked of childhood and treasured memories were revived amidst much humour and wine. Herbert was kept occupied with his golf, which gave my mother and me the privacy to rediscover our extraordinary closeness. We visited Marbella and sat in the nostalgic atmosphere of the Orange Square beneath the fruit-laden trees drinking big cups of coffee laced with brandy. We walked along the miles of beach collecting polished marble pebbles, exotic-looking shells and removing bags full of the rubbish left by thoughtless visitors. We drove to whitewashed inland villages and bought ridiculous quantities of fruit and vegetables, seduced by the wonderful colours and textures piled high on wooden market stalls. We tasted honey and goat's cheeses, and filled our bags with almonds and walnuts so amazingly cheap we were unable to resist them. We came back to the villa and cooked together, never running out of things to say. We daydreamed about persuading Herbert to buy us an orange farm so we could have a wonderful outdoor life creating a place where Martin would always be cared for and have work. We thought about all the things we would make and sell in the markets. Mum decided she could always go down into the jetset port and sing for our supper if our finances needed boosting.

We reminisced about the only holiday we had ever had alone together since she married Herbert. We had stayed near Marbella with a great friend who had a wonderful holiday penthouse flat overlooking the sea. Her husband was working so it was women and children only. What a time we'd had. In one of the finest restaurants on the coast Mum had stood up and sung with the owner, who had been a well-known tenor. The audience went wild and the encores went into the early hours of the morning. Our table was covered in champagne and roses. I became her agent, fielding all the questions and dinner invites. A large Middle-Eastern party were throwing five-thousand peseta notes into my lap. They asked if the beautiful lady would sing for them the next night – it was a birthday party. I was told the name of a yacht moored in the stylish Puerto Banus. We both remembered standing the next night looking at an enormous boat, the entire width of its wooden polished stern deck supporting a massive table laid for thirty people. Flowers and champagne on ice; white-suited and gloved staff and crew running around some very important-looking guests. We had hovered on the brink of a great adventure but in the end my dear mother had lost her nerve. 'That husband of mine would NEVER forgive me,' she had whispered fiercely. 'Get me out of here before I change my mind . . . and my entire life.'

Standing in the kitchen crushing garlic we wondered what would have happened if she had sung that night. Her voice was extraordinary and for me it was a tragedy she didn't make more of it. She told me about one of the few times she'd sung publicly with Max in South Africa – one of the sopranos in the show had laryngitis but the show was saved because Mum had sat in on all the rehearsals and knew all the songs. She received such glowing notices after the show and in the next day's papers that Max had gone into a screaming rage and cut all her clothes into shreds and had blacked both her eyes. It had, she explained, put her off public performances. Now her appearances were confined to charitable works, the odd restaurant with a pianist and a group of very dear and faithful musical friends. They would meet up in local pubs and have impromptu sessions together – this she felt would not be too much of a threat to anyone. Listening to her singing as she prepared a Spanish supper, I still felt sad that the world had missed out on a great star.

My mind wandered back to a time in the late fifties. Martin and I were standing on tiptoe looking over the banister of our London house into the large marble-floored hall, where Max was practising a tricky piece on the trombone. He was rehearsing for a big show. My mother was on the hall stairs vacuuming the carpet and singing along with the music at the top of her voice. Distracted by the noise, Max in a flash rage ran screaming up the stairs, ripping the plug out of the socket on the way. He took the vacuum tube from our speechless mother and proceeded, with all the strength of madness, to wrap it around her neck. She began to splutter and turn blue. Wide-eyed Martin looked at me, 'I don't fink he should do that to our mummy.' I nodded in silent agreement, whereupon he ran down to the landing and, without a trace of fear, tapped Max on the shoulder. The shouting stopped. 'Juey and me fink you're not allowed to kill our mummy so you'd better stop now, Mackie,' he said as he rolled his sleeves up and took the stance of a boxer, shaking his little fists. 'If you don't stop I'll kill YOU, Mr Wall.' Max glared at the ridiculous-looking knee-high figure. I held my breath. Suddenly Max was laughing – Mum was laughing – I was laughing – we were all scooped up in a big heap together laughing. Martin had the last word as he took Mum's face in his gnarled hands. 'Muvver, I don't fink Mackie likes it when you sing.' He had a point.

I asked her why she thought she made sane men become so possessive. 'No matter how much those scrubbed-faced flat-chested feminists fight,' she whispered over her full glass of red wine, 'men, Julie, do not like women to outshine them.

You have to make a choice.' I told her I could never compromise my life in such a way. She put her glass down and took my chin in her hands. 'That, my darling girl, is probably why you are in your thirties and do NOT have a husband.' I blew a raspberry knowing I would never in a million years swap my position for hers. She knew that I knew she hid her light and enormous sense of fun for the sake of a quiet married life.

With such open and relaxed days together I was, surprisingly, having sleepless nights. Something was wrong, but I could not translate the feeling into thoughts. What was it that so desperately wanted my attention? After two nights of staring at a white-washed ceiling I was so exhausted that the third night I prayed for sleep and some clue as to what was keeping me awake.

I fell straight into a really strange nightmare. TC was the star, which was not surprising since he was in my thoughts a great deal. With all that had been going on in the last few weeks I guess it was inevitable that my subconscious would scramble things up and give me the sort of dream Jung would have loved.

I dreamed I returned to the cottage unexpectedly. On entering the kitchen I saw TC pinned across the central work-surface by a scrawny woman, whose face was so blurred I could not recognize it. She was naked, and held a carving knife against his throat. She hissed and spat at me like a wild animal, gloating and cackling that he belonged to her now. I was amused, even though it was not a pretty scene. I explained laughingly to her that TC was free to be with whom he wanted in life, and perhaps this was not the best way of making him love her. At that point, she started to attack me.

I woke up with sweat pouring down my back, which for a terrifying moment I thought was blood. I was shaking from head to foot, and wide awake, so I went to get a drink. It was a perfect night for a nightmare; a spectacular electric storm was lighting up the sky; the Mediterranean looked sinister with its inky black swell.

Walking into the lounge I saw Herbert silhouetted against the large french windows.

'Couldn't you sleep either?' I whispered. 'Can I get you a drink of something?'

He turned quietly to face me. It was not my stepfather. My gaze froze on this strange pyjama-clad man and my heart thumped with terror as he faded into the walls. I was too scared to ask who he was and why he had come.

I wondered what the hell was happening but, although very frightened, considered myself far too grown up to wake 'mummy'.

The next day I phoned TC. He seemed fine, about to set off to London for a weekend workshop, the culmination of the second course. I did not want him to go, but with the money running out in the call box and Mum and stepfather hovering, waiting to go to dinner, I said nothing of these thoughts and hung up. Inside me there was the feeling that I might have made a terrible mistake. Was not telling him of the nightmare somehow putting him in great danger?

Malaga Airport

March 10th

I sat in the overcrowded departure lounge of Malaga airport. It was no surprise to learn that the flight to London Gatwick was delayed for several hours. Charter flights to and from anywhere in Spain seemed to be subject to frequent hold-ups with infrequent explanations. Enquiring in one's best Spanish when we might be allowed to take off only encouraged looks of contempt with replies in heavily accented English: 'H'yew h'wait h'over h'there.'

Speaking a foreign language and getting a reply in my own tongue always felt like a put-down. I bought an overpriced coffee and a stale doughnut and reflected on my five days spent on Spain's Costa del Sol.

I had worked so hard for the last six months setting up my own business, and it was building up well. I should not really have taken the time off but I needed a break badly. Progress had been good work-wise, but I was feeling troubled and was questioning many aspects of my life. Living with someone I loved, but only as a brother and friend, was an easy compromise, and although unspoken, we both knew something was missing. I wondered whether it was sensible to be establishing a business from a home that was not mine, and from a relationship that was not really fulfilling for either of us. I also questioned my business set-up. Did I really need my business associate? By the time everyone else had taken their cut of my work the net result was not much for me, which seemed to be a familiar pattern in my life. I knew some changes would have to be made, and putting space between myself and my everyday environment had made getting an overview easier. It had definitely helped to be away, although it may have been a mistake to stay with my mother and stepfather.

My mother, always astonishingly intuitive, had known immediately that beneath the surface all was not well with me. The last thing I had wanted to do was to worry her, which was why I could not discuss the nightmare. She knew I was troubled, yet the subject remained closed. There was nothing to hide and equally nothing to say. TC and I did not have any problems, there was no one else, and in fact most aspects of my life were alright. The wonderful song from the musical *Oliver* – 'I'm Reviewing the Situation' – summed up my state. I was tired of being alright – I wanted to feel wonderful. The Mediterranean climate and colours stirred a restlessness so deep within me I had to force my mind away from the orange-farm daydreams.

It had been wonderful to spend the time with Mum – in fact we had all got on very well together, which had been a relief. I did not have an easy relationship with my stepfather, and was delighted we had laughed and had some fun. I smiled as I recalled the arrival of their friends who brought the news that he had become a grandfather for the first time. They had been kind enough to allow us to give their telephone number as a means of contact. We were all so happy that night and enjoyed a celebration dinner with all the joy that a new soul brings into this world.

I was, however, very perturbed at my mother's behaviour on my departure. To insist on coming to the airport to see me off

when I had my own hire car was most unlike her. I could feel
the weight of her gold cross and chain, which she had begged
me to wear. I had shrugged it off, joking that it was not my
style to wear such a thing, but the tone of her voice was so
insistent I had agreed reluctantly to take it. My shoulder was
still damp from her tears as she had placed it around my neck
and hugged me.

'Please don't go back, Ju,' she had wept.

I explained quietly that I had to and really could not afford, in
more ways than one, to take further time away from my embry-
onic business, adding that I had several important appointments
the following day I did not want to cancel. I tried to make her
laugh by making her promise to tell me if she thought the plane
was going to crash, and in return I said I promised to believe
her. She shook her head.

'No, no, it's not the plane, I just feel so sad, I don't know why.
Probably too much Rioja last night,' she laughed – but not with
her eyes.

I had often doubted and teased her about her psychic ability,
and yet her premonitions were usually extremely accurate. I
reminded her of the time she had called me at my London
flat, waking me up in the middle of the night, telling me I had
to phone Buckingham Palace and tell them the Queen was in
terrible danger and was going to be shot at. She had seen Her
Majesty's horse rearing into the air in panic. For some strange
reason she felt they would listen to me – can you imagine the
phone call . . . 'Excuse me . . . er, I hope I have not disturbed
you . . . Yes, I do realise it's four o'clock in the morning but,
er . . . Well my mother, who lives in Warwickshire, well . . . she
has just had a dream that the Queen is in danger of her life, and
would like you to tell Her Majesty preferably to stay indoors
today, and not take part in the Trooping the Colour ceremony,
or if she feels she must go, perhaps she could walk?'

I could not believe that my intelligent mother had woken me
up, seriously expecting me to phone Buckingham Palace. We
had both collapsed into laughter at the absurdity of it, and
needless to say I did not make the call. The following morning
I was at my desk on a Fleet Street newspaper when the news

screamed in that Her Majesty Queen Elizabeth had been shot at as she was on her way to the Trooping the Colour ceremony. I went very cold, and felt as though it was all my fault. I imagined a great neon sign flashing over my head for all to see: 'She could have stopped this!' I vowed always to listen to my mother in the future.

However, standing in the check-in hall, I could not consider staying on without any clear indication from her as to why she felt so sad and anxious.

'I just think you should go back later,' was all she would say. Walking through passport control I felt a lump in my throat and could sense her tears even though she was out of sight.

I boarded the plane with a degree of trepidation. I did not enjoy the flight, and my relief was enormous when it landed safely. My business associate, JR, was there to meet me and in moments I was catching up on all the news and back in the swing of my working life, all thoughts of Spain temporarily forgotten.

My mother and stepfather had returned to their villa, in which they were expecting to stay for another fortnight. Unbeknown to anyone, my mother started quietly to pack. It was Monday evening, March 10th.

The Cottage

March 10th

'Hi, TC, I'm home,' I called as I entered the kitchen.

'Jules!' He got up from the table. 'Good to see you,' and kissed me on the cheek.

'So, how's it all going, "Guru T"?' I teased, tossing my holdall onto the floor.

'Exhausting, but brilliant.'

His face still looked pale and tired but his eyes were shining with enthusiasm. He had just completed the full weekend workshop with SA.

'Are you learning a lot during all these long sessions?' I enquired.

'It's incredible, Jules. This sort of knowledge could transform the face of medicine in the future.'

He pursued passionately many types of alternative therapies, always convinced that disease could be treated in many different ways, and more importantly, he believed deep understandings within individuals could actually prevent disease.

I picked up one of my ginger tomcats who was weaving around my feet.

'Have you missed me, Thomas, or is it supper time?' He nuzzled into my arm purring softly. I loved that cat. I put him down gently next to Ben, my other feline friend. They sat bolt upright side by side. 'My two little sentinels,' I whispered.

'They will protect you from "Der Spook",' TC answered absent-mindedly.

'Whatever made you say that, TC?'

'What?' he answered without looking up.

'Der Spook!' I reminded him.

'I don't know,' he laughed. 'It just came to me.'

I ran upstairs to the bedroom, and pulled my favourite Louis Feraud dress from the wardrobe. It was ten years old, and in permanent ink on the inner hem the words 'Der Spook' were handwritten. I had always wondered how they got there. I carried it downstairs and showed TC. We looked at each other shrugging our shoulders at one of life's apparently inexplicable events.

JR put the kettle on. 'Fancy some tea, JC?' she interrupted.

'Of course!' I said. 'The British answer to every traveller's thirst.'

She stayed for supper that night, and we all chatted animatedly; she about our work, TC about his course, and me about Spain.

JR left at 11pm, and by the time the supper things were cleared away, and I had unpacked and put a wash on, I felt pretty tired. My head hit the pillow and delicious relaxation melted my tense muscles. It was good to be in my own bed. I kissed TC goodnight, thinking we were more like an old married couple than the two people who had shared such passion in our early times together. In those days he had told me how if during the first year of a relationship you put a bean in a jar each time you make love, and for the rest of your time together take one out every time you engage apparatus, the jar would never empty. Sadly our jar was the only thing full of beans. I turned over and fell asleep immediately.

I awoke reluctantly to the sound of the telephone filling the bedroom with its unwelcome warble. I groaned and glanced at the clock, it was only half-past seven.

'I thought you weren't on call today?'

'I'm not,' replied TC with deep weariness, reaching out from under the duvet for the offending telephone.

'Yes, mmm . . . Yes, I'm Dr TC, what's the problem?'

He was sitting up in bed already fully awake. His remarkable ability to emerge from deep sleep into alert consciousness with such speed never failed to amaze me. Years of practice, I thought.

I was now also wide awake and sitting up, wanting to ascertain whether we were on full alert, and would have to get up, or if I could slide back into sleep.

'Penny, Penny who?' TC queried, looking puzzled and shrugging his shoulders to let me know he didn't have a clue what it was about.

'No, I haven't got a patient with that name . . .

'Yes, that is my address . . .

'Ahh, yes . . . in that case her name is Black . . . Helen Black.

'Yes, she has suffered with depression . . .

'Mmm . . .

'I see . . .

'No, that's not possible, I've got a full surgery booked this morning . . .

'Yes, I understand, could you take her to her home? . . .

'OK, I'll hold on.'

He placed his hand over the receiver, still looking puzzled, told me he thought it was something to do with Helen Black. I tried to make sense out of the one-sided conversation, without much success.

'. . . yes, hello . . .

'Mmm . . .

'I see . . .

'Well, has she committed any offence? . . .

'Right, then why are you holding her? . . .

'Yes I understand, and how is she now? . . .

'Yes, I know Cosmo Greene and the Self-Awareness organisation.

'She's on one of his courses at the moment . . .

'No, I can't. I've already explained to your colleague, I've got a surgery this morning . . .

'Good. Can you keep her there and bring her down to the surgery later this morning? . . .

'Yes, that would be fine, it will give me a chance to clear the morning patients . . .

'No, not at all, see you later. Bye.'

He put the phone back in its cradle.

'Who was that?' I enquired anxiously.

'The police at Guildford,' TC answered quietly, as he yawned and shook his head.

'Well, what did they want? What has happened? Is it an accident?'

'It is Helen,' he confirmed. 'She's been taken off a London bound train this morning because she was behaving oddly. Apparently she would only give them my name and Cosmo Greene's. They couldn't get hold of Cosmo.'

'What was she doing on the train?' I asked softly.

'They didn't say, other than she hasn't done anything illegal, but she seems depressed, and so they don't like to leave her on her own.'

'But why are they calling you?'

'She said she wants to talk with me, and realistically it's easier to leave it like that because I understand much more of what she has been going through these last few weeks. The police don't know her background, and they don't know what to do with her.'

He paused, looking at the two cats lying at the foot of the bed beginning reluctantly to stretch themselves.

'This course brings up a lot of gremlins from the subconscious and some of these experiences can be painful.'

'Yes, I guess you are the best man for the job.' I got out of bed and reached for my dressing-gown. I felt very uneasy and again irritated by this strange woman who seemed to be encroaching more and more into our life.

'TC?'

He looked up. He had a tousled boyish look which made him seem incredibly vulnerable.

'Promise me you'll take care . . .?'

'Of course I will.' He smiled impudently as he spoke. He treated my intuitive outbursts with cynicism and a lot of teasing.

'No, I'm serious, TC. Don't be alone with her. Don't trust her.'

He looked at me quizzically. I decided not to say anything else, but wondered why she had asked for the course leader and TC, and not her own family or friends. If she wanted medical advice, she wouldn't have asked for Cosmo, so she must have wanted to be with either of them for personal reasons. It seemed to me her ovaries were bouncing in TC's direction, and I felt convinced her depression was linked in some way to the fact he didn't want to know. A fleeting image of the nightmare I had in Spain stopped my thought-processes dead. Was TC in danger? In the harsh light of our morning bustle my fears looked ridiculous – besides, I was far too busy to entertain such horror, so I buried my troubled feelings and bounced into action.

Just over an hour later I waved him off to work from our small porch with its brand-new front door.

'I did it for you,' I said to the sky, patting the newly hung door as I imagined my great-grandad looking down on me.

I wanted to sob but didn't know why.

'Sometimes, Julie, you are ridiculous,' I chided myself.

Lighting my first cigarette of the day I sat down with a mug of coffee. A busy day lay ahead and I wasn't too sure where to begin it. My London flat had recently sold and the small financial surplus was being transferred to me, plumping up my current account into a rare healthy balance. I was due at the bank at 11 a.m. to discuss what to do with my nest-egg. I chuckled at the lovely feeling of, for once, having some money

– I liked my manager and was looking forward to seeing him, particularly as he had been so supportive when my account was bouncing around in the red.

I checked my diary, the page was crammed with things to do and business calls to make. Savouring a mouthful of coffee, momentarily I missed my *cafe con leche* in the Spanish sunshine, sighing as I noted the most important items:

11.00 Bank. Take savings account details.

Query Invoice No. 210 from The Boss re VAT.

Post Self-Employed Personal Accident Scheme Ins Proposal Form.

Meet JR for résumé on our three magazine copy dates.

Do invoices for Feb.

Speak with Mike re product placement deal with Philips.

Practise piano for Friday lesson.

The truth was I did not feel like doing any of it except playing the piano. I had that early morning fuzzy feeling and the disorientation one seems always to experience when first back from holiday. What a pain to have been woken up so early – I could have done with another couple of hours in the land of slumber. Wondering how TC was getting on I lit another cigarette and reflected that we hadn't yet really had a chance to talk about anything. These days something always managed to get in the way of any quiet times together.

After a board meeting with myself I decided to spend the time before my appointment pottering around the house – a decision which cheered me up enormously. I went upstairs and dressed in my favourite pottering clothes, all casual and comfortable. I was not really a business-suit person at heart. Now more relaxed I watered all the plants, and quietly set about tidying up the disarray of a week's absence. My cats, pleased at some unexpected company, were playfully skidding across the floors weaving in and out of my feet, chewing and pulling mischievously at my laces.

'You are not that hungry, you poor starved creatures.'

I lifted Thomas into the air on my foot, he dangled helplessly, a big ginger blob.

'What a weight, Thomas.'

Dropping him down gently I picked up Benjamin as his huge green eyes were glaring jealously at me.

'I love you too, you gorgeous creature.' I nuzzled into his fluffy fur. He purred immediately. Catching a glimpse of myself in the breakfast room mirror I announced to my feline audience, 'I think we will all go on a diet this week, chaps.'

I laughed as I put him down. They had both perfected the art of acting starved. TC and I think their record was six meals in one day. I fed them in the early morning, our home help, convinced by their plaintive cries they had been forgotten, fed them mid-morning, then TC, who could never remember whether they had been fed or not, gave them a generous lunch; a neighbour took pity on them and gave them afternoon tea, TC gave them supper and I fed them again at midnight, having returned late from London. The next day, they both lay helpless, like crashed hot air balloons unable to move even towards their food bowl; only the occasional distinctly unsavoury odour wafting from their rear ends indicated they were still alive. We discovered their tactics and vowed to resort to large signs indicating the time of their last meal.

I finished dealing with my post; nothing very exciting. No juicy orders or fat premium bond wins enabling me to take early retirement in sunny climes. Just the usual round of circulars, credit card bills, and tedious administrative matters that probably only served to keep someone in a job. I cleared the cluttered table and walked around the central work-station into the kitchen. The recently completed open-plan kitchen and breakfast room was a huge success. We rarely used the other rooms these days as everyone always seemed to congregate in the kitchen. The washing-up done, I hung my holiday washing out with TC's shirts, wrote a shopping list, sorted the fridge out, and fell back into the routine of daily life. I noticed it was nearly 10 a.m. so I collected my papers together and went upstairs to get ready for my business day. As I got to the bedroom door the phone rang. I ran back down into the breakfast room area and, slightly breathlessly, answered it.

THE POINT OF NO RETURN

'**H**ello, Jules, it's TC.'

'Yes, I guessed,' I laughed at his "doctor's" voice.

'Jules?' He cleared his throat. 'Helen is here with me in the surgery, she was waiting at ten to nine and we had a chat then and we need to talk some more, but she's decided she doesn't want to wait around here while I finish seeing the last few patients. She wants to know if she can come down to the cottage and wait with you, as she would like to talk to you.'

He paused waiting for my reply. I knew she was sitting in with him as he sounded so formal.

'I realise you can't speak, TC, but listen, I'm really busy this morning, is this really necessary?'

'Yes, yes it is. It will only be for fifteen minutes or so and then I'll be home. OK?'

'OK, send her down – but please – don't be long?'

'I'll get one of the receptionists to drive her down. Thanks Jules.'

'OK, TC, see you later. Bye.'

'Bye.'

'Bugger!' I thought, turning off the portable phone. 'That's all I need.'

I ran up to my attic office and called JR on my business line. 'Hi, JR, it's Jules. Listen, TC has just called and he's sending someone down to the cottage. It's that funny woman on the course – you know, the one who stared at me so much.'

'The one from the Guildford intro talk?' JR asked.

'Yeh, that's the one. She's depressed or something and TC said she wants to come and talk to me. I suppose he doesn't want her left on her own. She was taken off a train this morning in Guildford, apparently in a pretty distressed state, poor thing. The people on these courses seem to go through a lot of experiences don't they?'

'You are telling me!' JR retorted, 'And YOU, who had the cheek to make ME sign on. Well, JC, I think you should be paid for running the surgery annexe! We'd probably make more money than from advertising!'

'I know, JR, I know, but how could I say no, when she was sitting next to him, probably feeling suicidal . . . it's part of the job of living with a doctor, and anyway, baby-sitting a depressed patient is easier for me than the usual lot hanging on the doorbell bleeding to death. Ugh. You know how I hate the sight of blood. It's only a pain because I'll have to get onto the bank and postpone my meeting. Anyway, I thought I'd warn you in advance in case you need to call while she's in the house. If she wants to have a chat, it's best for her to have my full attention and I wouldn't want to explain in front of her why she is here with me in the cottage. People seem to get hyper-sensitive when they are depressed and I don't want to make her feel any worse . . . In any case, knowing my family history of manic-depressives, can you think of a better qualified baby-sitter?'

She laughed.

'You've got a point there. OK, Jules, thanks for telling me, we'll catch up later.'

'Alright, JR, I'll call you as soon as I know what I'm up to and we'll have a meeting sometime this afternoon. Tarra-fur-naa, chuck.' I delivered my best brummy accent.

'Bye, Jules.'

I phoned the bank and cancelled my appointment. What irony that one of my main reasons for getting back from Spain was for the meeting with the bank manager, and here I was cancelling it, much to his secretary's annoyance. Cancelling it in order to sit with a neurotic woman. I pondered the fact that I couldn't cancel it to stay in Spain and have a good time. My priorities were definitely arse-about-face.

'Oh well, *c'est la vie*,' I said quietly to myself as I heard a car pull into the drive.

THE UPSET . . .

I ran down the stairs, and opened the recently hung new front door to welcome Helen. She and Jill, the head receptionist, stood in the drive.

'Hello.' I nodded towards a rather anxious-looking Jill.

'Helen – come on, in you come.' I held out my hands to the white-faced and darkly clad woman. She looked drawn and frightened.

'I must talk to you,' she blurted out as she hurried towards me. 'I want to tell you how I set things up with John and TC.'

I knew John was another man on the course with her. I put my arms around her to reassure her. I could see she was jittery and I wanted her to feel welcome. Waving goodbye to Jill, I shut the front door and we walked through the small hall into our kitchen/breakfast room.

'Would you like a hot drink, Helen?' I asked immediately. 'Some tea or coffee? I was just about to make one for myself, the kettle boiled just as you arrived.'

She stared at me for a long time, without answering.

'Perhaps a cold drink then?' I said brightly, bustling in the kitchen making my own coffee.

She had knelt down on the floor next to the Calor gas fire – which was off.

'Are you cold?' I asked walking towards her. 'I'll put the fire on for you.' I did not wait for her reply.

She looked up, her pale eyes far far away.

'Water,' she whispered, oblivious to my second question. I lit the fire and walked back into the kitchen to fetch her some water. Our tap water was always rather tepid so I put ice in the glass, carried it over to her, and knelt on the carpet beside her.

She was shivering. She took the tumbler from my hand, and fished the ice out with her long thin fingers, putting the cubes onto the bamboo stool next to her. I pretended not to notice.

'Oh, Helen you are cold, aren't you?'

She nodded meekly.

'How about a hot-water bottle?' I suggested.

'Oh, yes please.' She managed a faint smile, and I felt relieved to have got a response out of her. Her hunched body looked so sad. I knew very little about her, and wondered what it was that so obviously troubled her, and what she wanted to tell me. Maybe it had something to do with her feelings for TC, and this man John. I felt I could sense her desperation for someone – anyone out there – to love her. Perhaps desperate to the point of a total lack of discrimination, thus making a fool of herself with all sorts of unsuitable men? I was aware of feeling great compassion for her. I knew so many women who did extraordinary things in the wake of unrequited love. I'd done plenty of stupid, humiliating things myself. I sensed this lady kneeling before me was no different.

I told myself to get her warmed up first to enable her to relax a little bit and hopefully to communicate. She was rocking and trembling. The switch of the automatic kettle clicked off, and I went over and filled a hot-water bottle for her. She had bowed her head, and was swaying slightly. I handed her the warm red fluffy bottle which she placed ceremoniously on the stool next to the now melting ice.

'That can wait,' she mumbled, still shivering.

I took a deep breath.

'So, Helen, what do you want to talk to me about?' I asked as gently as I could.

Her head slowly turned sideways, and she looked at me out of the corner of her eyes. In that moment her mannerisms reminded me enormously of my autistic brother and his friends.

'Do you believe in Jesus Christ?' she blurted out in a deep voice. I was somewhat taken aback to hear this noise after the silence, and thought for a moment before answering.

'Yes, yes, I certainly do.'

'Well, what do you think of him?' she questioned impatiently.

I replied without hesitation.

'I think that Christ was a truly remarkable man, filled with love and wisdom, a man who had the ability to heal the sick, and perform what we consider miracles.'

I was not a religious person in the conventional sense. In fact, drawing on my own experiences, I saw little to recommend most churches, or formal religion. I did, however, know a few great characters who were priests, and thanks to my mother's teaching I grew up with the absolute conviction that there exists 'something' I would call God, and that a man called the Christ walked our earth two thousand years ago.

'And what about Cosmo Greene?' she then demanded.

'I don't really know him that well,' I answered. 'But, from what I saw of him at the introductory evening in Guildford, I would say he is a very interesting man.'

She focused her gaze onto her knees. Her skin was white and covered in goose bumps. I noticed her over-washed sweaters were acrylic, and therefore would not help her to get warm. I asked her if she'd like another sweater. She seemed not to hear me. 'Helen, would you like a warm sweater?' I repeated.

She looked up and blinked several times before responding. 'Yes, yes I would.'

'As I walked towards the stairs she called after me, 'It must be pink.'

I possessed only one pink sweater, which had been hand-knitted for me by my mother. It was very precious, and I did not want to lend it to her. Lifting it out of the bedroom chest I hugged its softness next to my face. However, not wishing to add to her distress, I decided to let her wear it.

Time seemed to be hanging heavily, moving very slowly. It was not an easy task sitting with this far-away waif. I could see that she was exhausted to the point of not knowing what she wanted. I ran down the quite narrow and steep stairs which were walled on either side, and jumped the last three which turned the corner at the bottom and opened directly into the kitchen.

'Here we go, Helen – made for me by my lovely mum.'

I handed her the sweater. She stood up. She was tall and

angular, and her appearance was very unkempt and unwashed. I regretted my decision to let her wear my freshly laundered sweater. Much to my surprise she started slowly to remove her own worn-out tops. She wore no bra, her shapeless body was still shivering. I looked away, knowing her gaze was once again fixed upon me.

Then quite suddenly I became aware of a deep-throated growl coming from under the sofa, and saw four saucer eyes staring transfixedly at Helen. Thomas and Ben were cowering, their fur puffed-out, evidently terrified. I have great respect for the intuition of animals, and wondered if they felt threatened by her presence. It was most unlike the friendliest two cats in Hampshire to behave like this. I walked around her as she was pulling my jersey over her head, knelt down and reaching under the sofa lifted the growling ginger bundles out. Strangely they did not protest at all when I put them out of the french windows into the rain. I turned the key in the lock, and placed it behind a plate on the dresser, deliberately hiding it from her. 'Now they are safe,' I thought and felt a sense of relief.

'You are frightened of me!' a deeper and very different voice stated from the other side of the room.

'No, I'm not, Helen,' I answered. 'If anything, I think it's the other way around.'

I walked across to where she was once again kneeling, and put my arms around her bony shoulders, wrapped in the softness of my sweater. This time, I was reassuring myself silently. Her swaying presence was disturbing me. I tried to remember she was just a cold and helpless human, who needed some tender loving care.

'When did you last get a good night's sleep?' I asked.

She replied immediately. 'Three nights ago, I am so tired.'

'I think the best possible thing for you is to lie down in our spare bedroom. It's very cosy and I can sit with you and we can chat, or you can close your eyes and try to sleep until TC gets here. You can stay as long as you like, you know.'

Her eyes lit up, and she blinked several times as if to wake up. Her harsh staring expression softened, and she quietly nodded her head. 'I'd love that,' she sighed, visibly relaxing.

'Good!' I said. 'That's decided then. I'll pop up and put the blanket on. I've got to make a couple of quick business calls from my office, and then we will get you sorted out. If you change your mind about a hot drink, just help yourself.' I pointed into the kitchen. 'Coffee, tea, sugar, milk, mugs, cutlery. Just make yourself at home. I'll only be a couple of minutes.'

As I walked away the guttural voice returned and muttered after me, 'I want to be alone.'

I did not reply. I felt bemused and wondered where on earth TC was.

I ran up the two flights of stairs to my attic office, putting the electric-blanket on as I passed. I sat at my desk and on my business phone made a quick call to a leading advertising agency regarding a promotional idea which was waiting for a go-ahead. Still no decision, behaviour I found typical of many agencies. The client was all for it, but the agency was making a meal out of it, to justify their worth, no doubt. I decided to try TC to find out how much longer he would be. The surgery number was engaged. I went down the stairs hoping that he was on his way. For no apparent reason my heart was thumping against my chest walls, as if I had been running flat out. Pausing at the first floor's little landing bedroom I caught my breath. Everything looked so pretty and inviting; I knew Helen would feel safe there. Anyone would. My big teddy bear was sitting silently in the corner by the bed. I waved playfully at him, my heart now violently out of control and my entire body trembling. This was ridiculous. I took a deep breath and tried to ignore my extraordinary bodily quivering.

As I turned to go down the kitchen stairs, I heard the cutlery drawer rattle. I was pleased at the thought she was making herself a drink. I was about to make my usual jump down the last three stairs into the kitchen when suddenly the dark figure of Helen appeared coming up to meet me with her arms raised above her head. Something hit me in the solar plexus.

My entire body was racked with an excruciating pain.

I gasped. The screaming apparition of Helen now blocked the entrance to the kitchen.

'JESUS CHRIST!' she spat hysterically, climbing further up the stairs to within inches of my face.

'THIS IS IN THE NAME OF JESUS CHRIST!'

I could not make out what was happening.

I forced myself to look down at my body, and, to my horror, I saw the black handle of my biggest and bluntest carving knife sticking out of my lower chest. Her clawlike hands were wrapped around the bloodied handle, twisting and thrusting it into my flesh – deeper and deeper it went. She was driven with a rage that was demonic. A tidal wave of nausea hit me, and my twitching body turned to liquid and started to seep into the staircase.

'HELEN!' I screamed. 'HELEN . . . FOR GOD'S SAKE . . . STOP! H-E-L-E-N!'

Her eyes were wide, glazed and only inches from mine, glaring and brimming over with utter hatred. She heard nothing, lost in her own world.

'JESUS CHRIST! JESUS CHRIST!' She was chanting with each twist of the blade. 'THIS IS TO SCOURGE THE WORLD IN THE NAME OF CHRISTIANITY!' Her voice, masculine, venomous, thundered all around me.

'Oh dear God . . .!' I screamed. 'Please – not again!'

In a flashback of ancient memory, I knew this was not the first lifetime someone had tried to kill me in God's name.

'No!' I cried, feeling myself starting to drift far, far away.

There appeared before me a misty mountainside. A voice calling out into infinity. I WANT TO LIVE . . .

I WANT TO LIVE . . .

DEAR GOD . . .

PLEASE . . .

LET ME LIVE!

My eyes snapped open. I felt her spit on my face.

I wrapped my hands over her blood-drenched, blood-warm, slimy fingers, and started, as delicately and gently as I could, to try to pull the knife out. I felt violently sick.

It all seemed so ridiculous . . . so futile . . . to die at the hands of a screwed-up woman, in the name of the God I so loved.

I inhaled deeply, and a part of me was mentally shouting at myself:

'WAKE UP! COME ON – KEEP AWAKE! DON'T PASS OUT –
KEEP TALKING, KEEP TALKING . . . TALK! TALK! – WAKE UP!
. . . COME ON, JULIE . . . WAKE UP, FOR GOD'S SAKE!'

I was panting short painful breaths. My mouth filled with
the taste of blood and bile. My arm muscles had gone into
spasm with the strain of pulling the knife out, and they shook
violently.

'H-E-L-E-N! YOU DON'T NEED TO DO THIS, THINK OF YOUR
FAMILY, THINK OF YOUR CHILDREN!'

I didn't know if she had any family or children, but was trying
desperately to jolt her into the memory of some sort of normality.
My words fell off her, as if arrows against reinforced steel.

The knife jerked awkwardly out of my gut, blood spraying the
cream walls as she fell backwards. She was considerably taller
than me, and my arms were now above my head. My red-stained
fingers worked frantically on loosening her vice-like grip of the
knife. The rusted tip swayed dangerously from one to the other
of my eyes.

'DIE! DIE!' She was snarling and spitting the words at
me.

'FOR JESUS CHRIST . . . DIE! FOR COSMO GREENE . . .
COSMO . . . COSMO . . . DIE! THIS IS FOR JESUS!'

'Jesus is for love . . . not violence,' a thread of my consciousness whispered.

'I am going to kill you,' was her gleeful response.

Suddenly her image faded. The searing pain was gone.
Everything became still.

I was on a trapeze, swinging amongst the most brilliant stars I had
ever seen, suspended in a vast, black velvet night sky. I rocketed
back and forth, through the heavens. The speed exhilarating
– the vision intoxicating – my entire being exploding with the
excitement of its new-found freedom, beyond the straitjacket
rigidity of its earthly overcoat. There was no sound except
the rhythmic beating of a heart. Time did not exist. Nothing
mattered. I knew some tiny part of me was being stabbed, and
it did not seem to be of any consequence. I was flying. I was
free. I was so incredibly alive. I saw nobody and yet I did not

feel alone. I became aware of thoughts, calm, loving, soothing, beautiful thoughts.

> Be still, beloved.
> You are safe.
> Breathe deeply and slowly.
> Be still and know.
> All is well.

I was watching the surreal scene of my attempted murder from a place where pain did not exist. I could still see Helen's wolf-featured face, with its contorted mouth, foam gathering in the curl of her lips, as she fired venom-filled expletives into the exquisite stillness. I watched her mouth move, fascinated; the sounds leaving her blue lips became a pulsating vibration which I could see, feel and hear. It was a heartbeat – hers, mine – the entire planet united and breathing as One. She was simply a distorted face peering madly down a camera lens. A bolt of delicious heat ricocheted up my spine. My body relaxed. I sighed. I somehow knew I could not die. I was so much more than that crumpled little pile of flesh. I looked directly into her eyes.

'You cannot kill me, Helen,' I whispered.

'I LOVE YOU.'

THE AWAKENING

'I love you,' I whispered.

I did not know where the words came from. She looked shocked. Yet in that moment I felt an overwhelming sense of love and compassion for this person called Helen. I was no longer frightened of her, just incredibly calm as I observed her with total detachment.

So, this was it, was it? This was the dreaded death. The 'D' word that we are not supposed to talk about. The only thing all faiths, colours and creeds can guarantee they are going to experience, yet the very thing we invest the least of our time preparing for. As I witnessed my own 'dying swan' performance, I felt distinctly amused; the scenario was so bizarre, even I, the co-star of the show, found it hard to believe.

With the feeling I had all the time in the world, I surveyed the scene of my own murder. A grey and drizzly Tuesday morning, with me just about managing to stand upright on the steep stairs of TC's cottage, my professional chef's knife in the hands of destructive desolation and a gaping wound spurting and gushing hot blood everywhere. As I looked dispassionately into the face of my would-be assassin, her eyes became doorways drawing me into the world within her.

Immediately I felt as if someone had plugged me into a giant switchboard in the heavens. Every conversation taking place on the earth was moving through me, and I could understand every single sound. The space I was swinging in became a vast screen on which worldly dramas were playing simultaneously. I watched it all – fascinated by the dance of humanity. Transfixed by the immensity and brilliance of creation. To my amazement I found that if I concentrated on any thought I was instantly transported within it. I could watch the screen, and take part in it at the same time. It was as if I were in charge of a zoom lens, and could focus it on anything I wanted at will. An entire planet scuttling about its business lay before me; past, present and future. I thought of the Christ, and immediately found myself kneeling on a rocky hillside looking up at the cross from which he was hanging.

'Master, where are you going? How will we find you when you are gone? Where will you be?' My heart splintered with shards of desolation.

His head lifted, His eyes washed with a blue light, a light radiating from His entire being. A light which flooded the whole landscape, transforming all things solid into shimmering mirages.

He spoke.

'Everywhere you look you will see Me.'

The sound of His voice echoed across the skies.

I understood.

I flew back into the heavens, the screen before me was now filled with a light which shone with a brightness beyond anything I had ever seen. All the images of life blended into a sea of dazzling points of light, trillions of multifaceted gems reflecting a million suns. The cacophony of earthly sound exploded into one crystal-clear note and reverberated throughout the star-filled sky. It was breathtaking. Somehow everything was me. In me and out of me. Light and dark, good and bad, right and wrong. All encompassing. I was part of a magnificent whole. No thing was without meaning. It all made perfect sense in a sea of no-sense. No one was excluded. All was One. For one exquisite moment I saw what was behind the physical masks.

'Helen ... I ... LOVE ... YOU.' I cried out into infinity.

My tiny earthbound mind protested, with sarcasm dripping from its logical passageways. 'Are you totally bloody crazy too?' it demanded angrily. 'You are being murdered, and if I may suggest, this is neither the time nor the place to be declaring your love for your murderess. I can assure you she is not impressed!'

I did not care what my mind thought, in that moment it seemed so tiny. I closed my eyes and floated, at will, back into the vastness of space. I felt myself descending, and I landed gracefully in a magnificent garden filled with exotic blossoms. Divine fragrances and colours filled my senses. The intensity of the light was initially almost too bright to focus on anything. I waited, and became aware of two eastern-looking boys practising some sort of martial art. An elderly man was with them, his orange robes shimmering with a luminosity no earthly fabric that I knew of could match. He waved at me, laughing, and greeted me as if he'd been expecting me. Having left my body being stabbed in rainy England, I wondered what and who exactly he was waving at. I could not see myself, but whatever 'I' consisted of 'I' was able to wave back at him. He laughed again, and told me to watch his class. He did not use words, but I could hear clearly his instructions.

'Move slowly. No need for harm. Always use the attacker's energy against him. Always use the energy against them. It is so simple. So very very simple. Anyone can do it.' He looked in my direction, and nodded. 'You have no need of weapons. It is very simple. It will get you out of any situation.'

One of the boys lunged at the other, as if he was about to thrust a sword, or knife, into his body. The defendant raised an arm to deflect the force of the blow, and moved swiftly out of the way. The attacker fell over. The master bowed low and laughed, pleased with his students. His hands still together, he bowed once more but this time in my direction. 'Very simple, no?' He shrugged his shoulders and laughed once more. The class was over.

A sharp thud crashed into my groin as a knee jerked repeatedly upwards, the knife's now broken tip peppering my upper chest with ragged slits. Our locked arms shook uncontrollably as our combined muscle force waxed and waned. I held her gaze, and sensing the next kick, put theory into practice. I suddenly let go of her hands, ducked, and half-fell, half-stumbled from the stairs and landed on my knees in the kitchen, having turned three hundred and sixty degrees in the process. Without my weight against her, she lurched forward, and fell up the stairs, the knife embedding itself in the carpet instead of me. I scrabbled into a sitting position, and using the wall for support, I started to slide upwards, my shoulders and back squarely against the cold surface, and my blood-stained white leather sneakers wedged against the central kitchen unit to the front of me. My legs trembled and shook, the muscle-power nonexistent, the mental and physical effort so huge, my sweat ran as freely as my blood. The skylight above me swirled and spun like a gaudy fairground ride. Grinding hurdy-gurdy music seemed to screech out of the walls. My knees buckled under the strain, and I started to slip towards the floor again.

'BREATHE! DEEP BREATHS . . . WAKE UP! . . . YOU HAVE TO LEAVE THE HOUSE NOW.'

Clear powerful words sounded in my head. I stopped panting and deliberately drew in a deep breath.

'Who is this speaking to me?' I cried.

Out of the corner of my right eye I glimpsed a blurred movement and sensing the malevolent presence I flung my head to one side, only just avoiding the blade which smashed into the wall, pinching my hair on the way. She was back with a vengeance. My mind was clogged with the mud of fear, and I was at a complete loss what to do next. Being back in my physical body was no fun.

I knew my only chance was to get out of the house, but realised the wound in my chest was very serious, and I doubted whether I would have the strength to get outside. I weighed up the options with a speed which surpassed any computer. I knew I'd locked the french windows, and the hidden key would be impossible to reach without opening myself to further attack . . . and anyway, if I did make it into the back garden, where would I go from there? Fenced in on all sides, and the neighbours probably out, I would still be trapped, albeit in a slightly larger space. I would have to get to the front door. It was my only chance. I felt as if I was about to embark on a hundred-mile assault course. My sweater was heavy with the weight of my own blood and the sickly smell surrounding me was akin to an abattoir on a hot summer day. Revolting as this was, I knew that to pass out would be a tactical error.

Instructions once again arose in my awareness.

'GET UP! GET UP NOW! THAT'S RIGHT . . . REMEMBER . . .
REMEMBER . . . YOU MUST REMEMBER TO BREATHE . . .
DON'T HOLD YOUR BREATH . . . COME ON! . . . GOOD! NOW,
SLOWLY START TO WALK BACKWARDS TO THE FRONT PORCH
. . . HOLD HER AT ARM'S LENGTH . . . USE HER STRENGTH
TO HELP YOU.'

The command was so authoritative there seemed no option
other than to obey. I grabbed both her wrists, and using her
forward lunging power once again, I allowed myself to be
propelled backwards across the kitchen, through the corridor,
up a step and into the tiny hall. Her strength carried me all the
way. I was amazed it had worked a second time, and could hear
the gentle reprimand of my inner voice, 'YE OF LITTLE FAITH!'

Through the hall window I caught my first glimpse of
normality; at the end of our drive, there was a world charging
about its daily business. It was all so ironic, people in their M&S
raincoats out there buying their bread, whilst I am in here being
murdered. I was cheered with the thought that at least when they
find what is left of my body, they will see I had clean, good quality
knickers on . . . I felt that would offer some modicum of comfort
to my family and friends.

I was awakened from my idle daydreaming by the sound
of a butcher's hatchet cleaving a rib of beef. I crashed onto
the stone floor of our tiny entrance hall, the knife embedded
in my mouth. My taste buds recoiled as metallic-flavoured
blood oozed through my teeth. Using both hands she yanked
the offending instrument out. It felt as if all my teeth departed
with the blade.

I closed my blood-filled eyes and was immediately standing
over my body, watching. Eerie whispers reverberated off the
walls. No light. No music. No saviour. No choirs. No angels.
No friends. No voices. No space. No screen. No hope. No thing.
No apparent way out. Perhaps, this was hell.

As I hovered over my body, I recalled the time when I had
attended the Catholic convent. As I was not 'of the faith', the
nuns filled me with tales of what happened to the non-converted
when they died. I remember being terrified of being a 'lost soul',
condemned to 'wander in the mists of time' until I repented.

Their warnings were all the more frightening as I knew I was not christened, and they did not. My five-year-old mind had been filled with nightmarish images of blindly wandering in London smog, sulphurous yellow street lamps illuminating ghosts and ghouls and me crying out for my mother and Max. These nightmares recurred for years even after I left school. However, lost as I was in this moment, I still could not believe in such a fate. The assumption that not being christened means not being a believer is ridiculous. I realised I was taught to love God with a greater understanding and devotion than many of my baptised contemporaries.

I tried to will myself back into the brilliant light. Nothing happened.

'I am dead,' I thought gloomily. 'This must be it.'

I looked disbelievingly at the leaden lump of flesh slumped and bleeding in the hallway. Like a bolt of lightning a question hit me.

'Who is this thinking it's me? I am down there in the hall. Dead.'

'You are not ... please go back,' came the immediate answer.

If I had been in my body I would have jumped out of my skin. As I was already bodiless, this was rather difficult.

'I don't want to go back!' I informed the voice as I searched around me for a way out. I looked everywhere, but there was nothing, no arrow pointing to heaven or hell. What was I expecting? Perhaps an angel, or at least a dead friend or relative to come and meet me and show me the way. I tried again to go back to my vast space, but seemed to be stuck hovering in the hallway, forced to look down on my unconscious body which was still being subjected to the wrath of Helen-from-hell, as she stabbed, kicked and punched it.

What on earth was going on? I was not in a physical body because I could see it on the floor below me, but I knew it belonged to me. This 'me' doing the watching did not seem to have any definable shape but I knew it was still 'me'. It was all so crazy.

'WHO AM I?' I had no voice but somehow I cried out.

'My friend . . . you must go back,' came the immediate response.

'I do not want to go back into that shredded body. I'll be a cripple, I'll be a vegetable, come on . . . NOBODY can survive that!' I answered angrily.

'You will survive . . . and you won't be a vegetable . . . Go back.' The loving voice I heard was neither male nor female.

'How can you be so sure?' I demanded.

'Because . . . my friend, I am you.'

'I am so confused . . . I don't understand.'

'You will.'

'Why can't I go back into the light? Why can't I stay in the vastness, the place where I know, the place where I understand. Why do I have to go back into that horribly limited body and life?'

> Go back, my friend . . .
> And remember . . .
> I love you.

Instinctively I put my arm across my face, devastated to find I was once again in my torn and battered body.

'THIS IS IN THE NAME OF COSMO . . . COSMO . . . C-O-S-M-O . . . COSMO GREENE . . . FOR JESUS . . . I WILL SAVE THE WORLD!' She was still chanting in time with each savage stab, kick and punch.

I lay on the cold hard tiles looking up into her wild face. The soft green curls of the fern given to me for my birthday, neatly placed on the antique hall table, offered a striking contrast as they silhouetted her black shape. Suddenly it felt such an incredible waste of my life, to lie here and die in the constricting web of a stranger's insanity. A parade of loving faces marched in front of me. Friends . . . family . . . Tears started to stream down my cheeks. I never really told them how much I loved them. What a ridiculous life I had lived. Most of it had been spent trying to please people who did not even like me, and in truth I did not much like them. I had tried to fill their pits of desolation. What a fruitless and thankless task. I had hated most of my career. My dreams were lying unfulfilled and empty in broken pieces on the floor next to me. All the unfinished business of my short life crowded into the tiny space of the Hampshire hallway. I had been given the chance of another life by those in mission control. I had to make it.

The thought of TC arriving home any minute and finding the bloody bits of my body blocking his path stirred my leaden body. I began to feel incredibly angry.

'THIS STUPID PATHETIC SCRAWNY OLD BAG . . . DARES TO COME INTO MY HOUSE . . . AND SCREAM HER FILTHY ABUSE . . . WEARING MY FAVOURITE SWEATER . . . USES MY KNIFE TO SAVAGELY TRY TO DESTROY ME . . . IN THE IGNORANT BELIEF THAT THIS SORT OF OUTRAGE MIGHT PLEASE GOD. WHAT SORT OF GOD DO THESE IDIOTS BELIEVE IN?'

She was viciously pulling at my clothes with one hand, and stabbing relentlessly at me with the other. The anger created a surge of strength, and enabled me to divert each potentially lethal thrust of the blade. In the struggle my mother's gold cross flew out of my sweater. At the sight of this, she stopped dead in mid-stroke as if frozen by some invisible force – her head rolled to one side, her eyes glued to the crucifix. This was my chance. I could easily have taken the dripping knife from her hand and turned it against her, but in that never-ending moment I absolutely knew that even faced with such a horrendous and painful death, I could not use violence . . . I could not harm her.

THERE HAD TO BE ANOTHER WAY.

The pain suddenly abated so, seizing the chance, I grabbed at her legs, knocking her off balance. As quickly as I could I slid my back up against the door, my left hand groping behind me for the latch to use as a lever to help heave myself onto my feet. The trance which had held her suspended broke, and seeing that I might escape she let out a high-pitched scream and hacked at my left wrist, cutting into it several times, in an attempt to stop me.

'YOU ARE GOING TO DIE!' she reminded me once again.

Another wave of energy rushed through me and I stood fully

upright, momentarily immune to the state of emergency my body was in.

The knife speared towards my face.

'Intercept it with your right hand,' came the now familiar whispered instruction.

'I CAN'T DO THAT . . . I AM RIGHT-HANDED . . . I NEED THIS HAND! WHO ARE YOU?' I pleaded.

'You know who I am . . . Your hand will still work . . . I promise.'

I lifted my hand. The plump palm absorbed the blow as though made of butter. Using two hands and her entire body weight she pushed against me with all her might. I blinked in disbelief as the solid steel blade bowed like a boomerang. I knew it was impossible for a knife blade to bend . . . but everything happening was impossible . . . the whole bloody morning was impossible.

Everything was beyond my comprehension. I closed my fingers around the blade, and started to twist it out of her grip. It felt as if I had plunged my fist into a jar of acid. My left hand fumbled frantically with the brass latch behind me. The door opened slightly. As she freed the knife from my ripped palm, nerve endings in my hand, arm and shoulder contracted instantaneously, making movement impossible. She kicked the door shut.

I was terrified, overwhelmed and exhausted. I screamed.

'Dear God . . . Get me out of here. Don't let me die like this. Get me out of here! GOD! I know you exist. I beg you . . . Get me out of here.'

'Who do you think got you into this?' whispered the soft voice.

'I don't know, I don't know, I don't know. Just get me out.' I gibbered.

'Why?'

'BECAUSE IT'S HELL . . . THAT'S WHY!'

'It only seems that way. It is, in reality, bliss.'

'You call THIS bliss?'

'Yes, I do.'

'I don't understand.'

'You will.'

'What the hell is going on? When will I understand? When will I wake up?'

'Sooner than you think.'

I half-turned towards the door using my right hand to support me, my left hand yet again pulling at the lock. There was a loud crack as the parsley-chopping weapon split into the back of my right hand, pinning me to the door.

I heard her screaming at me, 'DIE, YOU BITCH.'

Using my left hand I managed to free my right hand. I flung the door open, knocking her off balance, and fell wildly into the open air. Her bloodstained hand lurched after me – I slammed the door on it. I called out with all the strength I could muster, my voice choking with blood and terror, the tone shrill and panic-riddled.

'HELP ME ... PLEASE ... SOMEBODY ... ANYBODY ... HELP ME!'

I looked down the drive to the distant mirage of the busy road, and managed to focus on some passers-by. For a wonderful moment I thought one of them might rescue me.

'HELP ME, PLEASE?' I begged of them, my arms outstretched. 'In the name of God somebody help me?' The intensity of my scream was deafening to me.

They ran away. All of them ran away.

My legs collapsed and I fell to the wet gravel, sobbing in total despair.

The inner voice started again.

'Come on, Julie, come on ... you've got this far, don't stop now ... get to the road ... you can make it to the road.'

I started to crawl and wriggle on my belly towards the distant horizon. A thump in my shoulder blade sent my entire right side into the air in a spasm of grotesque contortions. I was not alone.

I tried to call out again, but my voice had gone. People were still running away, and my will to live was ebbing away as fast as my blood. There was no stillness now, no guiding voice. Everything was fading into blackness as the sun of my life appeared to be setting. She was trying to pull the knife out of my shoulder blade. The pain woke me up once again. The muscles in my back had clamped around the cold metal. It was stuck. I continued to crawl along the sheer rock face of the drive, my feet finding enough purchase to slide me along inch by inch. Her foot thudded into my spine as she heaved the blade free. The relief was so huge I was able to stagger to my knees, and then wobbled violently to my feet as if totally drunk. With the very last trickle of physical effort, I threw myself into the entrance to the road, rolling helplessly onto my back. I had nothing left. I knew a car must stop now, or run over me. I was wrong. They drove round me.

I watched lifelessly as she slowly took the tip of the blade in one hand, and the handle in the other. Her movements slow and deliberate. The animal senses within her knew it was time for the kill, and she was squealing with delight, 'Now you die, scum.'

She stood astride my shaking body. I was enshrined in blackness.

The knife see-sawed towards my throat.

'DIE ... DIE ... DIE!' she sang. Her lyrics were rather repetitive. I closed my eyes. There was no more pain. A ridiculously optimistic thought popped up. 'Look at it this way, kid – from here on things can only get better.'

'Off with her head,' said the King. The crowd gasped.

THE RESCUE

The Driveway

'**P**ut the knife down, love.' A quietly spoken man's voice drifted onto the edge of my nightmare. 'That's right, put it down, love.' It must be time to get up, I thought, rolling over to look at the alarm clock and reaching out for TC. I screamed. I was lying in a bath of razor-blades and blood steeped in a pain beyond belief. I could not work out where I was. TC was not there. My eyes could not focus. I forced them to open wider, and the blur became a grey sky. My face was wet with the mist of drizzle falling towards it. Strangely distorted white faces were peering at me. I tried to speak to them, but no sound came out, just a stream of red warm liquid. I heaved.

'No, love . . . don't do that!' came the calm voice again. 'Put it down . . . that's it, love.'

My vision cleared and I could see the tall skinny figure of a woman dancing a grotesque jig in the entrance to our driveway. She had an enormous carving knife in her hand, and a young man was trying to take it off her. She did not resist.

He came towards me. I shuddered.

'It's all going to be OK, love.' He sounded frightened. His lovely face was inches from mine. 'I'm going to go and call an ambulance.' My memory returned. This was no dream.

I remembered the portable phone which had been in my hands when I came down the stairs and managed to splutter a few words to this young man indicating it was somewhere on the floor of the kitchen. He ran towards the cottage. The prancing dancing madwoman returned and started to attack me again. She had a small vegetable knife in her hand. My young hero returned and disarmed her once more.

I was bleeding profusely. Muscles in my back and chest were

violently pumping and throbbing; it felt as if I had ornamental fountains inside me, shooting my blood in every direction. Lying on my back, I was choking, and my neck felt adorned with a necklace made of ice. I could feel the cold air probing into the ragged slices in my throat. I slowly heaved my reluctant body into the emergency position, pushing my chin down into my chest to stem the flow of acidic liquid, frantically trying to remember my Red Cross first-aid course. Of the considerable crowd now gathered, no one helped. I could hear terror in their voices ... 'Don't move her ... Don't touch her ... We may say or do something wrong ... We may get blamed ... We may kill her ... She's going to die anyway, why ruin a good jacket keeping her warm?'

It was so dreadful, the whole surrealistic scene became funny. It was comforting to know that my sense of humour was not yet dead. I considered the most sensible thing I could possibly do was to remain as still as possible, and keep my mind off the subject of pain. I imagined the wonderful Barry Humphries standing over me, dressed in drag as Dame Edna. 'Her' heavily made-up face grinned above my head, 'Save your juices, darling,' she giggled. John Cleese ducked and weaved furiously behind her. 'Come on, it's only a flesh wound,' he encouraged. I laughed. I listened to all the conversations babbling away over my head, and mentally took part in some of them in order to stay alert. I did not have the energy to speak, so in the ensuing moments I composed letters to the people who were gathered in the driveway. It kept my mind off the fact I was bleeding to death surrounded by a lot of squabbling people and helped find an outlet for the utter frustration I felt with them all.

As my body lay dying I began to feel rather relaxed. The worst had happened, and I had glimpsed a magnificent ocean of consciousness beyond the clutter of daily life. The knife had pierced a hole in something deeper than my flesh. Inadvertently I had found a doorway into another part of me. It was not a question of death as an absolute end, more a feeling of moving dimensions and new beginnings. However, whatever it was I had experienced out there in the vastness, it was evidently not the moment to pack my earthly bags. Even though the odds for remaining in my physical overcoat were heavily stacked against me, I knew that I would live. After all, something, someone out there on the other side of the door marked 'death' made it very clear I had to return. It appeared that I was the only one around who thought so.

Knock knock . . .
Who's there?
DEATH . . .
Can't you see I'm busy right now?

The Driveway

Dear Crowd Of Onlookers,

Whichever one of you it was who told me that the ambulances were on strike – thanks a bundle. As I was aware that I might be heading for imminent departure from the planet, I did not feel this was the sort of thing someone in my condition should be hearing. It did not help my morale.

I suppose that it is a fact of this interesting life of ours that accidents always attract a variety of types of onlooker. I guess that I was just unlucky today, as none of you seemed to know what to do.

As for the man who did not want to help keep me warm with his jacket, as 'the blood might ruin it', I promise, I would have bought you a new one.

All I really wanted was one of you to hold my hand and tell me everything was going to be fine and maybe stroke my hair, or even encourage me. Perhaps while you were all arguing amongst yourselves you forgot that loving and positive behaviour goes a long way in times of stress.

I am also aware that it took some of you great courage to stop, and that you had a wonderful desire to help. Thank you.

This victim's guidelines for potential AO's (Accident Onlookers) are as follows:

Dying people are not usually deaf.

Dying people are not always going to die – and even if they do, they are not as dead as you may think they are.

When the victim is trying to get into the emergency position – help her/him.

Don't tell them anything negative.

Be gentle and loving.

And lastly . . .

If you cannot help . . . then fuck off!

Thank you for your attention,

She Who Survived In Spite Of You All.

The Driveway

Dear Policeman,

I know that I probably looked and felt dead to you, but the fact of the matter is, I was still alive.

Telling the gathered congregation 'She's a Gonna' did nothing to motivate them, or me, into the urgent action required to save my life.

Perhaps in the future you could add a clause to the policeman's manual?

'Gonnas might still be Goers.'

Gottit?

Good.

Yours,

The Little 'Goer' In The Driveway.

The Driveway

Dear Well-spoken Lady,

I don't think it occurred to you that it took seemingly every last drop of concentration and effort on my part to give you the phone number of my closest 'person to contact in case of an emergency'.

I was deeply grateful to you for going to telephone him for me, and equally dismayed that you came back to me, as I was lying bleeding to death, to tell me the number was engaged. Thanks!

Yours, in utter frustration,

The Woman Lying In The Drive Entrance of a Small Cottage in Hampshire.

PS – Next time you witness an accident, I suggest that the

most helpful thing for you to do is to run like hell in the opposite direction; almost everyone else did.

I recognised the familiar purr of TC's BMW and a slight screech of the tyres as it abruptly stopped. Moments later I heard him shout my name, with all the intonation of a thousand questions.

'J-U-L-I-E ?-!-?-!'

I tried to answer him, my heart leaping for joy at his arrival, but the vocal chords did not want to play.

Quickly he assessed the damage, talking quietly to me, and explaining what needed to be done. It was such a relief to be treated in a positive and loving manner. I could not let him know I was conscious of every word he uttered. I prayed he could see that I was 'in'.

'I am going into the house to find a blanket to wrap you in, so that we can get you to hospital. I will only be a few seconds. You are seriously injured and need emergency treatment, but we'll get you there, and I won't leave you. Keep as still as you can, and concentrate on your breathing . . . it's going to be OK, Jules.' His voice trailed away.

I heard him running off down the drive. I could feel my shoulder blade still thumping and pumping blood out onto the road. It was hard to believe there was anything left to come out. I tried to recall some basic biology on how much blood the average human could lose before passing out, or on. Fortunately I could not remember.

TC slid onto his knees next to me, somehow rolling me into a blanket.

'What news of the ambulance?' he demanded without taking his eyes off me.

'Well, we called one, Dr C, but they're on a go-slow, so it will be at least twenty minutes,' a slightly nervous and high-pitched man's voice answered.

'Let's get her in your police car then,' came TC's immediate reply. His voice different. Strong. Full of hope.

'We can't do that, it's against the rules to carry accident victims,' answered the unmistakeable voice of the law.

'Then help me get her into my car then,' he shouted with obvious frustration. 'I want a police escort front and back.'

The now familiar well-spoken lady's voice piped up. 'Don't you think you should wait for a second opinion.'

'Yes, wait for a doctor,' added another do-gooder.

I groaned inwardly, and wished fervently I could have stood up and punched them all on the nose, but TC did it for me.

'JUST GET OUT OF THE WAY . . . ALL OF YOU!' he implored. 'I am a doctor, and I don't need a second opinion to know she won't last twenty minutes, we've got to get her to casualty . . . so if you won't help me, just FUCK OFF!'

I cheered.

His words shook the onlookers out of their apathy, and the mumbled negative comments faded away. I couldn't believe people could be so thick. I felt as though I was in the middle of a Monty Python sketch.

'I'll help you,' a young man's soft voice whispered. 'We'll put her in the back of my car. Even though it's against the rules, I'll take the consequences.'

'You take her feet,' TC instructed, not wasting time on niceties. I felt myself being lifted into the air.

'Gently now . . . that's it . . . very gently.'

I hurt everywhere, my eyes forced open with the pain. I could see a large police Volvo with its blue light flashing hypnotically.

There were other cars parked haphazardly in the drive entrance, and quite a few people hanging around. I could just see the outline of the cottage, and wondered if I would ever see it again. I prayed that this bedevilled woman had not discovered the cats. It was all so unbelievable. I blinked hard several times, hoping I would wake up, but I was definitely being lowered into the back of a police car, and TC was holding me in his arms. The car door slammed as I embarked on one of the longest and most uncomfortable journeys of my life.

I felt incredible nausea as the police car sped off. TC had his arms wrapped around me, I could feel the warmth of his body and the accelerated beating of his heart. His hand was held firmly over the hole in my chest. It felt as though a hot-water bottle was strapped to me.

'Come on, Jules ... keep breathing ... IN ... OUT ... IN ... OUT ... that's it,' he encouraged me as best he could.

'This is not the way to Guildford,' he blurted out to the driver, his voice once more showing its earlier signs of panic.

'No, I'm heading for Cosham,' the policeman replied quickly. 'The traffic is tailing back for miles on the A3 into Guildford. I've just come from there, so I know we will never make it ...'

'... in time to save her life,' were the unspoken words which finished the sentence.

'I can get you to the hospital at Cosham much faster. I'll get the emergency department on the carphone and you can tell them what you need.'

TC took the intercom from the driver, and proceeded to speak with the accident and emergency department of Cosham Hospital. He described my injuries. The list sounded endless, and I was reliving each stab while he spoke, an icy blanket of fear crawling up my body. Death itself no longer frightened me – pain and suffering however was not an attractive proposition. Lying in the back of this speeding car, the pain was almost unbearable. It seemed so unfair that I should still be conscious.

'No, no, we don't need to meet the ambulance, it's too late for that. Her veins have collapsed so they won't be able to give her a transfusion ... it will have to be a cut down. No, I don't know her blood group.' He coughed, and asked the driver how much longer before we arrived.

'Five minutes should do it, Doctor,' came the reply.

'Five minutes,' TC told the hospital. 'Yes, fine ... OK ... over and out.'

He leaned forward, passing the receiver back to the driver, glancing anxiously at his watch.

I felt myself lurching forwards as the car screamed to a halt.

'The ambulance, Doctor ... shall we transfer her?' asked the driver, unaware of the conversation of moments earlier.

'NO ... NO,' TC replied impatiently. Winding down the window he called out to the ambulance crew, 'It's too late for a transfusion, we cannot move her again so we'll keep going. Thanks anyway.'

I fell back into the rear seat as we accelerated away, and found myself hurtling down a long black tunnel. There was no air and little light. I was panting and gasping for breath. From some far away land I heard the faintest whisper of TC's voice.

'Come on, Jules . . . we're almost there . . . don't give up now. Come on, breathe . . . IN . . . OUT . . . IN . . . OUT . . . come on, Julie . . . you can do it! I want you here . . . Don't go . . . Please don't go!'

I tried to will myself away from the gravitational pull of the black hole, but it had no effect. Every part of my physical and emotional body was totally exhausted. I couldn't be bothered any more. I'd had enough for one lifetime, even the instructions to stay meant nothing. 'They' could all get on with it. Everything went dark and silent.

A Doctor's Tale

'I'll see if she's still at home,' I told Helen as she asked if she could spend the rest of the morning with Julie. A 'Yes' instead of a 'No', and all our lives profoundly changed.

Jill's face at the consulting room door was white. My patient suddenly invisible. I turned, rose and followed her into the corridor. I could hardly hear her words.

'A patient was driving past your house. She said, "Does Dr C know there is a woman lying dead in the gateway of his drive?".'

It is true, time and the world *do* stop. In that moment I could see it all. Oh no . . . not that. Anything but that. Please God, oh please, no . . . We ran for the car, bleak emptiness in the space where my heart should be.

I could see it wasn't Julie, but just a pile of clothes. But then . . . it was a body, the life-force gone, the shrunken form of someone I didn't know. Thank God, not Julie. I bent over, of course it wasn't her, but then she spoke to me.

JULIE.

It is a strange thing to be split in three. The small self, paralysed, overwhelmed, despairing and in shock, in total disbelief. Then the doctor, taking in the pallor of the skin, the shock, the veins too collapsed to take a drip. The wounds, the pool of blood, the ebbing life. The feeble pulsation of blood vessels exposed to the air in a jagged slash across the neck. She wasn't going to make it. Far from the nearest help, there was no line to life. But then a voice within. 'Twenty-three minutes,' it said, clear and sure. Something came alive.

I ran into the house. Helen was squatting by the patio doors, rocking gently, staring out through the glass, somewhere far

93

away. I ran on, out into the garage. Against the wall a pile of old blankets. And an axe. Coldly, I saw the blow, her head spiralling from a single running backhand as I retraced my steps. But I could not reach for it. Not right, no time, who knows? 'What have you done?' was all I struck her with.

'I want a police escort front and back, we can't wait for the ambulance – we've got to get her to casualty.'

'Get into the back with her,' the young police driver said. 'It's breaking the rules, but . . .'

Then blue lights, 120 mph on the dial, blurred town and countryside. Voices on the car radio – exchanging information. I cradled Julie. 'Don't go,' I said. 'I want you here. Just shut your systems down.' I did not question how. A lifetime passed. As the hospital gates appeared Julie slid away. The minute hand said 19. 4 more left. Helping hands. Her dead weight. Struggling up the steps. Please, God, hurry. I watched as the surgeon worked the sharp metal tip of a long plastic cannula through her chest wall, searching for the superior vena cava just above her heart. Lifelines connected. The minute hand said 23. The miracle began.

Overcome, I flung my arms in gratitude around a slightly bewildered, suddenly pink-cheeked police driver. After all this, I knew Julie had to be alright. I somehow sensed that I was playing merely a small part in something much greater, even though I had no conception of what it might be.

THE INTENSIVE

'JULES! JULES!' I heard a familiar voice call. 'We are there. We've got you there. You're safe now, Jules.'

Someone was stroking my head. It was TC.

Ah yes! I regained my consciousness, which unfortunately involved regaining my memory. Tuesday morning, minding my own business, got stabbed, crawled away, got stabbed lots more, people ran away, danced through the heavens, some bright spark put me back in the cosmic lift and pressed 'Ground Floor – Exit 10: Extra Loving Care For Souls In Distress', lift doors opened, lying in the drive, busybodies staring, policemen, voices, rain, cold, damp, pain, excruciating pain. Oh yes. I remembered.

The door opened, whitely clad arms reached into the back of the car in which I was lying. Soft drizzle fell onto my upturned face as I was extracted expertly from my cocoon and carried towards the dark entrance of the land of needles, knives and nasty smells. I shuddered violently. The warmth of TC's loving hold had been ripped away, and the biting cold seeped into my bones. Softly spoken voices issued commands as an army of worker-ants crawled all over me, prodding and probing.

I watched attentively as the medical team worked on my broken body. They squeaked and slid over the shiny floors, often bumping into each other on the way. I hoped they knew what they were doing. In that moment I regretted having lived with a doctor, recalling the many horror stories he had told me about his days as a houseman working in casualty. This did me no good at all, so I directed my thoughts to *Dr Kildare* instead, and contemplated how, at the age of five, I had found Richard Chamberlain so gorgeous. This demonstrated clearly that my ability to fall for the wrong type started young.

A fresh-faced nurse waved a large pair of scissors under my nose. 'I'll have to cut them off,' she declared to her colleagues. I recoiled at the sight of the open blades, which moved off in the direction of my feet. They crunched through the denim of my jeans, the icy air following in their wake, eager to attack my vulnerable and exposed flesh. My sweater was also deftly removed.

Scrubbed fingers removed the cross and chain from my ripped neck, and handed it to an ashen-faced TC, who was still at my side.

Hospital Accident and Emergency

Dear Emergency Staff,

Thank you, with all my heart, thank you all for your efforts in the face of duty.

One of the strange things about your jobs must be that you have no time for judgements about the life you are fighting to save, other than the necessary medical observations. The bodies laid out in front of you, in their various states of disrepair, could belong to some real A1 shits. Perhaps there are times when you would be doing the world a favour if you went about your emergency work a little more slowly than usual, although I have no doubt you could be sued for even thinking such thoughts.

A casual observation, guys, which you may find helpful in the future is, you all seem to suffer from the same problem as accident onlookers. JUST BECAUSE I HAVE MY EYES CLOSED DOES NOT MEAN I AM DEAF. Those little 'medical speak' asides do nothing for my waning spirit. I can hear them all . . .

'She's lost almost all her circulating blood.'

'If we don't get some in her soon we'll lose her.'

'I'll have to take a sample.'

'Her veins have collapsed, we will have to do a cut down.'

'No . . . too late, get a cannula into her.'

'Severe internal damage and bleeding, we'll have to open her up.'

'Her jugular is exposed, keep her head still!'

'Looks like her liver's the problem.'

'We are losing her!'

I can see your point of view – I realise you have got to speak to each other and that there is no time for pleasantries, but can you see mine? Perhaps you don't realise I am conscious, and still able to feel pain? Finally, my friends, I am not intending to go anywhere, so you won't lose me. I have travelled light years already this morning, so I am simply resting my eyes, and to be frank, I prefer not to see what you are up to. It would seem that I have no choice but to leave my body in your clinical care. If I could, I would cross my fingers, cross my heart, and hope not to die.

She On The Slab.

'Jules,' TC whispered, his face next to mine. 'How can I contact Jenny?'

My thoughts immediately jumped to Spain and for one magical moment I could feel the heat of its winter sun, and was sitting on a flower-filled terrace gazing out into the blue, blue sky. My mother's voice was giving me a phone number, 'This is for emergencies,' she had explained. 'Write it down in case you need to get in touch with us.' I told him it was in my address file, although I couldn't remember exactly where I had written it. I knew it was the number of the kind souls who had arrived at our villa bringing the news of Herbert's first grandchild only days earlier. They would shortly be facing my parents with news of a very different nature. What an irony.

'Who else shall I call?' TC asked gently. I breathed in deeply, closing my eyes. It was such an effort to think and speak. I told him to get Hank, my uncle.

'Name?' a starched white voice demanded impatiently, interrupting us.

''Ooee 'Imes,' I spluttered in response, barely able to open my mouth. I retched.

'Julie Chimes,' TC repeated quickly.

'Self-inflicted, I assume,' the 'Lemon-Lips' from behind the clipboard continued, barely waiting for the reply. She looked as if she was holding a wedge of sharp citrus fruit in her mouth.

Unable to voice my outrage in that moment, I used all my strength to give her my 'Pram-Look'. When I was a baby, strangers would ask my mother to turn my pram away from them, as they didn't like the way I looked at them. This became known in my family as the 'Pram-Look', and definitely disconcerted people. I imagined her sitting on the toilet, farting ... childish, but a great way of dealing silently with pompous people. I dictated another letter and I felt a lot better. My, what a busy morning I was having.

Accident & Emergency Dept

Dear Casualty Sister with the Clipboard,

I understand fully that, in your difficult job, it is necessary to make fast assessments of injuries to us poor souls being carried in to your sterile world. I also appreciate the fact that you have probably been working for far too many hours, and tiredness is colouring your view of life. I do not, however, understand how you could begin to think that my wounds were self-inflicted, and, even if they were, to voice your opinion in my hearing was not the most tactful day's work you have ever done.

You must witness some very determined suicide attempts, 'Lemon-Lips', to have allowed this instant diagnosis of my situation. I will always remember your frost-bitten reception on my first, and I hope last, hospital visit.

I do agree, in the calm sea of contemplating my highest truth, that all that happens to the individual in this lifetime is of their own magnificent creation.

Right now, however, I am in no mood for such expansive thoughts, and therefore feel unbelievably pissed off with you. Is this what I have stayed alive for?

Yours most sincerely,

Admission 246, Day 1.

'You'll have to leave now, Doctor,' one of the nurses announced, taking TC's arm.

I called out, not wanting his loving presence to be removed. 'I'll be right here,' he reassured, trying to smile, as he was ushered out. I felt very small, very cold, and incredibly lonely.

I lay naked and shivering on a hard, narrow trolley, in a fluorescent-lit corridor outside the see-through doors of the operating theatre. I could not believe it was possible to be so cold, my body started to tremble violently, so totally out of control I thought I would fall onto the hard squeaky-clean floor. I could almost hear the newscaster's serious voice report, 'Julie Chimes died this morning in a Hampshire hospital after falling from a stretcher whilst awaiting surgery. Her death was caused by head injuries, and had nothing to do with her multiple stab wounds.'

Accident & Emergency

Dear Person with Hot Hands,

I have no idea who you were, possibly you were a member of the medical team, or just someone who happened to be passing.

You held my feet when I was lying in that strange disinfectant-filled corridor shivering to death. I could not believe that it was possible to feel so cold, so frightened, and so utterly alone.

The warmth that flowed out of your hands into my blood-less body was incredible. The heat of your compassion and love washed over me. I felt as though I was wrapped in a shawl of the softest material, woven with magic.

I begged you not to go away, but my mouth could not form the words. For all of the medical attention my smashed body received, I will always remember your touch.

Love is a transmittable ease.

Yours, truly with thanks,

Cold Feet.

'What is your name, Julie?' A bright-young-thing asked me.

''Oolee,' I answered quickly.

'Very good,' he encouraged, wrapping me up in what looked like aluminium foil. 'This will get you warmer.'

It didn't, and I continued to shake, rattle and roll, my entire body convulsing in its oven-ready wrap. I entered the twilight zone. What a cold and lonely place. All the latest technology whirring away, but the most important life-saving device missing. The medical profession does not yet realise that love is one of the most important things to help us to return or cross the bridge called death. The milling white-coats are obsessed with the fact that I might have forgotten my name. I have been asked at least twenty times, and each time I answer correctly, although it sounds odd, ''OOLEE 'IMES.' Secretly, I've got no idea any more who I am, but I'm not going to let them know that, as I do not think it will help matters if we are all confused. They should realise that I have more important things to worry about than my diction and my given name. Little matters like maybe I'm going to die, and I haven't even begun to live.

'She's going into shock,' I heard a voice behind me yell. Well yes, I suppose that was a fair assessment of my condition, I was indeed shocked, and stunned, at the events so far this morning. I tried to focus on the masked figure hovering over me. 'We're taking you into the operating theatre in a few moments, where we'll soon have you sorted out. Now, can you tell me your name?' he enquired with the patronising tone of voice so prevalent in the professions. I was slightly anxious that he did not seem to know who I was. It was not a good time to remember jokes about good news and bad news. The bad news is we've removed the wrong leg ... the good news is the other one's getting better. Once again I repeated my name as best I was able between clattering, chattering teeth. Just a label which did not belong to me anymore.

'Well done,' he droned. 'Now I'm going to ask you to count to ten.'

I never realised this hospital business was so intellectual.

'ONE ... TWO ... THREE ... FOOOOUUUURRRR ... ZZZZZZZZZZZZ ...'

With great difficulty I opened my eyes, and tried to make some sense out of the darkness. The heat was incredible, and I became aware of groans and moans all around me. I tried to move, but it appeared I was strapped down. A searing pain ripped through my body. I cried out, the agony bringing me out of my drowsy state. I idly wondered if this was hell, although on reflection, it was probably heaven. As a child I had often dreamt of heaven being a large hospital, with thousands of rows of iron-framed beds filled with groaning occupants being tended by nurses with enormous wings. After all, people die due to bodily dysfunction, and it seemed obvious to my four-year-old mind that heaven would get them well. My dream job had been to cheer up the ranks of wounded, who were always wrapped in blood-stained bandages, and wanted me to find them cigarettes. I often woke up exhausted – heaven didn't have many tobacconists.

I could make out the odd blurred shape, seemingly floating past my feet, and was becoming so convinced I was in hospital heaven, I half expected a four-year-old kid looking like me to pop up and ask me if I wanted a smoke. I heard the muffled sound of a telephone ringing, accompanied by a great deal of high-pitched bleeping. Heaven was evidently a place of high technology. I couldn't move my head, so I turned my eyes to the left. There was a wall. I looked to the right and saw a bright green ball bounce across a screen.

Blip . . . Bounce . . . Blip . . . Bounce . . . Blip . . . Bounce . . . Blip . . . Bounce . . .

Another wave of pain racked my body.

BLIP . . . BOUNCE . . . BLIP . . . BOUNCE . . . the green dot wobbled. It was reflecting my heart rate . . . I panicked. It showed.

BLIP! BLIP! BLIP! BLIP! BLIP! BLIP! BLIP! BLIP!

A stampede of running feet and bleepers was heading straight for me. My tongue was super-glued to the top of my mouth, so I was unable to ask where I was, as the angels of Emergency Ward Heaven fluttered around me. I decided to try and ask for a drink. I was parched. The sound came out as though I had a severe speech impediment. 'OUGHTA.' Someone must have understood, because a lemon-flavoured lump of cotton-wool was dragged along my lips. I threw up immediately.

An eastern-looking man stood over me. I demanded to know

where I was, why, and what had happened. No sound came out
of me, but fortunately he could mind-read.

'Yew er en op-ital. Yew er nut welly rell. Dam-adge river,
foatscut, rotsoff uvver plobrems. Yew er welly ruckie tubby
arrive. Yew er member?'

I told him I was not a member, had no intention of becoming
a member, and that I wanted to leave, but only unintelligible
grunts left my lips. My only chance of freedom shrugged his
shoulders, looked more confused than I felt, and left.

I was once again alone in my twilight world. In that dark
hothouse environment my memory cranked back into motion.
Nothing in my life had trained me for this. It seemed incredible
that Helen had so desperately wanted me dead . . . and, to do
the deed with my own bloody great carving knife. That really
got me. I've always hated knives, even the sound of one being
sharpened sets me on edge – the reason my carving collection
remained blunt. The thought of what extra damage she could
have achieved had the knife been sharper was abhorrent. Given
the choice, I think I would have preferred to be shot. I didn't
even have the comfort of knowing her motive. Did she just
want me out of the way, her cuckoo-mentality wanting my
life with TC? Or was she locked in another reality, some sort
of time-warp where I represented something which had to be
destroyed? Maybe when she put my sweater on she thought she
was me and therefore believed she was annihilating everything
she hated about herself? Had I become the equivalent of Dorian
Gray's portrait? I wished I knew – the mind tends to relax when
it can explain the actions of others, but there was no relaxation
for my mind. It was turning somersaults.

What had I done in my life that was so dreadful I deserved
this? Had I done anything? Was I guilty of some heinous crime,
or was I an innocent victim? And, if this was punishment, who
had passed sentence on me? My mind reeled with the force of
so many unanswered questions. Would I ever again be able to
access the wondrous experiences that lay beyond my physical
body, or would I have to wait until I died again? Why had I
been made to come back?

My thoughts were interrupted when two nurses stood at the

side of my bed and took my temperature and blood pressure, studiously plotting the results onto a clipboard chart.

'Very good,' the scribe muttered to her companion as they walked away, squeaking on the institutional floor.

My senses were becoming more awake; the light got brighter and the sounds around me sharper. The strange ripples of acute discomfort also became more frequent.

'Intensive care ... yes ... can you tell me your relationship with the patient? ... Fine ... Her condition's critical, but stable,' I heard a woman's voice announce. Paranoia perhaps, but I had the spooky feeling they were talking about me. The phone rang many times, with almost the same response on each occasion, but sometimes 'comfortable' replaced 'stable'. It was an unorthodox way of finding out how I was doing, but better than nothing. Had I been able to answer the phone, 'comfortable' was the last word I would have used to describe my condition.

Intensive Care

Dear God,

Today I called for You to save me. I don't think I've ever really asked for anything from You with quite such passion. In fact, I was getting so desperate I called for Your Son too. Looking back on the events of this morning I can see there were conflicting messages beaming their way to You. On the one hand, there was that rabid fruit cake, carving abstract geometric patterns into my torso ... in Your Name just for good measure, and come to think of it JC's too, and on the other hand, there was me asking Father and Son to rescue me. These occasions must make Your job difficult. I suppose it's normal for us humans to contemplate Your existence seriously when faced with death, but then, I always did leave my homework till the last minute. I admit, it all seemed a little late to be thinking about the meaning of life.

Perhaps it was You who filled my being with the strongest feelings of love and compassion for this pathetic woman doing her utmost to destroy me. I can't imagine anyone else putting such thoughts into me, and even if it wasn't You, who else would believe that I could tell my own would-be murderess that I loved her and that she couldn't kill me? I couldn't even believe myself, but the words just popped out. Unfortunately she did not seem to hear me; she was too intent on making a human colander out of me.

I suspect I have many things to learn from this morning's events. After all, I am still here, lying in an overheated twilight zone called intensive care. I feel dreadful, so I am not really sure whether to thank or to curse You for my continued presence on this planet. Strange as it seems, somehow, somewhere, deep within my being I know all is well. Perhaps, one day, You will help me to understand?
I still love You,
Julie.

Intensive Care

My dearest Mum,
Today you have been much in my thoughts. I had an accident this morning. Don't panic ... I'm still in one piece – just!

The most important things to tell you are that I am going to survive, and that I had clean underwear on. I made it. I've got more stitches in me than Frankenstein's bride, but I am told the surgeons got grade A in needlework. Don't worry – the worst has happened. What a way to find out your airport fears were founded!

Mum, I have the strangest feeling no one could have stopped what happened to me – for some reason it was meant to occur. I do not begin to understand why, but I pledge the remainder of this thing called life to finding out.

I hope you get here soon.

Did I ever tell you how much I love you?
Julie

Time had no meaning in this grey world. I tried to keep tabs on it by remembering the blood pressure and temperature checks that took place every fifteen minutes, but I was adrift in a nauseous sea of lime-green consciousness, and the iron-framed hospital bed was but a flimsy raft, bucking and tossing me around. I realised time was rather a comforting peg on which to hang the mind; without it, everything swirled into a cauldron of bubbling nonsense.

'How are we?' A smiling face interrupted my force ten sea-of-life crossing. She could see, evidently, there was more than one of me, which made the fact I saw four of her less worrying.

'You've got some visitors, dear,' she continued, her face inches from mine.

I squinted as I tried to focus on her swaying white hat, and the two blurred shapes standing behind her. She moved away, I blinked away the cling-film cover on my eyeballs and saw TC. Behind him, upright, white-faced with a clenched jaw, my greatest friend, my uncle Hank. Two of my favourite men. It was so good to see them. They both looked pretty shattered as they stood, unable to speak, their eyes trying desperately not to reflect their feelings as they quickly scanned my mummified body for the visual confirmation of the morning's damage. They gave nothing away as they spoke softly to each other and to me. The only thing I learnt from them was the time. It was 8 p.m., but I was in no fit condition to describe the last ten hours of my day, nor could I hear about theirs. That did not matter, it was a great comfort to know they were there, forming a bridge of love for me to walk across, back into the world of physical reality. They left after a short time, promising to return the next day.

I lay staring at the ceiling, wide awake. An intense purple-coloured light hovered over the length of my body, slowly moving towards me until it melted into the white sheet that covered me. An intense heat was seeping into every cell of my body. I started to cry, but everything was so numb, externally nothing seemed to move; internally my mind was racing and my heart breaking. My nose blocked as the tears filled my eyes and back-washed up the nasal passages. I started to choke. As sorry for myself as I was, the crying would have to wait. It was a long and pain-filled night.

*　　*　　*

'We do love you, you know,' a familiar voice whispered in my ear, waking me up. 'We can't believe this has happened to you,' it continued, the words charged with the energy of utter disbelief. I opened my eyes, focusing on the now familiar ceiling of my intensive care cubicle. Everything was brighter, and it definitely felt like a sunny morning, especially as Sophie was sitting there, chattering away. Gorgeous, normal Sophie banter, guaranteed to bring anyone back to earth with a bump and a laugh. Sophie, mother of three, doctor's wife, political campaigner and full-time working woman, had somehow managed to arrive at my bedside, stroke my hair, kiss me and tell me I was loved, before the day had even started. I thanked God for her vivacity, feeling her explosive use of the word 'fuck' peppering the conversation as verb, adjective and solution for most of life's problems was far more comforting than the massive shots of pethidine racing through my veins.

A Colombo look-alike wearing a mackintosh and an 'I'm only doing my job' expression carried a chair and sat down between Sophie and me. We watched silently as he produced a notebook and pencil, introduced himself as a police officer, saying nervously he required a few details from me, and read out in a flat voice a few words telling me I was accused of attempted murder.

'I need you to answer some questions and then we can get this matter sorted out,' he muttered apologetically, looking at the floor.

My heart missed a few beats as my swollen brain cells tried to assimilate this piece of information.

'YOU ACCUSE ME OF WHAT! ARE YOU BLIND? LOOK AT ME! LOOK AT ME! YOU CAN'T BE SERIOUS?' It was not possible to speak, but my electronic monitoring equipment displayed my rage. Almost instantly several nurses came dashing to my bedside in response to the noise and hastily escorted both of my visitors away.

'I'll come back later when you're feeling better,' the nervous law-enforcer assured me over his shoulder.

I spent the next few hours in a confused fog. A never-ending stream of doctors and nurses attended to my bodily needs. I could hear the sound of ripping velcro as my upper arm was bound, a little rubber bladder methodically puffed until it squeezed the rubber bandage tightly against my skin, pulse taken, watches checked, puff-ball released, blood still circulating, albeit too quickly. Plastic bags filled with burgundy blood and innocuous-looking fluids that knocked out all feelings and topped up my fuel tanks swung gently overhead, the perfect mobile for a bored patient. I watched them empty; it took forever. Charts were filled out, temperature taken, forehead felt, eyes peered into, conversations bounced across my netted body, but NOBODY spoke to me.

My soaring blood-pressure and restless condition had little to do with yesterday's surgery, the source of the heat burning through my body was linked directly to the absolute belief that life was totally unfair, triggered by the astonishing accusation from 'Colombo'.

I sank into the hard bed, pushed by an invisible force, my teeth clenched together, my body shaking. The whole bed started to vibrate. My vision clouded, the sounds of hospital life faded rapidly. I was standing in a classroom. It was large. The male teacher sitting at the front looked hot and harassed. Tie askew, hair dishevelled.

'Come here!' he barked at a petite, very blonde girl. 'You know what happens to cheats?' he questioned the trembling child now standing before him.

'But, sir, I didn't cheat, sir!' she pleaded.

'How dare you answer me back,' the red-faced teacher shouted.

'Sir . . . please, I promise, I did not cheat. They were trying to copy me. I was only telling them to stop. Please, sir.'

His cane sliced into the back of her chubby legs, leaving a huge red weal. Her little knees buckled. She started to cry.

'What do we do with cheats and tell-tales?' he asked the silent class.

'We send them to Coventry, sir,' they chanted in unison.

'Good. No one will speak to our little Miss Cheat until further notice.' He hung a sign around her neck, written in red pen, 'IGNORE ME'.

'This is for your own good, madam,' he explained, wagging his nicotine-stained finger at her.

I stood in front of the little girl, and confronted him.

'She was not cheating. She's telling you the truth. You know she is. Why are you doing this to her?' I was screaming at him. He did not see me. The girl looked at me. Her blue eyes filled with tears.

'Life's not fair, you see,' she whispered. I gasped.

She was me.

I remembered the incident. I was accused of cheating in a mock examination with the result that, at the age of ten, I was sent unceremoniously to the school kindergarten and put in 'Coventry', where I spent an entire week as punishment for a crime I had never committed. The dunce of the class had turned around and begged me for an answer, and feeling sorry for her, I helped. At the sound of the headmaster's voice she had immediately turned the tables and quick as a flash she had accused me of trying to copy her. She was convincing, and I carried the can, crying with humiliation and disbelief every day and night until my release. Weighing up my current predicament, I had a definite sense that history was repeating itself.

Lying in a bed, surrounded by starched strangers, pipes, tubes, plastic bags and pain, the sense of hopelessness led me very quickly into a state of deep depression. I caught a glimpse of my reflection, distorted in a nurse's glasses; a swollen scabby face with eyes like saucers, matted hair, naked shoulders and a throat covered in plasters and cotton-wool. It was horrible. A black shadow hovered over me, and for one dreadful moment I thought I was back in the driveway. I braced myself for the cut, but it never came, so I opened my eyes and slowly brought the black blob into focus. It was a priest. He mumbled a few words which I couldn't hear. I think they were supposed to be of comfort to me. I remembered when TV celebrity Jimmy Saville had arrived at the hospital where my family and I were keeping a twenty-four-hour vigil at my critically injured Uncle John's bed. Mr Saville had just flown in from the Channel Islands and had got a few presents for 'his girls'. It was in the middle of the night and his arms were filled with fresh flowers which he placed on the beds of all the sleeping women. He had a kind word for everyone and was so full of care and fun and love. I wished he would turn up at my bedside now with a bunch of freesias for me. This was a definite reaction against seriousness and nothing against priests *per se*.

The white-coated army came around to check my progress. In their view I had improved enough for Inspector 'Tact' to return, and after his interview, I could be moved. I was not thrilled at either prospect. I mumbled a confused statement in reply to the police officer's questions, the information from the brain's memory banks exiting through my mouth in hot torrents of scrambled words. He smiled encouragingly and seemed to understand. The compassionate line of questioning and his bedside manner were very different from his earlier performance, so it did not seem necessary to ask him whether I was still a potential murder suspect. Within minutes of his departure I could scarcely remember anything I had said to him, yet my recall of the previous day's events lay etched in vivid technicolour on the screen of my mind, playing over and over and over again. My contemplations were interrupted by two men with brown teeth, fingers and coats. I was about to make my first move on the road back into the world. It did not go as planned.

Intensive Care

Dear Porters,

I realise that I carry a little too much weight for my height and frame, but not enough excess to forgive you both for dropping me whilst lifting me onto your trolley.

When you were trying to put all the tubes back in the right places, it reminded me of a time in childhood when I broke my grandmother's favourite vase. I frantically scooped up all the pieces and shoved them back together with the wrong glue, desperate not to be caught. Had I confessed my crime, the vase could have been repaired, and no one would have seen the join. As it was, the patchwork lump left on the shelf attracted immediate attention, 'Who did that?' Shock, gasp, horror! Strange what one remembers, but I now have a degree of empathy for that vase ... I know what it is like to be a patchwork lump left on the shelf.

What was really funny, even though it hurt, was the fact that you seemed to forget I was there. As you whispered in panic, 'Quick, get her up before Sister sees,' it was apparent to me that you were not bothered at all that I noticed you had dropped me! Your behaviour was no surprise – I realise that all people involved with accident victims seem to think that they are brain-damaged and deaf. This was very nearly true after your services.

I admit I was glad you were on a go-slow, because if you had dropped me any quicker it could have been even more painful.

I have been trying to lose weight ever since.

Thanks for adding to my complexes.

Yours Painfully,

Crossed Tubes,

Bed 27, Intensive Care Transfer List.

A ROOM WITH A VIEW

The room was incredibly bright; early spring sunshine flooded through the large windows to my right, which occupied the entire width of the room. Much to my surprise I was alone and not in a ward, yet to my knowledge I was not a private patient. At the foot of the bed a large chart was clipped to the iron frame, beyond which was a wardrobe. I wondered what was hanging in there, as in the rush of yesterday I forgot to pack. In any event, having never been in hospital other than in very early childhood, I had no idea what one wears in such places. The memory of yesterday, when my clothes were ripped off me, made me shudder. I felt deeply embarrassed at the thought of my bloody nakedness – there was nothing dignified about nearly dying. It was a relief to see I was covered with a thin white sheet and wearing something which I guessed was a hospital gown.

It was impossible to tell which part of my body was which; all I could feel was intense, cutting and crushing pain. The room was as hot and stuffy as a sauna full of maiden aunts, and I lay imprisoned in this overheated hell, itching, prickling, foul-smelling and nauseous. No part of me knew peace. I longed for fresh air and the freedom to move around in my own body. All I was able to do was groan and sigh. Although alone, I could hear others making the same noises – poor sods.

I was so angry. The smart-arse voice which guided me out of the house had told me I was going to function as normal. Glancing down at my mummified body I found it very hard to believe. I was beside myself with misery, drifting in and out of fitful consciousness. Giggling nurses who looked far too young to be responsible for human life came and went. White-coated doctors came and went. Chris, lovely husband of Sophie, came and went. Even the walls of the room bounced in and out in time with my breathing. Everything was coming and going. On each occasion I was asked how I was feeling I replied, 'Dreadful', only to be acknowledged with sagacious nods accompanied by 'Well, that's to be expected' type comments. I wondered why they asked. I had no experience to measure this one against, so I had no idea how I was supposed to feel. My thoughts were repetitive, their vocabulary limited to sex, excreta and male genitals. In all my life I had never felt so miserable. Someone was whispering in my ear.

'My friend – if you would but work on the fissures and wounds within your mind – your body would heal. It is that simple.'

I looked around, but the room was empty. Smart-arse was back. I did not understand what was meant by the fissures and wounds of my mind. All I could understand was the intense pain. I was finding it very hard to breathe and was sweating with the effort of trying not to faint. My heart was pounding. I called out but was unable to make a sound. Everything faded into darkness.

Naomi's determined face came into focus. 'How could they have not noticed the pain-killer was off? I can't believe these people.'

She stroked my hair, and asked softly, 'Are you OK now?'

Luckily for me, my friend had seen the film *Airplane*, and recognised that my pallor, sunken cheeks and crossed eyes meant there was something amiss. Thank God she was not afraid of making a fuss and insisted that a doctor must see me. I understand that after much protesting one was found. It had been four hours before anyone noticed that a pair of agency nurses had managed to disconnect the pain-killer.

I opened my eyes and managed to splutter a few words, my powers of speech returning, and my body relaxing its guard for the first time in twenty-four hours, knowing it was in safe and highly sensible company.

'Don't try to speak, it's going to be alright. I wanted to come as soon as I heard, but other than close family they wouldn't allow visitors until today.'

She noticed my puzzled expression and laughed. 'You're never very good at knowing what day it is, are you?'

I tried to smile, without success as my tight mouth formed a crinkled grimace.

'It's Wednesday afternoon,' she continued, 'and you have been transferred from Intensive Care to this room. Sister told me that they decided not to put you in the main ward, as they think it's better if you have some privacy, as the other patients are bound to ask questions, 'cos it's all over the local TV and press. Can you remember what happened, Ju?'

'Yes, everything,' I whispered.

She looked at me for a long time, 'It's so good to see you.' Her voice broke with emotion.

'It's good to see you too. It's good to see at all.'

'You made it.'

'Yeah, I made it.'

I closed my eyes, aware the pain was starting to ease. I wiggled my toes, and clenched the muscles in my legs. They felt as if they had run a marathon, heavy and aching, but I knew they had not been damaged. As I opened my eyes I noticed for the first time my hands, which were two bandaged clumps. I had no recollection of my fingers being hacked off. I tried to wiggle the stumps, and found, much to my relief, the signs of life and thumbs. There was an assortment of tubes coming out of both arms and disappearing behind my head. I rolled my eyes to try and see around the sides of the bed but as I was wedged between some very hard pillows I couldn't move my head at all and therefore could not discover what was going on behind me – perhaps a good thing.

On my left was a cabinet with an envelope on top. Vaguely I recalled that earlier in the morning, someone had shown me the cross and chain my mother had given me, explaining that 'It was on the side if I needed it.' I didn't know what exactly I was supposed to do with it in my trussed-up state, explaining as best I could under the circumstances that my mother was the religious one, and really it belonged to her.

Naomi was sitting very still on my left-hand side, as though on guard, when two bright faces appeared behind her.

'Just come to check you, Julie,' one of them smiled, taking my pulse as she checked the watch pinned to her ample bosom. Next the 'velcro' treatment as the little rubber bladder puffed up to check my blood-pressure. The other nurse swung my mobile of liquids into view as she checked them all. I could tell that these women knew exactly what they were doing as they worked quietly around me, the unsung heroines of the secret world within hospitals.

Naomi told me that her husband Leo was absolutely furious with TC. I asked why, genuinely puzzled by her remark.

She shrugged her shoulders, 'Well, for sending that woman to the cottage.'

I reflected on her words, not knowing that her husband was to be the first in a long line of those who would blame TC. Unable to move my lips, thus sounding like a bad ventriloquist, I defended TC.

'But he couldn't possibly have known she was going to do this . . . she was like a bloody mouse . . . No one could have predicted this outcome . . . we were all trying to help her. Oh for God's sake, Naomi, please don't start blaming TC, that's all I need.'

'No, no, don't get me wrong, I don't blame TC, neither does Leo really, it was just all such a shock, Ju.'

She reassured me by kissing my forehead and promising to return as soon as she could.

'We'll all be thinking of you tonight,' she said as she left the room.

Shutting my eyes, I began to try to make sense of the events of the last weeks. I could see the medium in Belgrave Square banging his fist down telling me to change the door. I saw the new front door being fitted, and remembered how baffled and irritated I had been by my great-grandad's message from the world of spirit. So much had been left unsaid.

I wondered why he didn't tell me the whole story, reasoning that if he could concentrate all that energy into communicating so powerfully and convincingly through a strange medium, a person I did not even have an appointment with, and tell me about the door, surely he could have added a line about not letting any woman behaving strangely enter our home? Without a doubt, hanging the new door was one of the most significant factors in enabling me to get out of the house. The way the old one opened would have made it virtually impossible for me to escape. I would have been mincemeat.

So, was this meant to happen to me? Was it part of some plan – to be attacked but not to die. Was this some sort of punishment, and if so, what had I done to deserve it? Why was someone in the world of spirit allowed to assist in my survival, but not stop the event? I could not believe that such hatred, such physical strength, such relentless violence could exist in anyone, let alone a woman. She had seemed so pathetic when I met her. I really believed she was likely to harm herself . . . or the cats. My antennae had picked up the warning signals, but my translation was dangerously out of sync. Wherever had that destructive force come from?

There was so much I did not understand. I felt overwhelmed by the enormity of the task of sifting through my memory-banks in order to draw some sort of conclusion from the events leading to this moment. As my mind whirled, building up a vortex of unprocessed information, I heard the word:

'Meditate!'

I opened my eyes and looked around. There was no one else in the room. I must have imagined the voice and sank back into my thoughts. I recalled a book of TC's on meditation. I had read the first couple of chapters and convinced poor JR we should give our minds a break and have a go at meditating. We had sat on the patio following the instructions in his book. There were hundreds of migrating birds chattering away in one of the trees, filling the air with an incredible level of noise. As I started to take deep breaths I experienced almost immediately a sinking feeling, as if I were being pushed down into the chair and floating onto the floor. Everything seemed to freeze-frame. In unison the birds stopped their racket, as if a film editor had given the signal to cut the soundtrack. I had opened my eyes very slowly, only to find all the birds and JR staring at me. We were both so spooked by the experience, we reached for our cigarettes, made two huge mugs of instant coffee and vowed never to try again. It was eerie.

Lying amidst the smells of incinerated bandages, dried blood and disinfectant, experiencing extreme mental turmoil, I decided to break that vow and try it once more – I needed to do something to quieten my mind. I took a deep breath and exhaled slowly. I sighed out loud as the screaming tension in my muscles relaxed slightly. I inhaled once more, as deeply as my physical limitations would allow. As I held the inbreath, once again the feeling of floating and light-headedness returned. I exhaled very noisily, feeling no need to breathe at all. The image of a white-marbled courtyard came into my mind. It was filled with flowerpots, baskets and tubs; tumbling exotic colours and textures filled the canvas of my mental image. Intensely bright, warm and so incredibly peaceful. I saw myself sitting on a low wall which surrounded ponds and fountains. I sensed there was someone else sitting with me, but I could not see them.

Welcome home, dear One.
Where am I? What is this? Who are you?
You are always asking so many questions ... endless praying and inquisitive chatter.
Well, yes, I suppose I am ... but it's only because I'm trying to fathom what is going on. It's not every day a virtual stranger sticks a carving knife in your middle and tells you it's in the name of God to save the world!
My friend, you will never find out if you do not wait for a reply.
What do you mean by that?
Your mind, look at it. Chattering, thinking, analysing, puzzling, pondering, debating, comparing, criticising ... non-stop. Thousands of thoughts every day. Negative, repetitive thoughts. Thoughts which mould and produce your reality and earthly experience.
Are you telling me I created this mess with my own mind?
It is not a mess ... it is a perfect lesson. And yes, you did create it.

Well, I don't like what I'm creating . . . how the hell do I stop this mayhem? My life has been unbelievable.

Your life has been necessary. Every last detail of it.

But how do I understand it? How can I learn from it?

The thoughts – watch them! Watch this mind of yours. These wayward, negative, destructive thoughts will start to steady if you would but watch them. That is the start of meditation.

That simple?

Yes, that simple.

Then what?

As you watch, you will become aware of the space between these restless creatures. And, in that space, you will be amazed at what you know.

But between my thoughts there's nothing . . . silence?

Exactly! You learn fast.

You speak in riddles.

You think in riddles.

So, I'll watch them.

Yes.

All of them?

For starters, take just one of the most negative, and change it for something wonderful. Something that delights you. Something positive.

OK, I'll start when I'm feeling a bit better.

No! Start right now.

What difference will a few days make in the big scheme of things?

Why wait? What is the attraction of remaining in your self-imposed hell one second longer than necessary, when paradise is only a whisper away.

Please . . . whoever you are . . . can you answer a few more questions for me?

The image started to cloud, and then fragment. I had the sense I was the one clouding and distancing myself, as I floated back into the hospital bed. I called out.

*　　*　　*

In Spain ... did you send me the dream as a warning? Was it you I saw that night? Were you behind that spirit-message about changing the front door? PLEASE ... was it you who guided me and spoke to me when I was attacked in the house? I heard a deep throaty chuckle, followed by whispering echoes.

Find out!

In that moment, amidst all the craziness, I was reminded once again of the part of me sitting in the eye of the storm, watching it all, as if it was just a film, and nothing to do with me. I prayed with all my heart. 'Whoever you are watching over all of this, please don't give up on me. I have got this far, and although I'm drugged and confused, please help me to see through the chaos. I know you are there. I love you – whoever you are and whoever I am.'

My peace was disturbed by women's voices. I opened my eyes and once more faced the stark reality of the hospital room.

'Good afternoon, it's time for a little exercise.'

I explained I was not in the mood for jogging to the athletic-looking duo standing over the bed. They were not impressed, and flipped back the sheet with menacing energy.

'We're from Physio,' the one with blonde cropped hair informed me. Looking at the crisp white trousers, tops and shoes, coupled with the dangerously pronounced biceps, I rather thought they were from some very healthy land where flabby torsos were treated with contempt. I was right. Rolled onto my side before I could protest, I screamed out with the pain, loose flesh draped over broken glass – my innards were definitely amiss.

'Now don't be a baby.'

I pointed out as politely as possible that it would be wonderful if someone would be kind enough to explain to me what had happened since I entered hospital. They softened immediately, and rolled me gently onto my back.

'You are a very lucky woman,' the smaller woman began. I contemplated the last few hours of my life, and thought that to be a matter of opinion.

'You are in the Q A Hospital near Portsmouth and you had the best medical team working on you yesterday. It was nothing short of a miracle all the right surgeons were there – you've got the *Hospital Watch* programme to thank for that.' The older woman laughed. 'They were all on duty because they all wanted to be seen on TV.'

'Another piece of luck was that the camera crew were busy filming something else when you arrived, so you've been spared stardom, and anyway, the consultant wouldn't have let them film you, it was too much of a panic. You haven't even got admission notes,' the blonde crop added.

I asked why I hurt so much and felt so sick. They explained that, because I had been under anaesthetic for such a long time, I was reacting against it. After all, I had had major surgery, not to mention the shock that multiple stab wounds bestowed on the physical and mental systems. Well, I could have guessed that much. 'Surgery for what?' was my question, but they didn't hear me.

'Now come along – let's try again – over we go – good – there we are.'

I screamed again; their scant explanation made life no more comfortable, in fact I considered their actions were adding to the shock. There was not enough air to satisfy the needs of my lungs as I wheezed and gasped.

'Thought as much,' Blondie muttered. 'Smoker, are we? We've got to keep all that fluid off your lungs, so let's try a cough, shall we?'

I flushed with guilt as I regretted every lungful of smoke and noxious fumes I had ever inhaled. The only cough I could manage lightly tickled the back of my throat, leaving me in tears, agony, and deeply dissatisfied, and now aware of another physical problem – the sticky brown gunge coating my breathing apparatus. I never thought I would miss the ability to expand the chest and squeeze out all excess liquid. The mere thought of inhaling a cigarette was so revolting, I heaved.

'Now the other side,' they chorused as I was rolled sharply over again.

'The doctors like us to get patients moving again as fast as possible after their ops because the quicker you move, the quicker you mend,' Blondie explained. Such positivity did nothing to ease the pain. They wedged me back into the cement-bag pillows, heaving me up into a slightly more acute angle. They left a perspex cup on the bedside cabinet with the instructions, 'Anything you cough up spit it into there. We'll see you in the morning.'

It was a rendezvous I did not look forward to.

I was beginning to wonder where TC was, when a petite lady doctor entered the room. She seemed genuinely delighted to see me awake and when she asked how I was I had the feeling she really meant it. She talked as she checked the charts and fluids. A different nurse also came in carrying a bag of plasma, which was immediately hung on my mobile. As the tube was reinserted into my arm I felt mildly repelled, watching the liverish-coloured fluid draining into me. I cheered myself up thinking about the comedian Tony Hancock and his 'Blood Donor' sketch, and pondered upon whose blood I was receiving.

'How's the pain?' the doctor asked.

'Pretty raw,' I replied.

'Because of this morning's little problem,' she sighed, looking up to heaven in the way over-worked under-staffed people do. 'We've got you on the maximum dosage pain-killer, but you see, pethidine is addictive, so we will try to wean you off it as soon as possible, but at the same time we must keep your pain threshold as high as possible because the lower the pain, the faster you will heal. You can help us keep the balance by telling us when the pain eases. We've got you on intravenous fluids at the moment, but you can try sipping a little water now, and in the morning you can probably have tea and juice, we'll see how you go through the night. Your body is very strong and healthy, and your skin has a lot of elasticity, so I will do all that I can to get you well and out of here.' She patted my arm reassuringly.

'One other thing.' She hesitated.

'If you could talk about it, it would help. Don't lock it away.'

I thanked her quietly as she left the room, although I felt like shouting at the top of my voice, 'THANK YOU . . . THANK YOU . . . THANK YOU . . . BEAUTIFUL LADY FOR REALLY CARING . . . THANK YOU FOR TREATING ME AS AN INTELLIGENT HUMAN BEING . . . THANK YOU FOR ACKNOWLEDGING THAT

I HAVE SOME PART TO PLAY IN MY RECOVERY . . . THANK
YOU, THANK YOU!'

Nurse 'Plasma' did the routine checks, and was filling out
the charts when TC and Hank walked in. They both looked
shattered and Hank looked angry. Knowing how hard he worked
in the world of film and theatre props, with deadlines similar to
those of advertising and marketing, always 'I want it yesterday',
I felt dreadful that he was having to take time out for me.

'I've got in touch with Jenny and Herbert,' TC said, sitting
down. 'They're on their way back. They couldn't get on a flight
today, but managed to find seats on one for tomorrow. They
will get here in the evening but probably too late to visit you.'

I so wanted to see my mother and hear her voice. To absorb
some of her strength, and feel her love. I realised there was no
one else who would understand what I was going through. Only
she would know. It was so disappointing to know I wouldn't see
her for another whole day. Time moved incredibly slowly in the
environs of sickness.

Hank ran his hands through his hair and pulled up a chair
next to TC.

'How are you, Ju?' he asked.

'I'm not sure, Hank. I can't believe this has happened to me
– I mean . . . was it something I said?'

They both laughed and the 'he who speaks first is bound to
say the wrong thing' tension broke. TC was staring at me as if
he couldn't believe I was alive. I longed to hold them both but
couldn't even take their hands.

TC spoke quietly. 'We've been to see Cosmo Greene at the
London centre, that's why we're late, as I thought I should be
the one to tell him. He's in a bad way about all of this. He sends
you his love, and wants you to know that he's really with you.'

I winced at the thought of the awareness teacher. This was the
man in whose name, alongside God and Jesus, I had been knifed
repeatedly and I didn't give a stuff for how he was. I suspected
that was why Hank was looking impatient. I knew he would
have wanted to see me first, before having tea and sympathy
with others. I looked at TC, momentarily disappointed that he
had not come straight to see me, but I realised that Mr Greene

and his course would come under scrutiny and TC was the only one who could give him the full picture. My hurt dissipated as I saw the haunted expression on his face; he was operating on his reserve tanks, relating mechanically to me all the people he had managed to contact, but behind his façade of efficiency I could see that he was in a terrible state of shock and exhaustion. I was worried about him. He needed care too.

'Oh my God,' I gasped.

'What?' Hank and TC answered in unison, leaping to their feet in panic.

'The cats,' I cried. 'Tell me she didn't find the cats.'

'They're fine, she didn't touch them, really they're fine,' TC reassured me. 'They just want you to come home.'

What extraordinary things humans are. TC couldn't tell me he wanted me home, but had to hide behind our mutual love of Tom and Ben. And here was I, coping with the fact I had been hacked about and even able to find some compassion for the woman who did it to me, but the thought of her harming one of the cats made me want to tear her limb from limb. Feelings of rage poured out of my mind and my body responded instantaneously, prickling and burning as if it were covered in freshly chopped chillies. How quickly the physical reacts to the mental. I remembered The Voice telling me to change my thoughts, so I shifted them from rage to something a little cooler. I pictured the cats playing in the kitchen and immediately felt soothed. Suddenly I was aware of just how much my state of mind could help to speed my recovery – perhaps The Voice had a point.

'TC, where is she now?'

'Holloway.'

'I couldn't stop her, I tried everything I knew. She was like a killing machine. I just couldn't stop her. I couldn't get through to her. I tried. She was in a different world. Why did she do it? TC, why did she do this to me?'

He stroked my arm, bringing his drawn face close to mine.

'The police told me she thought you represented a different God, and she had to kill you to save the world,' he replied, rubbing his eyes absent-mindedly, as if in total disbelief.

'But why? She was so meek when I met her ... all she

talked about that night at the party was how much she hated violence.'

'Julie, she's a paranoid schizophrenic!' The words shot out of his mouth and hit a wall of silence. It took a few moments for the impact of this statement to sink in. Images from the old Jekyll and Hyde films came to mind. Split personality. Dangerous. Unpredictable. Cunning. Helpless.

'Oh dear God,' I managed to utter, stunned with this new piece of information, as the implications began to percolate.

'She's your patient, TC – didn't you know?'

'I don't treat her for it, Julie – her psychiatrist does – he prescribes her medication. I've only seen her a couple of times in surgery . . . and then nothing to do with her mental condition. Look, we'll talk about it more when you feel stronger.'

'What's the damage then, doctor?' I enquired, changing the subject.

'I don't know, but I'll find out. Who's in charge of you?'

'TC, I've only just found out where I am,' I protested. 'He was wearing a white coat,' I added as he left the room in order to find one of the medical staff and clarify what lay beneath the bandages.

Popping his head back around the door TC managed a smile. 'I'll be back in a minute.'

'Hank, look after him for me. Don't let him go back to the cottage.'

'Don't worry yourself about all of that, Ju. You just concentrate on getting out of here. He's staying with us. He's shattered but doesn't realise it – we all are. I suppose his doctor's training is keeping him going.' Hank smiled, his steady presence bringing me enormous comfort. I did not need to explain things to him. He knew.

'God, you should see some of the things TC has to deal with – if he wasn't detached he would probably go mad. He had to go to a suicide last year . . . an "under-the-train" job. He had to go to certify the death. Can you believe it? They needed an official cause. He came home and drew me a diagram of where he found all the bits. He was in a dreadful state and had to talk about it. He found a man's balls placed perfectly on one of the sleepers. What a job.' Hank winced. We both drew in deep breaths with the shock of such an image. I wondered what thoughts that man had had on his mind as he leapt under the London express train.

'Hank,' I added urgently, beginning to feel myself drifting out of consciousness.

'What, Jules?'

'Remember, he saved my life. TC saved my life. Never forget that!'

It was night-time. The room was washed with the overspill of fluorescent light from the corridor. Outside, the horizon was black, with no signs or sounds of life. Far away I could hear my mother singing to me. I guessed it was very late. I had no recollection of TC and Hank leaving and deduced I must have fallen asleep while they were still here. I began to stretch myself, having momentarily forgotten my physical condition, and gasped as searing pain wasted no time in reminding me. A nurse appeared immediately.

'Well, hello. How are we tonight?'

I still found being addressed as 'we' somewhat disconcerting.

'We're all doing fine,' I joked. As the words left my mouth I realised I was displaying all the signs which had probably led to the schizoid label my assailant had acquired. Strange voices speaking to me, and now, I was answering as 'we'. It was all very worrying.

'We have had a hard time, haven't we?' the nurse clucked as she rearranged my body and its various tubes. 'We might feel better if we spoke about it?' she added, with the energy of curiosity rather than comforter. I remained silent. 'Was it a boyfriend?' she enquired casually as she drew up a chair. I did not reply. 'I said to my husband only the other night, the world's not what it used to be. All this violence. I myself personally blame the telly, and videos, I mean, it must have an effect on young minds, not to mention old ones . . . as I say, drink and drugs have their part to play . . . if you could see what we have to see, you'd never touch a drop again. Was he a drinker?' I looked at her. 'Your boyfriend, was he a drinker?' she repeated, nodding knowingly in my direction. 'Yes, as I say, it's the drink that sets them off, I said to Fred, my husband, we should count our blessings that none of ours have these addictions. If one of our girls had something like this done to them,' she nodded at me, 'there's no saying what my Fred would do. He's a mild man, but I wouldn't like to vouch for him if he was crossed. He's a bit of an 'eye for an eye' man between you and me . . .' And so she continued for the next hour, presenting me with a monologue of her and Fred's view of life, to which I made no comment. It was interminable, and I had nowhere to hide, lying wide awake and hurting watching her mouth contort itself into an amazing array of shapes as she emphasised various points. I was beginning to feel very sorry for Fred, when she made a move.

'Well, dear, you'll probably feel better for having talked about it.'

She got up and put the chair back against the wall. 'And don't worry.' She smiled a knowing smile looking over her shoulder as she left the room. 'They'll have him behind bars for life for what he's done to you.'

I began to realise what I was up against.

The day dawned grey and insipid, as was my first cup of hospital tea. It struck me as rather odd that I could be pumped full of drugs to ease pain and induce sleep and relaxation, only to be shaken awake for a cup of lukewarm water, fatty milk and tannin. Furthermore, it was considered a treat. Balancing the cup in my bandaged hands was quite a feat, and provided my first exercise of the day.

'If you keep it down you can have another one later this morning,' the tea-trolley assistant cheerily informed me. Weighing up the options was depressing, but in the event tea and I did not remain friends and, thankfully, I was returned to water.

The nurses had gone but I was not alone. The bed was flanked by a number of men and women. A well-groomed man introduced himself as the consultant surgeon and in the manner of one who has no time or patience, gave a staccato explanation of the others present – registrar, doctors and trainees. I forgot the names as quickly as he gave them, his aura of intimidation affecting all of us. There was a definite pecking order, those in the lower ranks not speaking, eyes lowered, tired and drawn, hoping not to be picked on. His number two answering with brisk efficiency all the questions which were directed at me. This game of medical tennis bounced back and forth across the bed, Pomp trying to outmanoeuvre Circumstance on every serve, with the occasional retrieval of an out-of-court question thrown back by a junior, eager to win approval. I did not exist.

I studied the faces of the people who had saved my life, the senior personnel masters at avoiding eye contact, the trainees still new enough to meet my gaze and show warmth and compassion. From their furtive manner it was apparent that kindness equated with weakness, and I had little doubt that any signs of empathy would be eradicated by the end of their training. I likened it to a prize-winning gardener who could nurture, nourish and treasure his onions for months, show them, discuss them, only to eat them in the end.

'Have you passed wind yet?' All eyes were now on me, as Pomp asked his question. Farting was not something I would normally admit to; however, I could see he was serious – he was staring at me, awaiting my reply with obvious impatience. I shook my head.

'Well, tell someone when you do,' he instructed, with which he and his entourage swept out of the room.

Shortly afterwards my favourite lady doctor entered the room, accompanied by several nurses whose arms were filled with flowers. 'These are for you,' they informed me as they arranged them in an assortment of containers, holding the cards up for me to read the messages. I was touched deeply by the loving thoughts and prayers of my family, somewhat surprised that they knew I was in hospital – I was only just beginning to come to terms with my situation myself.

Dr Kindness checked the charts with Pomp and Circumstance's new instructions, shook her head in weary disbelief, writing her own notes as she discussed my medication and treatment with the nursing staff. Her enormous dark eyes lined with the bruise-blue of not enough sleep surveyed me with approval.

'You're smiling,' she said, 'that must be a good sign.'

I told her how the consultant wanted to know if I had broken wind. She and the nurses laughed. One of them waved her hand in the direction of my nether regions explaining that passing wind indicated that 'down there' was functioning as it should. I realised with a sense of panic that 'down there' had not functioned at all, and with even greater panic I was at a loss to know what to do when all the water I was taking on board needed to exit. Sensing my dismay, the doctor patted my arm and told me to ask for a bedpan when the need arose.

After they had left the room I felt very vulnerable. I had always been a person of independence and privacy, and to find myself exposed, helpless and likely to wet the bed was not my idea of a good time. The sound of the door opening woke me up and JR walked in. She looked pale and dazed.

'JC,' was all she managed to say, as she sat down, not removing her gaze from me for one second.

'Hi, JR, what time is it?'

'It's just after three. Christ – your eyes are like saucers.'

'So are yours.'

She relaxed noticeably and smiled. She took a notebook and pen out of her handbag, cleared her throat. Dear beautiful JR, ever helpful, wanted to know what I needed. As I had absolutely nothing with me, I realised I needed quite a few things. I watched her hands shaking as she wrote down instructions on where to find everything in the cottage. I was exhausted with the effort of thinking and talking practicalities. That done, she told me a few things about business. I was in no shape to take anything more in, and suggested she took a break, knowing she was probably longing for a cigarette. 'Have one for me,' I said as she left the room, although in truth the thought of smoking was so revolting my lungs contracted in horror and I added more fluid to the perspex cup at my bedside.

I heard footsteps in the corridor. Footsteps that were different. Footsteps I recognised. Footsteps with a bounce – a sense of purpose. I turned my eyes as far as I could towards the door and waited. They stopped short at my room. I smelt the perfume. I knew she had arrived.

'Mum?'

'Ju?'

She appeared in the doorway. Her beautiful face shone like an angel.

'I knew.'

'I know.'

'I've always known.'

'I know.'

She walked to the bed and took my face in her hands.

'My darling Ju . . . how could they have done this to you? You were too lovely . . . evil wants only to destroy such beauty.'

She moved the lank hair away from my face and kissed me on the forehead. Her cheek rested against mine as her tears splashed against my flushed skin.

Walking over to the sink she filled a kidney-shaped bowl with water. Opening her travelling handbag she rummaged around the many pockets, producing cotton-wool pads and various tubes and small plastic bottles. Squeezing something into the water, she picked up a towel, came over and sat on the edge of the bed. Gently she washed the hair that framed my face, strand by strand dipping it into the warm water and squeezing out the debris and stains of violation, patting each lock dry and combing it back into shape. She then cleansed my face, washed it, and smoothed and patted moisturiser into all the parts without stitches. Quietly she spoke as she performed the cleansing ritual.

'I walked all the way here from Spain.' I looked at her quizzically.

'I paced up and down the plane – the hostesses were wonderful. They understood and let me pace. It made me feel better . . . but it's a bloody long way!'

We laughed. From her make-up bag she took some mascara and kohl pencil, and worked on my eyes with the care of a fine artist. 'When you were little, you would never let me do anything for you . . . you were such an independent little bugger . . . now I can wreak my revenge for all those meals you threw over me.' I smiled at her, and told her to do her worst. She threatened to put pink bows in my hair and I, in turn, promised to die in her arms if she so much as tried.

She explained how when she had returned from saying goodbye to me at Malaga airport she'd heard a voice telling her to pack and be ready to leave the villa. It had been a nightmare for her, forcing herself to leave everything in place for the owners, when her heart had been bursting with the pain of unknown fear. When my stepfather returned from his golf, having received the news, my mother had been on the doorstep waiting for him – with their suitcases. Not getting on a plane that day had been terrible and not knowing any details other than I'd had a serious accident and the name of the hospital was a nightmare for her. Call boxes that didn't work, operators who spoke no English, and TC not at home. When they eventually arrived, having flown into London instead of the Midlands, they'd hired a car and driven straight to the hospital, not knowing what to expect. My stepfather had gone immediately to fix up a hotel nearby for my mother to stay in, tactfully allowing us those first precious moments together.

'Where's the cross and chain?' she asked suddenly.

I signalled with my eyes towards the envelope on the bedside cabinet.

'In there.'

She took it out and held it against her breast. 'It didn't do you much good, did it?'

'It gave me the time to get out of the house . . . it helped to save my life.' I told her how it had caught Helen's attention as it had flown out of my sweater and caused her to stop dead, enabling me to get up off the floor. Mum opened out her hand and we looked at the cross. There was a small gold-coloured medallion on the chain as well, about the size of a thumbnail.

'Where did that come from?' she asked.

'I've no idea . . . it's not mine. It's the right crucifix . . . but the medallion must belong to someone else.'

She tried to slide it off the chain, but the hole in it was so small it was impossible to move it over the loops of the catch. It was a permanent fixture. I was baffled.

'Ju . . . there's writing on it . . . here, you look, I haven't got my glasses on . . . can you see what's on it?'

She thrust it under my nose, I blinked to clear my blurred

vision. It was old, brass and worn. On one side was the face of Christ, on the reverse was the Lord's Prayer. My heart missed a few beats, for although its appearance on my chain was a mystery, it felt like it had always belonged to me.

'It's an apport,' Mum said with authority.

'Whatever is that?'

'A gift from the world of spirit. In times of crisis there are often enormous surges of spiritual energy, within which miracles can happen. Matter can be materialised from the astral planes into our physical world. This medallion is charged with that energy – I can feel it. You were protected.'

'Mum, I left my body. I left all the blood and gore behind. I was given instructions – so much has happened – I saw Jesus. I can't begin to tell you – I know I was protected and guided every step of the way but I still don't know why this had to happen.'

'Darling Ju, there is always a purpose behind everything, but you and I may never be allowed to know. I'll tell you something.' She lowered her head and whispered in my ear, 'I have been taken out of my body – it's more real than here . . . God, it was so beautiful I didn't want to come back.'

'Neither did I.'

'Ju, we must stay very strong.' She stopped talking and looked at me. Her eyes filled with tears. 'The pain . . . the pain must have been so dreadful. If it could only have been me. If only I could take the hurt out of your eyes. It's too much for a mother to bear . . . to see her child mutilated.' She shook her head in disbelief, tears rolling down her face.

'Hey, Mum!' I asked. 'What happened to the being strong?'

'Oh, fuck it!' she answered, breaking down and sobbing, 'I can't even hold you.'

Mum left the room to find my stepfather. I imagined JR was still puffing away on a fag in some corner of the building and I was once again left to contemplate my bandages. I still had no real idea of what damage lay beneath them and had the distinct impression nobody wanted to tell me. The hospital personnel made light of everything, their brusque manner leaving no room for questions – the general atmosphere was one of 'We'll have you out of here before you can count your stitches'. I realised the reticence was for my benefit, but images of Frankenstein's monster with his patchwork body would not leave my mind. Not knowing the extent of my injuries was very frightening. I could recall each plunge of the knife but had no idea of the damage inflicted. Perhaps everyone assumed TC, being a doctor, would be telling me all I needed to know. The most anyone would divulge was that I was lucky to be alive. I knew it was ungrateful but in the light of recent events, I did not feel overwhelmed with good fortune.

My mood improved the moment Hank walked in. He was alone. Drawing up a chair he sat at my side. The youngest of my mother's brothers, he was one of the few people present throughout my entire life, thus a trusted friend, and one who shared more of my inner thoughts than most.

'Hey! how are you doing, kid?' He asked.

'Terrific! I just love it here. Where's TC?'

'In the inquisition,' he replied cryptically.

I asked him whether he knew what my injuries were. He didn't, and explained how he preferred not to know. However he did fill me in on what was going on beyond the confines of my emotionally sealed quarantine. It was not good. Apparently everyone had gathered in the hospital canteen. My mother's sadness, frustration and anger had exploded, her shock manifesting in the shape of a someone-must-pay-for-this attack. She had taken a knife and held it against TC's chest, making it clear to all concerned that she felt he should be the one suffering. Hank and I both knew that she was one of the most gentle and harmless people but not a woman to be underestimated when it came to the defence of those she loved. Hank explained how she had been firing on all cylinders but he had managed to soothe and calm her down enough to leave TC alone. It was terrible to think of two people I loved affected in this way. Quite a scene had ensued. This in turn had upset my stepfather, who hated any form of confrontation and was, according to Hank, hell-bent on getting my mother out of the place as fast as he could. Mum had no intention of leaving me, resulting in further tension, now between her and her agitated husband.

'And what about TC?' I asked.

'He doesn't know what day it is,' was all Hank said.

Added to this, I learnt JR was experiencing difficulty in coping with the business, finding herself suddenly responsible for all of my negotiations. She was under pressure, with several publishing deadlines to meet, and had received rumblings that our clients could not wait upon my health and might terminate our contracts.

My heart sank. Keeping things from me in order to protect me only served to make me feel worse. Somehow all my visitors' fears, frustrations and unspokenness, although kept under control in my presence, were having a very deep negative effect on me. I was ultra-sensitive, perhaps through lack of food, drink and tobacco, and my heightened awareness meant I absorbed atmospheric stress immediately. I could see straight through people. It was most disconcerting.

'Hank.'

'Yes, darling.'

'Don't hide anything from me. Tell me everything.'

'I'll always tell you everything,' he answered, smiling.

'Have you told Nanny?'

'Well, no, not yet. Jen thinks it's best that we keep her away from the hospital. Especially after John . . .' His voice tailed away. John, the eldest of the three brothers, had crashed in a light aircraft he was piloting and suffered horrendous burns in the fire that ensued. This had been the last time our family had been gathered in a hospital – for a two-week bedside vigil. The horror we and the families of the three passengers witnessed had changed all of our lives irrevocably. To see four men's bravery amidst such suffering tore our hearts apart. John and one of his friends lost their fight for life. We were shattered. No, I agreed with Mum, I couldn't put my dear Nan through that kind of anxiety again.

'When you tell her what's happened play it down. I'm going to be fine. Tell her I love her.'

'I'll tell her,' he reassured me.

By the time my mother returned I could no longer hide my despair, nor she hers. Some part of me had believed that in the event of an accident everyone involved would rally around and love each other – perhaps the result of watching too much American television. I had a deep yearning for harmony. My mother stood beside the bed, her usually clear voice infiltrated with a hostile edge. Her jaw was set, her eyes clouded with a film of anger and bewilderment; the walls of her usual dignity and control were rubble at our feet. The room jangled with her presence.

'I'll kill him for this,' she said between gritted teeth, her pitch rising. 'I'll kill him,' she was shouting. 'My Julie, what have they done to you? And if I find her, I'll show her what she's done to my girl, my child, my gentle Ju. GOD, I'LL, KILL THEM.' She was hysterical.

'STOP IT! STOP IT – LEAVE HIM ALONE. JUST LEAVE HIM A-LONE! LET IT BE, MUM. I'M ALIVE . . . I AM ALIVE. I CANNOT STAND ALL THIS ANGER . . . ALL THIS BLAMING . . . I CAN'T BEAR IT.' Salty liquid streamed from my eyes and nose, burning my stitched mouth, finally seeping into the bandages around my neck and stinging like hell.

Mum softened immediately. 'I'm so sorry, Ju,' she whispered, dabbing my eyes with all her earlier tenderness. 'Please forgive me, I shouldn't be so angry, you're right, it will help none of us. Please don't cry . . . the last thing in the world I wanted was to add to your distress. Oh Ju,' she sighed, 'what a bloody mess.'

Circumstance entered the room with my stepfather hot on his heels, demanding with solicitorial directness and impatience how much longer I needed to remain in hospital, without even acknowledging my presence. Mum jumped up and stood by his side; extending her hand towards the doctor, she introduced herself as my mother. Her charm was easy and natural and the doctor softened his aggressive stance and directed his answer to her. I was so excited. I was about to find out how I was.

'. . . will be anything up to six weeks . . . It's still early days yet. There is the risk of infection . . . Her chest is very weak.'

They all became aware of my interest in the conversation and Circumstance led them out of the room, to continue the discussion out of my earshot in the corridor. Six weeks. Six weeks of suffering all that hospitalisation entails.

*   *   *

Well, my friend ... do you wish to add to the suffering of the world?

Oh ... it's you again.

Yes, it is you again.

I'm in no mood for conundrums. And no, of course I don't want to add to the world's suffering.

Then stop suffering.

What's that supposed to mean?

Your present experience ... your current circumstances ... do you wish to suffer, blame everyone else and be a victim for the rest of your life?

No ... I've told you I don't want to suffer.

Your last few encounters demonstrate how much you dislike being treated like a victim ... would you agree?

Well ... I can't bear all the tension and blaming TC when they don't know the facts. But what can I do about it?

Lighten up. See the humour in your situation.

I do not find it as amusing as you obviously do.

I do not laugh at you. Dearest One, have you remembered that you are far more than your physical wrap? When you were out of body consciousness flying into the realms of your Higher Truth ... were you that concerned with your body?

No, I wasn't interested in it. In fact, I didn't want to come back into it ... I suppose that's one of the reasons why I am feeling so pissed off.

The body you inhabit has a human destiny ... do not think so ill of it. Could you not instead have gratitude for what it has just endured on your behalf?

It got itself stabbed just for me?

For your learning.

The little cutie. And for today's lesson?

How not to suffer, you see ... for all of this incarnation you will always have a choice between being the victim and the symbolic spiritual warrior ... strong, poised, cheerful ... BUT ... you cannot be both. Choose one or the other.

If I choose the warrior, will my life improve? Warrior implies

fighting . . . I thought you spiritual guys were against that sort
of thing. Anyhow, how can I tell I'm not just kidding myself?
How will I know victimhood is over?

**It will have nothing to do with what happens to you.
Many have the misconception that spirituality means
nothing negative will ever happen – no, my dear. Your
attitude to any moment will be your barometer, for your
attitude to events will change. It will be a fight, a fight
in which none is harmed, no one wins or loses, for it is
a fight against wrong understanding – ignorance, if you
will – you even call it by the name of evil.**

Can you give me another clue?

**Yes. When you touch on truth instead of ignorance . . .
you will always have the pleasure of my company!**

But who are you?

No . . . WHO are YOU?

Suddenly the room was full of people, nurses, Hank, TC, JR,
plus my mother. My stepfather beat the retreat in double time.
Patting my head and muttering something about 'the office', he
left the room. If I'd had any degree of control over my internal
systems, I could not have chosen a better moment to release a
long noisy fart. There was a brief embarrassed silence, broken by
raucous laughter – mine. My mother, quick as a flash in perfect
American drawl announced, 'Hey, guys . . . the next one's on me!'
We were all laughing. Even though days earlier I would rather
have died than do such a thing in public, I no longer cared that
I was being laughed at . . . in fact it was wonderful to feel the
release of everyone's tension over such a ridiculous thing. As a
family we had always had wonderful humour, even in the midst of
terrible sadness . . . and in my heart I knew The Voice was once
again right: the tears of laughter were indeed preferable to those
of sadness. It also meant that 'down there' was working again.

'It's a really good sign, they tell me,' I told them.

'Nice one, Ju,' said Hank, 'I'll remember that for future use!'

He kissed my cheek and explained he was driving Mum to
her hotel. Mum then kissed me and told me she'd be back in
the morning.

'I think this calls for a brandy,' she informed me.

'Only one?' I questioned.

'A little drinkette in the face of a family crisis,' Hank replied, still laughing whilst raising his eyebrows feigning innocence.

'You lucky buggers,' I called after them as they left, big sister with her baby brother arm in arm.

JR also took her leave. I was aware she was still trembling slightly, her gentle nature unable to come to terms with such a violent event. I told her to drive carefully and not to worry about the business. I couldn't give my work any serious consideration – there were too many other things to deal with. She understood. I doubted if our contractors would.

TC was looking at my chart. He seemed very far away and distracted.

'TC, I'm so sorry Mum attacked you like that. Hank told me.'

'Jenny didn't mean it, Jules . . . I know that . . . any parent would be enraged.'

He sat down, his gaze towards the over-polished floor. Nothing was said for what seemed like an age. Several times he looked at me and cleared his throat, as if to begin a sentence, only to return to his contemplation of his shoes.

'What is it, TC?' I asked, unable to remain silent any longer.

He coughed.

'Jules, I want to continue with the course . . . I think it is very important that I see it through.'

I looked at him in disbelief.

'After this?' was all I could manage to say, looking over the bandages and plasters covering my body.

'Cosmo thinks that this is one of the most important decisions of my life . . . I have to do it for me . . . I have to come to an understanding about all of this.'

'Can't we do that together, TC, in the privacy of our own lives?'

'The whole course is really with us. They are phoning all the time, and praying for us . . . and Helen,' he added rather hesitantly.

'TC . . . I'd like you here. Is that too much to ask? When is the bloody course anyway?' I fought to control my anger, due entirely to the bitter disappointment I felt inside.

'Friday night and the weekend,' he replied. 'I'll be back to see you Monday,' he then added, as if that somehow made it alright.

'You could do it another time.'

'It wouldn't be the same ... the whole course are in this. Cosmo said it is a great learning opportunity for us all. Jules, he and his wife are devastated by what has happened.'

'TC, they are not lying here full of fucking holes. What sort of people are they not to see that I need some love right now? I want to know what has been done to me!'

I was crying. So was he.

'Please, Jules ... don't make it difficult for me. I just can't handle what has happened. You've got your family ... you won't be alone.'

'It's not the same.' I did not go on as I could not bear to see him so distressed. I told him to do his course. His face lit up.

'Can I give them a message from you?' He asked with such sincerity, I refrained from expressing the many expletives I would have loved him to deliver on my behalf. I felt such a long way from The Voice ... it had told me I would always have the pleasure of its company when I was not being a victim. My first real chance at choosing the warrior and I'd fallen in a blubbering mass of self-pity and hurt.

'Thank them for their prayers,' I managed to reply.

'I will. Thank you, Jules.'

The night sister came in, cheerful and bustling. She looked at us both and very kindly offered to find TC a bed in the hospital so he could stay near to me. He thanked her and, explaining that he was otherwise engaged, left rather hurriedly. Sister came and wiped away my tears.

'We'll look after you,' she said, her smile and nod indicating she knew how I was feeling. 'Do you want to talk?' she asked. I did and told her everything. She was wonderful, listening with all the patience, interest, encouragement and love of a lifelong friend. When I had finished, I thanked her. She stood up, cupped my face with her hands and to my surprise, she thanked me. The tenderness of that moment paved the way for the first real sleep since my arrival.

TWO LEGS AND A POEM

I was ravenous. I realised that for four days my only food intake had been intravenous and sipped liquids. Dr Kindness had told me I could try some solids. I was prepared to try anything to fill the gastric-juice-dripping cavern within. For the first time since my admission, I was aware of my internal organs. Everything felt sore, distended, not helped by the pressure created by my full bladder which was causing severe discomfort. I could hear the clatter of life beyond my open door and caught glimpses of uniformed figures dashing past. The professional carers were working so hard, I felt guilty asking them for anything, even though my call of nature was verging on the urgent. I tried to get some attention by asking for help in a soft, timorous voice – there was of course no response. I was building up a dangerous head of steam, so I called out with more enthusiasm. Still no response. The internal pressure was now so enormous, I yelled for the bedpan loud enough for the entire ward to hear. No one came and one of my greatest fears manifested. Hot, sterile-smelling pee flooded the bed, soaking my backside and inner thighs. I cried with the ambiguous mixture of guilt and delicious relief. As the last drop exited, a young red-faced nurse appeared.

'Did you want a bedpan?' she asked.

'I'm sorry . . . it's too late,' I mumbled in response, my head hung low.

'Oh!' she said, sighing with a weary resignation that implied this was not the first mishap she'd had to deal with this morning. 'Why did you go and do that?'

'Because . . .' I stopped short of a facetious reply when I saw her over-scrubbed and chafed red hands. 'I couldn't wait any longer. I called for help, but no one came ... and I just couldn't wait. I'm so sorry.'

'We'll have to change you,' she replied, leaving the room to find help. I wondered what for ... perhaps someone with greater bladder control? I lay in the rapidly cooling puddle, beginning to itch and unable to move. Eventually she returned with an older woman and the two of them attacked me and the bed amidst a flurry of talcum powder and starched sheets, with all the energy of acute irritation. Even amidst the pain of being rolled and moved, I had to admire the dexterity with which the sheets were removed from around my body. For some obscure reason it was reminiscent of train-commuting businessmen who fold their broadsheet newspapers in such a way as to be able to read them using only one hand in the crush of rush-hour.

I was sipping a cup of hospital-grey tea, trying not to think about whose lips had last graced the thick rim, when Mum walked in. She looked terrific, dressed in white cotton slacks and jacket, draped with her trade-mark scarves, bangles and brooches. I was glad to see her looking more relaxed.

'Good morning, darling. How are you feeling this morning?' she asked brightly.

'I slept for the first time ... I think I'm beginning to feel a bit more with it,' I replied.

She went on to explain she was staying in a local hotel, and she too had had the first decent sleep since the news and was feeling a lot better. We both agreed that, for healing and general well-being, sleep was one of the most underrated cures in existence. She told me that Herbert had gone back to sort things out at home and would return to collect her on Saturday. 'Don't be offended by his inability to say anything comforting – you know he's always hopeless at expressing himself ... he just doesn't know how to deal with this ... he can only be pragmatic ... he got the flight, hired the car, sorted out the hotel for me ... you know, Ju, remember he made it possible for me to be here.' She looked away, embarrassed at her need to defend him.

I asked her to fill out the meal selection card for me. She read out the choices but, hungry as I was, nothing really appealed.

For some reason I was longing for a baked potato, creamed with butter and black pepper, topped with fresh coriander – perhaps my body knew what it wanted to assist in its recovery. My mother offered to go out and get me food but the transportation of mash was not an easy task, even for someone of her ingenuity.

'I'll write down boiled potatoes with carrots and gravy ... it's the closest we can get,' she said, writing something else on the card.

'What are you saying?'

'I've told them it's your first meal in days, and that you are longing for creamy mashed potatoes and could they help as you've had a rough time and deserve what you want.'

'Oh Mum, I don't want them to think I'm a nuisance.' I was embarrassed.

'Fuck what they think ... You've just survived a diabolical attack, and if you don't ask for what you want, you'll never get it. You want mashed potatoes, you'll have mashed potatoes!'

'You sound like a Jewish mamma.'

'I am a Jewish mamma. I was just born into the wrong family ... they must have got my cot muddled.' I chuckled as she went on, her voice now serious.

'By the way, Ju, don't be surprised if you take up fishing when you leave hospital.'

'What?'

'Fishing. You could find you have a passion for fishing,' she repeated, her face dead-pan.

'Why?'

'The taxi-driver who brought me here this morning told me that you have in all probability got his blood in your veins. He's a regular donor here.' She was whispering. 'He's a fanatical fisherman.'

'Did he tell you what else he enjoyed?' I asked, wondering what other secret passions had been intravenously fed to me.

The women from physio walked in.

'Today's the big day,' Blondie announced.

'Big day?' I repeated quizzically.

'Yep, today is the day we are going to have you on your feet again.'

'You are kidding . . .' I said. I looked into their faces and could tell they were not. Light-headedness overwhelmed me and they had not even flipped the covers back. My mother looked on in mirrored disbelief.

'Isn't this a little early . . .?' she asked politely.

'Never too early to get mobile again. She'll thank us for it when she's walking again . . . and all the pain will be forgotten.'

Pain. I was frightened. I was so weak and hurt in so many places it did not seem possible I could support my own weight. Their deft movements and certain manner, however, convinced me they knew what they were doing. Their confidence gave me the courage I needed – they were, after all, only wanting to help me.

'OK. Let's go,' I said, taking a deep breath.

'Well done, Julie,' Blondie and her side-kick Robin chorused in encouragement.

We did a few warm-up rolls from side to side with the mandatory coughing-up session. Although all movements were torture, everything was definitely a little easier than previous attempts at mobility. I knew how much my smoking had been frowned upon, but never so much as during those moments. I heard my mother's sighs, knowing somehow, beyond the realms of scientific understanding, her body was probably feeling all my pain.

'Now, Julie, remember there is nothing wrong with your legs other than lack of use. They will feel a bit shaky to start with but they will be fine,' Blondie informed me as she brought me into the upright sitting position with several swift movements. I was panting and perspiring with the effort, the floor a yawning abyss threatening to swallow me into extinction. Blondie and Robin wheeled my mobile of tubes and plastic fluid bags alongside me and then swivelled me around so my legs could dangle over the side of the bed. My little legs. It was the first time I had seen them since the accident; they felt nothing whatsoever to do with me. They looked incredibly pale with slightly stubbly hair growth, and about as capable of holding me up as two condoms filled with aspic jelly.

I peered down the front of my oversized hospital gown as it

gaped open. I was horrified. Between my breasts and running down to my navel was a three-inch-wide band of bloodstained white dressing, held in place with abundant strips of pink sticking plaster. All I could see of my chest was peppered with scabs and encrusted blood and pus. It was not a pretty sight. I turned my attention back to the job in hand.

My arms were placed around the shoulders of the girls in white, who took my weight whilst I hung between them in the crucifix pose and screamed, convinced all the stitches in my body had just been ripped out. Mum jumped up. 'PLEASE . . .' was all she managed to say, her clenched fists and white knuckles giving away her tension. They ignored her, concentrating on balancing me between them as they took a leg each and guided it towards the floor, as if I were a delicate puppet with tangled strings. Very slowly they lowered their shoulders, allowing me to take the impact of my own weight. My knees buckled and I started to fall forwards in a sickly faint. They rescued me.

My friend! You're forgetting to breathe.

I opened my eyes and drew air greedily into my lungs, bringing an instant beneficial effect. Silently I thanked the guiding voice. Blood rushed and pumped into all the forgotten corners of my limbs.

'Shall we try again?' Robin asked gently.

'Yes, I'm ready,' I replied.

We repeated the process several times and on the fourth attempt I stood unaided. It was marvellous. I gave myself a gold star for achievement. 'Now we're going to try a few steps,' Blondie informed me. 'Don't look so worried, today we will support you but tomorrow you're on your own.'

Mum moved and stood a few paces in front of me, her arms outstretched, and with a broad grin on her face said, 'Come to Mummy then,' in her best coochee-coo voice.

'Don't make me laugh,' I begged her, still unsure of the control I had over legs and bladder. The process of walking a few steps was extraordinary. With a new sense of admiration I experienced the complexity of this everyday action, each movement deliberate, requiring intense concentration and massive physical effort. I would not have believed six faltering steps would provide me with such a sense of fulfilment. Mum, Blondie and Robin all applauded me, delighting in my joy. I was eased systematically back into the bed, and lay back, hungry, exhausted, needing the bedpan and increasingly aware of a raging toothache.

A gentle touch on my cheek woke me up. Lunch had arrived and my mother was sitting on the edge of my bed, her expression triumphant, a plate of mashed potatoes balanced on one hand, a spoon in the other.

'Open wide,' she said, as she informed one of the onlooking nursing staff how she'd had to wait thirty years for this as I had NEVER let her feed me when I was a child. I took my first mouthful. The potatoes were lukewarm, watery and slightly lumpy, but for me it was one of the best meals of my life – even if I did have to be spoon fed.

The afternoon was incredibly busy. The usual rounds of doctors and nurses came and went. I reported my toothache and Pomp's cold finger, inserted into my mouth, was miraculously able to diagnose that the swelling was nothing and was 'to be expected'. The throbbing only intensified. I was lowered and raised onto numerous bedpans, then patted dry and talcum-powdered, still to have a bodily odour resembling elderly ladies on a hot day. Flower bouquets and arrangements arrived by the armload, and the bare room began to look like a Mayfair flower stall. The fragrances were exquisite and all but drowned out the sterile smells of accidents and hospital life. The messages attached to each offering were full of sincere good wishes for my well-being. In the pulsation of the silence every bloom was whispering to me. I strained to hear, not believing that I believed the flowers were talking to me.

'R-E-M-E-M-B-E-R . . . R-E-M-E-M-B-E-R . . . W-H-O . . . Y-O-U . . . A-R-E . . . O-U-R . . . B-E-A-U-T-Y . . . I-S . . . Y-O-U-R . . . B-E-A-U-T-Y.'

Yes, it was as I feared, they were most definitely talking to me.

I had a steady stream of visitors, including my other uncle who'd driven several hundred miles to be at my bedside. He walked in looking pale and shocked, calling me 'Rice-pudding', my early nickname due to a passion for the home-made dessert. We talked of many things. It was uplifting to see him and a reminder that a healing environment is created by anything that takes one's mind off the horrors . . . and what better way than the laughter and love of one's family and friends.

'Ah . . . Miss Moneypenny,' I exclaimed as my secretary walked in clutching many bags.

'I've brought you all the things on JR's list,' she announced.

'You went to the cottage?' I asked.

'Yes,' she replied.

'And . . . how was it?'

'The cottage is as lovely as ever,' she reassured me. I wondered who had cleaned away all the blood . . . and who was feeding the cats in TC's absence.

Miss Moneypenny interrupted my thoughts. She was more than the efficient organiser behind my new business, she was also a valued friend. She opened my toilet bag and one by one removed the contents, explaining what she had brought me. When she placed the nail polish and acetone remover on the bedside cabinet, I winced. I did not hold out much hope for their use, looking at my still bandaged stumps.

I recalled a story about my uncle John. He had raced motorbikes, which led him to spend much time in hospital beds. TC had first met him whilst he was recovering from two broken wrists and various other fractures. TC was then a young duty doctor doing his hospital rounds and was amazed to find several of the prettiest nurses sitting on the bed of a mummified figure, turning over the pages of a raunchy magazine for him. TC figured that this man had some charisma and from then on he and John forged a lifelong friendship. In fact John had always wanted me to meet TC, but his match-making plans always failed and one or other of us wouldn't make the date. It was therefore ironic that when we did at last meet, it was in the hospital where John eventually died. Then TC was an incredible source of strength to myself and my heartbroken family. How strange the cycles of life are, that now he is, in their eyes, the villain of the piece. Explaining his absence to everyone was one of the hardest things I had ever had to do. It would seem that both my mother and I felt we had to make excuses for our partners' behaviour.

Miss Moneypenny was still producing the contents of my bathroom cabinet, exactly as I would have done had the roles been reversed, eager to ensure nothing had been forgotten, her bag full of 'just in cases'. My mind wandered. I tried to picture Pomp and Circumstance sitting on my bed, giggling and eager to please me, turning the pages of arty photographs of naked men.

JR arrived. She looked tired and anxious and was clutching a number of ominous-looking papers under her arm.

'JC, I'm sorry to do this to you but I've got to clear up a few things around work. I've been up to London today and had a meeting with the boss . . . She's not happy.'

The boss was our nickname for an old friend of mine who was our previous employer. We now freelanced for her but relations between us were somewhat strained – working with a friend had not been entirely successful. I dreaded the thought of dealing with the nitty gritty of my business arrangements; other than the details of being stabbed, it was the last subject I wanted to hear about. I forced myself to concentrate, as JR launched into a well-rehearsed speech. It transpired that I was being asked to resign as a director of the media sales company I had originally worked for. The company accountants had been informed by the Inland Revenue that, because I was still named as a director, I could not be classed as working freelance and therefore I owed thousands of pounds in tax and national insurance. The company was responsible for these payments, so the matter was urgent.

'This is your official resignation, which you must sign today,' JR added, thrusting a form under my nose.

'I left media sales six months ago and I work as a consultant for four other companies. You know as well as I do, JR, that the directorship was not worth a toss . . . not one share, nor one shred of remuneration against the company's success. It was a title given as a palliative. The only reason my name still appears on the notepaper is because none of us thought it important enough to change.'

'JC,' she pleaded, 'you don't have to explain to me . . . I was there, remember? I know it was a title without any worth but the Inland Revenue doesn't and the boss is panicking, because she's liable for the money. Just sign it. Treat it as a joke.'

'A fucking expensive one, JR,' was all I could say as she placed a pen carefully through the bandage of my left hand, which was easier to get at than my right one. With great difficulty I signed the paper, unable to focus on the blur of excuses which formed the text.

'Well done, JC. It's over,' she said sympathetically.

JR spent the next half an hour asking questions related to my negotiations. With great reluctance I dragged my mind back to before the accident and answered her queries to the best of my ability. I was so grateful she was there to shield me from direct contact with the world of business – the world where friendship is directly proportional to how useful you may be. I knew neither of us was suited to life within it – we were far too honest – but for the moment I wanted to give my dear friend all the help I could.

My past had a surreal quality and all that had seemed so important days before had no further value for me. I would need time to explain my new perspective to those around me, although I doubted that they would be able to comprehend all that had happened to me. For the time being it seemed appropriate to act as if nothing much had changed and that after my recovery life would continue as before. My mother and Hank were the only two people I felt I could tell about the experiences beyond my body and, of course, The Voice. I knew nothing in my life was to remain the same. A force, beyond my petty desire to control, had awakened.

By the time everyone had left, it was late evening. The duty sisters had told me I could have visitors any time, which certainly helped the time pass more quickly, although it was exhausting. I was given the medical once-over prior to sleep and pronounced well on the mend, all readings of fluids, pulse, blood-pressure and temperature returning to acceptable levels. I was congratulated on my efforts in taking my first steps and given an enormous amount of encouragement by those who guarded my health with such vigilance. During my incarceration I met many beautiful angels disguised as humans. I also encountered several humans who had, in all probability, trained under Mengele and had no disguise.

I was shown a long cord, with what looked like an old-fashioned light switch on the end of it.

'If you need the bedpan, press this,' one of the nurses told me, 'and one of us will bring it for you. OK?' She placed the buzzer somewhere by the side of my left leg and promptly disappeared.

As tired as I was even the drugs could not induce sleep. Left with my own company I dared to allow my mind to undertake the job of considering the future. It did not look good. I had to be realistic about what lay beyond the cocoon of my hospital room, and once again I had to face all that had been troubling me when I took off for Spain, several lifetimes ago.

Look yourself in the eye of truth and tell yourself what you see. You'll be amazed at what you will discover.

In my raw state it was not difficult to be honest. I knew I did not want to go back to the cottage – the memory of the violence was all too vivid. I felt I would always smell my blood and terror impregnated into the fabric of the walls. I did not know how I would ever be able to pick up a knife again without being reminded of its sinister uses. And then, there was TC. Whether his absence from my side was due to shock, or pressure from his course, or just the inability to cope, a future with him was looking bleak and lonely. Life as a doctor's partner in a small English town did not seem to be the right backdrop. I was on the wrong stage and it was getting painful. I could no longer see the point of remaining with someone just because it is better than having no one. I remembered my mother's impassioned plea to the newsmen of the fifties, about God not wanting people to remain together if they could not love each other. I realised how brave she had been and how right she was. I knew of many couples who remained together in varying states of misery. There were those who would rather die than admit their desire for improvement, let alone change. I wondered which state I was trapped in and what this love business was all about.

Freedom. True love is freedom. Loving someone enough to want the highest for them ... even if that means letting them go from your life. Loving yourself enough to want the highest for you ... even if that means letting them go. You see, all that you have been given is not yours – you are merely the custodian. Things will come and things will go. People will come and people will go. Holding on to anything with the attachment of possession can create pain for all concerned. Love with conditions is not freedom – and therefore ...

Not love.

Very good. What did you feel as you rocketed through the heavens?

Freedom ... incredible freedom.

And what did you feel for the woman who was wishing to inflict as much harm on you as is humanly possible?

Love.

Yes indeed. Love. So you see, you have had a taste of love in true freedom. You will never forget it again, my friend – that I promise you.

But can such exquisite love and freedom be experienced without dying ... or have I got to wait until I turn up my toes?

You can experience the bliss of all createdness any moment you are ready.

How?

Don't lie to yourself ... about anything. That will be a good start.

My honesty only served to depress me. My position seemed hopeless. If I chose not to return to life with TC, where would I go? The thought of spending even a few days with my mother, much though I loved her, filled me with horror. I considered my stepfather was a full-time job for my mother and my appearance on the scene would create acute stress for all of us. The Spanish holiday had worked because for a lot of the time Mum and I were on our own. During the evenings and when Herbert was not playing golf I was prepared to act the dutiful daughter who was happy to go along with everything my stepfather wanted to do. I was sick of the pretence and in my current predicament in no shape even to begin to feign niceness towards this man with whom I had so little in common. I knew my grandmother would welcome me with open arms and provide all the love and care I needed. Unfortunately she lived within only a few miles of my mother and that alone would create yet another set of problems. Once more I faced the no-win situation so prevalent in my childhood.

What little capital I possessed was about to be repossessed by the Inland Revenue and any future income was looking distinctly precarious. After a quick mental calculation, I knew I could not even afford to go away and convalesce. I had no idea how much longer I was to be incarcerated in this sterile cell, whether I would have the use of my hands, whether I would ever get fit again, whether I would have to go through a trial, what was happening to Helen-from-hell and what, if any, my rights were. For all my visitors, I felt unbelievably ill-informed. My lawyer stepfather and doctor-boyfriend had both absconded. Self-honesty was frightening ... it was indeed a bloody mess. I began to itch in every inaccessible square inch of my body and nature, once again, was calling.

Wedged horizontally between the pillows and bound and tucked so tightly between the stiff sheets, I was unable to move into a position to see exactly where the buzzer had been put. I extended my arm as far as it would reach without inflicting serious pain. I took great care not to pull out the long needle inserted into the back of my hand, dripping saline fluids slowly back into my debilitated system. I'd been told it was also very important as an emergency access for fresh blood in case of a second haemorrhage. Fortunately, I had no memory of the first. With full extension, I reached only empty space. I rested for several moments and then tried again. Still nothing there. I tried lifting myself up with my elbows. The pain of stretching was excruciating but I caught sight of the inoffensive little contraption alongside my knee. My cheeks were aflame with the effort of such strenuous exercise and my bladder bursting at the seams. I called out for help in a stage whisper, not wanting to wake the adjacent ward full of post-operative snoring women. Other than loud groans coming from behind my head there was no response. I tried once more to fling myself towards the buzzer, gasping and panting for air.

It was impossible, it was just too far away.

'OH FUCKETY FUCK FUCK FUCK!' I cried out in total frustration as once again my bladder shed its load into the squeaky clean bed.

'Very funny, God!' I hissed. 'I can't take any more. Let me die. Please just let me die.' I was furious. 'All this fucking humiliation . . . why? Four days ago I was a private individual getting on with her life. And now . . . Now . . . I've had my life flung into public view, fucking pompous-arsed strangers prodding and probing and telling me how I feel . . . police accusing me of attempted murder . . . my family is shattered . . . my mother can't stay . . . Hank's knackered . . . TC can't love and care for me . . . JR can't cope . . . and I've just wet the bed. CAN YOU HEAR ME! I can't fucking stand any more!'

'Who are you talking to, dear?'

I saw a nurse silhouetted in the doorway.

'I've wet the bed.'

'You should have pressed the buzzer . . . that's what it's for. We're short of staff, so you'll have to wait for a change.'

She had gone before I could explain. It was a very long time before she returned. A bad stomach ache prompted me to consider that I would soon have other 'down there' activity to contend with . . . which led me to consider the date. I realised the cramps and spasms were familiar, which was almost comforting – a pain I recognised, yes, it was THAT time of the month. The logistics of what would be required to facilitate ovary and bowel function did not bear thinking about and the night dragged itself into morning.

It was the weekend. Other than the increased traffic flow of anxious faces hiding behind hastily bought pre-wrapped flowers, it made little difference to my routine. Most passers-by could not resist staring, some even adding banal comments, 'Alright are you then, love?' I asked for my door to be closed.

The moment had arrived for an inspection of what lay beneath the dressings. I braced myself for the worst, my heartbeat lumpy with fear. First my left hand was unwound from its grubby-looking wrap. There were three horizontal lines of black stitches on the inner wrist, and my fingers were taped in as many places as a prize-fighter's. I considered I'd won the bout on points but sadly, other than the scars, had no trophy to show for it. The plasters were removed to reveal numerous scabby cuts and scratches. After wiping with lots of alcohol-soaked cotton-wool the hand was declared well enough to have no further bandages. One by one I wiggled my fingers, as instructed. They all worked. I grinned at the service team gathered around the bed. It was my first moment of happiness for hours. They all smiled back.

Then, after a lot of unwinding, the right hand emerged from beneath its surgical wrap. A clenched fist, red, angry and hunchbacked.

'Who bandaged that hand?' Pomp demanded.

All eyes present had an instant fascination with the floor.

'I asked,' he said with growing irritation, 'who bandaged that hand?'

I was feeling uncomfortable and wondering what was so wrong with the way it was dressed.

'Well?'

One of the housemen cleared his throat and replied nervously, 'H'hmm . . . er . . . you did, sir.'

Many throats cleared and I joined the rest of the team in finding the floor to be a source of great interest.

All credit to Pomp, he did not flinch as he barked his next order, 'Well, let's get these fingers working, shall we?' without the faintest trace of guilt in his voice. After much coaxing and uncurling, three fingers and my thumb relaxed their grip slightly on the invisible knife-blade they were still clutching. Those little digits had done so much to save me from death. I coughed back the wave of emotion I felt as I gazed upon the two battle-scarred hands. My right index finger remained in hibernation, bent double. The back of my hand resembled a Victorian corset laced over a bulging midriff. It could burst at any moment. The palm was also puckered with several inches of vertical stitching, the skin soggy and septic. The loose skin between finger and thumb was also embroidered. A sharp instrument prodded, probed and scanned the surface looking for response. There wasn't any. Then I was asked to move the fingers. I couldn't. Someone had super-glued them into a sculpture pose. I watched the doctors' faces. I detected concern. I asked when the feeling would return. Circumstance answered, 'In time' with all the ambiguity of a lawyer.

I was cold, shy, and nervous as once again I lay naked before a group of strangers, mostly men. I did not even have the comfort of being semi-conscious. They were all now staring at the metallic river of thick staples which snaked from the depths of my navel to the cleavage between my breasts. I was aghast. I had no idea the injury was so immense. What had she done to me? I thanked God the flesh-pinching clips were wide enough to conceal all signs of the attempted disembowelment. I was a person of squeamish disposition. The wound was peered at for some time and I was assured there should not be too much of a scar after a few months. It did not appease my secret distress. I was eased forwards onto brittle-skinned hands, as cold fingers pressed gently an area of my right shoulder blade. I cried out as a spasm of pain exited the deadlocked muscle. I was lowered back into a sitting position. Pomp caught hold of my left arm, and peered above the elbow. There was a large gash. He informed one of the doctors that it should have been stitched. It had been missed in the rush of life-saving activities. My neck was next to be inspected. Of course it was impossible for me to see what lay beneath the dressings. It was a good thing – I'd had enough shocks for one day, and of all my injuries, the memory of my throat being sliced was the worst. My entire body shuddered and began to curl into a foetal position.

'How the jugular could be exposed and not severed is quite incredible,' Circumstance murmured to himself, his face inches from mine. Incredible indeed.

They were all very pleased with the micro-surgery on my face and neck and informed me I was healing so quickly the fine stitches could be removed within the next couple of days. I observed their professional pride and recognised how they had taken a great deal of care to minimise scarring.

'Thank you. Thank you for all you have done for me . . . all your care. Thank you,' I said, as I saw each of their tired faces in the light of compassion. What a dreadful job they had. Tears of gratitude were running down my cheeks. Pomp and Circumstance smiled. For a moment they looked boyish and coy.

'It's what we're here for,' one of them responded, his voice soft. 'You are making remarkable progress. Quite remarkable. If you carry on like this, you can look forward to leaving us next week. You will be able to go home.'

A rush of excitement surged through me – until I remembered what had happened at 'home'.

'Have you got someone to look after you?' they asked.

'Oh yes,' I replied mechanically, 'my boyfriend's a doctor.'

'Of course,' said Pomp and they were gone.

Nurses cleaned me up and swaddled me in new bandages, as they confirmed how pleased the big guns were with my body's progress. I asked them about the groans coming from behind the party wall.

'Oh, that's Wilf, that is. He's in a coma. Been in it for months.'

'What happened to him?'

'He was stabbed.'

'Oh,' I said, somewhat taken aback. 'Poor Wilf.'

'Yes, poor Wilf. He was late for his Sunday lunch once too often.'

'Late for lunch?' I repeated, not seeing the significance.

'Yes. His wife stuck the carving knife in him.'

'Dear God.'

'She's on parole. Actually, she's a really nice lady ... she was just pushed too far ... went over the edge. She visits him every week.'

'On Sundays?' I asked.

'Yes. Funny that.'

Left to my own devices, I decided to try to access The Voice. There was so much to ask of this strange teacher. Closing my eyes, I concentrated on the image of the marbled courtyard I had seen previously. Nothing happened except the background din increased in volume. I sighed and prayed for help. No outer voice instructed me but I was aware of thoughts running on a different frequency from my usual frenetic ones.

Clench your muscles and then let them go. Keep your breathing steady. Deliberate. Feel the effect of the air entering and expanding your chest. Let everything go on the outbreath.

I sighed with relief as tension floated out of my body. Almost immediately I started to sink down towards the floor until I was falling through the tiles. I panicked, but could not stop the descent. There was no resistance. I called out as I spiralled down and down, my voice absorbed into the density of total stillness. I bumped to a halt. The cave was vast, its floor a lake of polished phosphates, the brilliance of the shine tempting me to skate across the surface in childish delight.

Welcome again, Dear One.

The entire cavern reverberated with the sound of The Voice. No recognisable form was in sight.

Welcome? Where am I?
You are on your way home.
What home? This looks to be a long way from Hampshire.
That is not your home.

You're telling me . . .

Before you drown yourself in the well of self-pity, let me remind you that no bricks nor mortar will ever be your true home. More a temporary shelter in a make-believe storm.

I don't want to go back there anyway.

You will return, my friend, for it is necessary.

But my life is full of problems, all the more complicated because of Helen's little outburst.

There is no better way of adding to someone's problems than to tell them they have problems.

So what would you say I've got?

What you have is the opportunity to discover solutions.

Solutions need problems.

Solutions arise within the heart of one who can say what they want, the one who understands about right action.

Well . . . Of course I know what I want . . .

And what is that?

Well . . . I want . . . I don't know . . .

Yes, you do know. Concentrate.

I want to get better. I don't want to have to . . .

No. The rules are you can only state that which you want.

OK . . . I want to be cared for by someone who can love me . . . I want to be loved. I want those around me to be kind and gentle with each other. I want to live in a world without hatred. Without cruelty. Yes, that's it. Dear God, why is it so hard to find?

It's not hard. Know that paradise exists, believe in it, yearn for it with all of your being . . .

I do believe it . . . but I can't find it.

Take heart . . . for how can you yearn for that which does not exist? There has to be a part of you that knows you have never left.

Which part?

The part which knows that impurity is the recognition of your own imperfection. Purity is the recognition of your own perfect imperfection.

You've lost me there . . .
**Whilst ever you are a stranger in Paradise . . . you seem
indeed to be lost, but I can promise you, you will find
your Self.**

The heartwarming sound of my mother's soprano voice lured
my awareness back into the hospital room. She asked if I'd had
a good sleep. I decided to tell her about The Voice.

'It's probably your guide,' she said after some thought.

'But I can't see anyone. I only hear it. Sometimes it is outside
of me, and sometimes it's inside me. I float away from everything
going on around me but I know I'm not asleep. Mum . . . it's
different from dreaming. It started to happen during the attack.
It seems to know everything I am thinking. Do you think I'm
going mad?'

'No, darling. You're not going mad. The world is mad . . .
not you.'

'Mum. I'm frightened . . . I'm out of control, I don't know
what's happening to me.'

'Ju.' She took my left hand very gently and rested it on her
upturned palm. Stroking my fingers she continued. 'Life has
to go on. The people around you will soon disappear and you,
well, you will have to face this on your own. You have to come
to your own understandings about it . . . no one can do it for
you. All the goodwill in the world cannot erase the memory of
what has happened, not for you, not for any of us. Time will
have to work its magic. The Voice will guide you. I will pray for
you and you must remember to say your prayers.'

'You sound like you are going away for a long time.'

'I am.' She was crying. 'I am a wife. My husband wants to see
his new grandchild. He expects me to be at his side. He doesn't
like me to be away. I have to get back for Mart. I told you, life
has to go on.' Her voice was brittle, her reasons for leaving
unconvincing. I looked at her for a long time and resisted the
urge to be sarcastic about her wifely duty. I could see she was
torn and I did not wish to add to her obvious hurt.

'And?' I asked quietly.

'You are so bloody psychic. Yes, you know there's more . . .

it's stupid to pretend. I believe the real trouble is he'll never forgive TC for this ... he hates him ... he's always hated him and now, well, there's no stopping him. I believe he wants to destroy him. Ju, you know what he's like when he gets a bee in his bonnet – it will be better for everyone if I can keep him away. I won't be able to come to you ... he'll never allow it, but you can come to us when you leave hospital. Please, Ju, let me look after you.' Her voice was soft.

'Mum, I can't stay with you because I know I won't be able to cope with the force of his negativity – I'm not that good at it when I'm well. What has happened to me is a nightmare but it is ridiculous to blame TC. It only makes things worse for me. I'm sorry, Mum. I'd love to be with you but I think it would kill me to have to listen to him banging on about everything over and over again, reading all sorts of things into the situation that don't exist. In any case, it puts you into an impossible situation, he'll only get angry if he thinks you don't agree with him and ... well, you're right, let's just leave him out of it. Are you leaving soon?'

'Any time now. I'm waiting for him to collect me. Don't be hard on him, Ju. I've told you he can't help it. It's his nature. Just pity me having to listen to it.'

'I know he can't help it, but you'd think just this once he might give some consideration to how we are both feeling. I do not understand how it is that, suddenly, all these fucking people who spend hardly any time with me or TC seem to think they know everything that happened last Tuesday. They are seeing what they want to see.'

'Hey, don't let it get to you. Come on, Ju ... over and out. Know that I love you, God loves you, your family loves you, all your beautiful friends love you. Even that daft husband of mine loves you ... in his way. Think about the good things. Some people have no one.'

He came for her and seeing her crying, was eager to leave as quickly as possible. His big frame loomed over the bed and he placed his opened hand on my middle and gave it a hearty rub. In muted voice, between clenched teeth, he growled, 'Now look here ... I've got to get your mother out of here. You understand, don't you ... she's too sensitive for this sort of thing? I don't want another "John" on my hands.' I all but passed out with pain as unthinkingly he ground and crushed my wound. His face was tense. I did understand taking my mother away was what he thought was best for her, but it was a moment of great sadness for me to realise how he had not the sensitivity to ask me how I felt. I heard her sobbing long after they had left and felt utterly sick of always being the one who did the understanding.

My mood was black. My visitors did little to alleviate the acute pains in my chest. My heart was hurting but I couldn't show it. Especially as some of the visitors were from TC's first course, and virtual strangers. I lay, not really listening to all the polite conversations. I was, of course, told repeatedly how lucky I was to have survived and how brave I had been and how well I looked . . . considering. I felt none of those things. Although well meant, for me the words were hollow.

Write one of your letters. It will make you feel better and remember, someone has to play the role of baddie in your play.

I was getting used to The Voice interrupting my mundane thoughts and knowing how to deal with my negativity. It was paradoxical – on the one hand it was frightening to feel I was being watched twenty-four hours a day and yet on the other, it was so comforting to feel someone knew what I was experiencing. As instructed, I considered the mental compositions of the last few days, and on reflection agreed, they did indeed make me feel better. Perhaps it was because I felt free to say exactly what I wanted without fear of repercussion, allowing full expression of my self-pity and thereby exorcising it. I wasn't too sure what was meant by the baddie in my play. I'd have to think about that some more.

'Pathos, darling . . . don't forget the pathos.' Max in full Professor Wallofkski regalia appeared before me, brought his face close to mine, and very slowly placed his tongue under his upper lip, pushing it out until he became Guy the gorilla. I giggled, just as the little girl used to do. 'It's all so bleedin' tragic,' he said with his unmistakable voice.

Hospital Room, Saturday

My Dearest Visitors,

Thank you all for taking the time and trouble to bring yourselves, and all that fruit, to my bedside. If I have appeared to be far away, this is not due entirely to all the drugs pumping through my system, but more to do with my mind being preoccupied with matters other than the weather and state of the NHS.

Now, I KNOW for my benefit you have all taken great care to eliminate certain words from your vocabulary. How do I know? Because without exception you have all let out the odd stab, cut, knife or slash somewhere in the conversations. You were all trying too hard. It has kept me amused in a macabre sort of way. You see, I have got a little competition running to see who can use the forbidden words most creatively. The prize will be the offending weapon hermetically sealed – yours for life. There are, to date, many contenders for the title.

The judge's decision will be final.

Thank you once again for the cabaret,

Your Captive Audience, who loves each one of you.

My catching up on correspondence was interrupted by two nurses wheeling a trolley into the room, sitting on which was a television.

'We thought you'd like this, Julie,' one of them said.

'It gets more like the Savoy here every day. Fresh flowers, ensuite bedpans, and now . . . a television. Wonderful. Thank you.' I did not have the heart to tell them watching TV was one of my least favourite ways of wasting time. I was famed for falling asleep in front of it – TC's sons used to take bets on how many minutes I would stay awake from the start of a video. I know the beginning and credits of more movies than I care to mention. The nurses were cheerful. It was so sweet of them to replace the noticeable absence of a loving partner with the box. Television . . . the surrogate 'something' for most people. I guess it was better than sleeping pills.

They turned it on, and left the room. The picture was

enormous. The colours were far too bright, and washed with an overlay of bright red. A well-known commercial was on the screen. God was most definitely testing my ability to see humour in the worst. A large carving knife sliced through the bloody joint with ease, as the voice-over said, 'BOOTIFUL.' Bootiful indeed. However, not all was bad. The evening film was not going to be *Psycho*.

Blondie came from physio and, as promised, had me up and walking without too much help. I managed to shuffle across the room and reach the wash-basin where I clung on to the little porcelain bowl puffing like a sixty-a-dayer. As I regained my composure, I lifted my head to ask for help back to the bed. Everything stopped. It was gruesome. The thing staring at me. I stared back, frozen to the spot. Blondie was speaking to me but her words were inaudible, drowned out by the beating of my heart.

'Who are you?' I hissed. Its lips moved with mine. The eyes were red-rimmed and enormous, the face distended, bruised blue, white and black, the lips thick and swollen, stuck in a snarl revealing upper gums and teeth. The neck was covered . . . in plaster . . . or some sort of bandage. I reached out to shield myself from the monster's fixed gaze. My right hand banged into the mirror.

'No . . . oh no . . . no. What have they done to me?' I was crying.

'Hey! It's not as bad as it looks,' Blondie reassured me, her arms suddenly around me. 'I didn't realise you hadn't seen yourself. I'm sorry . . . I know . . . it's all a shock but I promise you, it will all settle down and you'll never know . . . the surgeons here are marvellous. Now come on, let's get you back into bed.' She took most of my weight with her shoulder as she guided me back to the bed. I was still crying long after she had left the room.

It was agreed the intravenous pain-killer could be stopped and furthermore the saline drip was removed. The relief was instantaneous as the needles were taken out of my veins. Initially I was frightened my body would not function without them and lay very very still. I could feel my cells readjusting to life on their own. The early evening inspection team had also found the source of the terrible pain in my jaw. There was an abscess around a lower tooth. It was a great relief they had found the root of my discomfort, even if it had taken three days to convince them things were amiss. It was so infected, they advised me, nothing could be done until Monday. I was given a soothing paste, and oral pain-killers which I hoped covered all areas.

I managed to eat my supper unaided – which was lucky as there was no one around to help. Some soup, followed by more potatoes. The TV blared away and true to form, I drifted in and out of fitful sleep. Each time my awareness came back into the room, I jolted awake, temporarily unsure of my whereabouts. By the time the hot chocolate nightcap arrived, I was very tired. I forced myself up, it was worth the effort for the best meal of the day.

I reached for the cross and chain and took it from its envelope. The medallion was still there. Staring at it, I was consumed with love for the face looking back at me. No matter what in the darkness of ignorance man had done to him, Christ knew only love, compassion and forgiveness. What a great Being. What if there were others like him on earth now? I tingled with excitement as I considered what it would be like to sit at the feet of a spiritual master. Someone who knew what life was for, why we were all here, why it seemed such a struggle. I thought better of asking the tea-trolley driver where one might start looking for an enlightened master, which could have been a big mistake. Masters are known to turn up where you least expect them. I suspected The Voice had a lot to say on the matter, but I fell into dreamless sleep before contact was established.

I slept straight through and awoke refreshed, feeling stronger and happier after an undisturbed night. It was Sunday and the sun was shining. The morning shift of cleaners, caterers, carers, doctors and visitors were all in cheerful mood. I got out of bed by myself and had a little walk around the room. I did not have enough courage to venture into the corridor on my own. I decided I would have another go later in the day, with the guiding arm of a friend to fall back on. It was a miraculous feeling to be independent once more. I wished I could have danced and sung, but felt cautious about celebrating my new-found freedom too soon.

At the tiny sink, I washed as much of the front of my hair as was possible using only my left hand, without getting the dressing on my neck wet. It took a long time, but systematically I worked my way around my face, washing and towel-drying a strand at a time as my mother had done. The swelling and bruising in my face was much reduced and I was beginning to recognise myself once again. I put a little eye make-up on in anticipation of letting everyone know how much better I was feeling. I had never much liked the Holbein look of lashless women. As I manoeuvred the spiral brush I was reminded of a charming Irishman I'd worked with once. He used to call me Dusty, as in Springfield, and accuse me of disturbing papers on his desk if I fluttered the lashes too much. He also used to call me his 'Little Y-front stretcher'. In a department of over forty men, with two and a half women, I assured him it was no great achievement. His offbeat humour was always landing him in trouble; unfortunately he sensed if he got to anyone and would go for the kill. My lovely Murphy, always over the top . . . no doubt fuelled by slugs of poteen and mugs of tea with a lot more than sugar in. He would have loved the eyes staring out from the mirror. Dusty was back. A definite indication things were on the mend.

It worked. Everyone remarked on how well I looked. I spent the rest of the day out of bed, exploring the world beyond my room. My first major excursion was to the bathroom, which was opposite my doorway. I was told there would be no more bedpans . . . I was a big girl now and could make it alone. It was a very long way – the crossing of the corridor was akin to walking on a tightrope over the Niagara Falls. I lost my balance several times but eventually made the sanitised throne room with time to spare, clutching with embarrassment the enormous white hammock standard-issue hospital sanitary protection.

I called in on my neighbour Wilf on the way back. He was moaning as he lay comatose, wired for sound. If the story I'd been told was true, this was the handiwork of one insertion of a carving knife meant for the Sunday joint. I stood watching his chest rise and fall. I was crying again – perhaps I was lucky.

'Hey, Wilf!' I was certain he could hear me whispering. 'Don't give up. She didn't mean it. Come back, Wilf.' I jumped as a small neat woman wearing a prim smile and hat entered the room. Remembering it was Sunday, I said hello in a rather strangulated voice as my jellied legs managed to run out of the room.

Regaining my composure, I ventured once more into the land beyond my room. It was time to call my mother. I found my purse and with great difficulty my inexperienced left hand sorted out the necessary coins. I walked very slowly to the pay-phone, using the walls as support. There was a queue. The air was thick with cigarette smoke and gossip exhaled from the lungs of women clad in quilted housecoats and fluffy pink slippers. I could hardly breathe. The harshness of fluorescent lights bathed everyone in a sickly wash of colour; the creatures hanging around looked more as if they were awaiting auditions for the next 'living dead' movie than patients on the mend. Eventually I got to the phone and after much fumbling managed to get through to my mother. She answered after one ring. She was unable to hide her resentment at having to be at home and I found myself spending five pounds worth of coins trying to cheer her up. As my money was running out she shouted that she had sent me a letter explaining 'things' and that my stepfather said it would be 'alright' to reverse the charges the next time I called. I resisted the temptation of smashing the phone onto its cradle and walked unsteadily back to my room, repeating the last words of the call out loud, 'Alright to reverse the charges. How very bleedin' generous of him.'

Friends, family, course participants and working colleagues came a-visiting. I was overwhelmed with the kindness and love I was shown which far outweighed the use of forbidden words. I realised my condition was something being shared by a great many people, many of whom I did not even know. As I learnt how I was being held in the prayers and thoughts of so many I felt a great surge of well-being, and knew that somehow their love played a vital part in my recovery.

As expected, Monday arrived on time. The morning was action packed; physio had me all but skipping around the room, followed by the gentle removal of stitches from my mouth, neck and left hand. Using my make-up mirror, I inspected my newly exposed flesh. It was horrible. Five long red scars crisscrossed from below my left ear to my Adam's apple. When I turned my head to the right, all the scarred skin puckered into an unsightly lump, reminiscent of my own attempts at sewing bulky seams together. I found it hard to believe the reassurances that it would improve. Taking consolation in the fact that the scar on my mouth was almost undetectable with head-on light, I figured I could always wear scarves around the throat.

I was escorted to the dentist whose surgery was on a different floor. He confirmed there was an abscess in the lower left jaw. My mouth stretched open as he excavated and X-rayed. After a short while he explained there was nothing much he could do as the tooth was smashed, and the splinters and fragments were embedded in the jaw which was too swollen and pus-filled to enable him to pick them out. He told me there was no hope of saving the tooth, and my own dentist would have to extract it as soon as was possible. He asked me if I knew what had hit me so hard as to cause a tooth to shatter. I told him about the carving knife. He went very quiet and with extra care removed what splinters and pus he could. The pain was dreadful.

I returned to my room alone. It was the longest excursion I had made to date and I longed to rest. Arriving to find lunch waiting for me, hungry as I was I couldn't touch it. I nursed my aching jaw and dozed, tossed and turned, wondering what had happened to TC. He showed up eventually in the early evening. He explained he was delayed because he had stayed in London and he and another course participant had gone to Holloway to see if they could visit Helen. It was something discussed on the course and Mr Greene felt it was 'appropriate' behaviour. Not surprisingly they had been refused access.

'Has this man got some kind of grudge against me?' I asked.

'Of course not – he and Felicia think you are very special. Look, I've got this book for you. It's from them.'

He handed me a paper bag in which there was a book and

a card. The book was on spiritual matters and inscribed with a message about how special I must be and how much they were 'with me' – I was not convinced on either count and put the book on the bedside cabinet. These people were strangers to me and were encouraging TC to stay away. If they were teaching universal love and claiming they could improve the quality of one's life, they were not doing much for me. I could not see what was so wrong in the person I lived with being with me. I opened the card. The message was similar. I read it twice. It took a third reading to spot the mistake. It was not addressed to me. It was for Helen. I put it back in its envelope before TC noticed.

'Perhaps, TC, it's easy to be magnanimous when you are not lying in a body full of knife-holes . . . or climbing the bloody walls of Holloway charged with attempted murder!'

'JULIE,' he shouted back. 'Cosmo was gutted when I told him what happened. He's really supportive of us.'

'Well, I'm sorry, but I do not feel supported by you or your teachers. With me . . . really with me, excuse me, but I don't see them around. What's going on, TC?'

He put his head in his hands and rested it on my arm. 'I don't know, Jules . . . I really don't know what's happening. I'm so tired.'

He climbed onto the bed and lay next to me. I lay very still, holding him as he slept.

Why can't we help each other?
Because you do not know the true nature of help – you believe your actions are a measure of how helpful you are and thus, in the book of your life, no action means no help which means . . . no love. So . . . you judge yourself to be helpless and loveless which is not the truth.
Why do you always have to speak to me in cryptic clues?
Because you like crosswords.
I don't want riddles, I want answers . . . please.
I speak with absolute simplicity – it is you who thinks in riddles.
Oh really? Then I must be very thick.

172

Well, yes – your armour is at times.

Thanks a bundle.

My total pleasure – I will present you with a riddle if you wish.

Try me.

Your armour – this thing you have built up around your Self in the belief it will protect you. One has to observe it did not do you much good this week of your life.

What do you mean?

Well, there you are, living your life, pleasing everyone – observe the form your so-called armour takes. You and millions of particles of consciousness have been brought up to believe this is good, helpful and loving behaviour. You would do well to contemplate the parable of one's cup overflowing ... You see, my friend, one can only give, or receive, from a full heart – fear and expectation-based actions have no real value other than as teaching demonstrations.

But how do you give from a full heart?

Remove the armour. Stop trying to please others. Stop expecting others to please you.

I will become a tortoise without a shell. Very vulnerable and easily squashed.

Not quite. More a light bulb without its shade.

Bright?

Yes – very bright. And in that brightness all can see who they really are. Now that, dear friend, is giving.

You are telling me that we can't help each other because our hearts are not full.

No. If you hear me I am telling you that your hearts are overflowing with love. You are unable to give or receive because your light is dimmed by your wrong beliefs.

So all these people I feel let down by ... they cannot give me any support because they cannot see who they are and I cannot receive because I too am blind?

Exactly.

Well, who are they?
The same as you.
Who am I?
That is what you must find out.

TAKE AWAY THE FATHER AND MOTHER
REMOVE YOUR SISTERS AND BROTHERS
AND I
MY FRIEND
I AM
STILL THERE

DISMANTLE THE BRICKS AND MORTAR
CONSUME ALL FOOD AND WATER
AND I
DEAR FRIEND
I AM
STILL THERE

ERADICATE ALL PLANTS AND TREES
DRAIN THE OCEANS AND THE SEAS
AND I
MY DEAREST
I AM
STILL THERE

SNUFF OUT THE CANDLES OF HEAVENLY LIGHT
DESTROY THE STARS AND MOONS OF NIGHT
AND I
DEAREST FRIEND
I AM
STILL THERE

AND THEN TAKE ME AND YOU
DISSOLVE US IN THE CRUCIBLE OF TRUTH
AND I
DEAREST ONE
I AM
STILL THERE

I looked at the white cotton track-suit laid out on the bedside chair. White shoes, white socks and new underwear. The watch on the bedside table read 4 a.m. – I was wide awake and excited. It was Tuesday. The day had at last arrived. I could leave my hospital cell. The new clothes provided by the ever thoughtful Naomi gave me the feeling of first day back at school. New class, new teachers, new books and stiff new knickers. A new start. In the frenetic 'stitch 'em up and get 'em out' routine of the post-operative ward there had not been enough time to consider the implications of this second go at life. I had no real idea what I was going to do about anything. I'd had many loving offers of places to stay from friends and acquaintances and I had at least managed to make a decision about the next week of my life. I was to stay in a village pub, which Naomi and Leo ran. They were a couple I loved, we had shared many good times together. I knew in their company I would not be allowed to take things too seriously; also, I thought some of my visitors would appreciate the proximity of the bar, having endured a week of hospital canteen teas and coffees. As TC had to work, they were going to collect me in the late morning.

I lowered myself gently out of the bed, the metal clips and sutures all pulling tightly on my skin as I moved. The internal pain was now tolerable but I was still in great discomfort. In the midst of physical contraction it was so hard to remember a state without pain; I knew it existed but doubted whether I would ever know ease again. I walked slowly over to the handwash basin and performed the slow ritual of ablutions.

I longed for a bath with an intensity which made me

want to weep. I was not dirty, but I still felt the filth of violation clinging to me. A full, hot, perfumed bath was the only thing that would symbolically wash this feeling away. I wanted to feel squeaky clean and for my skin to be plump, pink and shining with vitality. In the grey morning light, however, it was pallid and loose, its hue anaemic-white dappled with patches of black bruise and flame-red scars. Dried blood and scabs encrusted my torso, flesh hung from my limbs, the underlying muscle tone having all but disappeared in less than seven days. My hair was lank and smelt of disinfectant. I surveyed the sorry sight as if I were in an overheated department store trying on a dress that was definitely 'not me'.

I put on the new track-suit. It took me the best part of an hour to dress myself, tying the shoelaces proving to be the most difficult task. I could not bend down, but I could manage to lift my leg onto my chair for very short bursts. Then I had to negotiate the laces, with my injured hands. With virtually no feeling in my right-hand fingers, swelling and bandages to contend with, it was almost impossible. I broke out in hot sweats, my face burning, my heart pounding with the effort. Resting between each movement, I eventually did it, falling into the chair. Knackered, and only 5 a.m. Still, it felt great to have clothes on.

I ate a light breakfast, and sat looking out of the window, waiting. As the hours came and went I was beset by childish fears. Perhaps they were not coming. Maybe I'd given them the wrong day. They could have had an accident. Maybe they had changed their minds. Perhaps my watch was wrong. I was working myself into a bad state. It was time to change the record. I got up and collected together the flowers. I placed some of the magnificent arrangements alongside my holdall, ready to take with me. The rest I rearranged and with the help of the nurses distributed them throughout the ward and public areas. I then cleaned the sink and tidied the room as best I could. Nurses, doctors, cleaners and fellow patients came in and out, wishing me luck, love and best wishes. Dr Kindness made me promise that if I ever had a baby I would let them all care for me. We both cried as we hugged each other.

Why do I keep crying?
It's a great sign.
Of what?
Your heart opening.

I was handed a brown paper bag and asked to sign for it. I looked inside. There were the remains of the clothes I had been wearing only seven days previously. I took out the sweater and laid it on the bed. I ran my fingers over its surface stiff with caked blood. I found thirty-two holes. I wondered, if I had died, whether this is what TC and my mother would have been given. I was crying again. I realised it was probably standard procedure to hand possessions back but I was not ready to awaken the memory contained in the innocuous-looking container.

Hospital Room

My Dearest Mum,

Remember I told you about the clean underwear? Forget it! Today a nurse handed me an NHS carrier bag with my possessions, including my bra and pants. It would seem that in the terror of what happened last week, I did unspeakable things in the lower half of the ensemble, and the top half has been cut up the middle and is now a delightful shade of dried blood-red. Perhaps I should offer them as a challenge to the biological powder merchants?

It would seem they had to hand me back EVERY-THING. Rules are a most interesting phenomenon – exactly who they protect is fast becoming one of life's great mysteries. I thought rules were there for my good, to protect me. With the benefit of a week's contemplation, I think this is a full bedpan. Many of our rules are born out of terror that someone might fiddle/cheat/sue or even beat the system, so the system must protect itself.

I am beginning to feel well enough to be terrified at the prospect of leaving hospital. 'The Voice' is still with me – I hope it sticks around long enough for me to get some deeper understanding of all this mess. I miss you.

Temple still undergoing rebuilding . . .

Soul intact.

Much love, always,

Pincushion.

The moment came to leave the hospital. I walked slowly out of the room, supported by a very cheery Naomi and Leo. Many faces lined the corridor wishing me well, the human battleship, patched and refitted, and about to be relaunched into the swirling sea of life.

I did not look back. I stepped out of the sterile hot-house into the watery sun of a March morning. The contrasting cold took my breath away.

Remember to breathe, my friend . . . it is known to assist the human condition.

Yes . . . I had heard something to that effect.

THE RETURN

The cottage looked so innocent squatting in the middle of a late winter garden. The drive was back to its original length, the front door looked innocuous and very new. Other than too many milk-bottles and the overfull dustbin, there was no clue to show it had been the scene of such a social breakdown.

My dear friend Paula led the way. She did not speak, and I appreciated her sensitivity in allowing me to take it all in, one step at a time. The house smelt of polish, bleach, fresh paint and new carpet. It was cold and un-lived in. I held on to the wall as I worked my way through the hall, passage and into the kitchen. I stood and looked at the stairs. I began to feel faint. In the silence I could hear myself screaming; the walls had absorbed the sounds of terror and were playing them back to me. I shook my head, trying to clear the echoes of horror ricocheting in my inner ears when the phone rang.

The next half an hour was spent listening to the shock-driven babble of Helen's sister, who was very surprised when I answered the phone. She was expecting TC to answer. She needed to speak on behalf of her sister who was desperate for me to know that she didn't mean it, would I forgive her and promise not to sue her? Yet again I was faced with one of those situations I had never been trained for. I could not hang up, feeling all the pain of this girl. I knew I would do the same if I had a sister who was so disturbed but I did not feel it was my place to offer forgiveness to Helen. First of all I needed to forgive myself for being stupid enough to have gone against my intuition. I wanted to be left alone to get on with my life. I told her this, and that I had just walked back into the house for the first time since the incident. It did not seem to register and on she went. I was very tired and could see Paula was getting pissed off. I scrawled who it was on the back of an envelope. It was almost worth the call to see the horror on Paula's face. She made frantic cutting gestures across her throat wanting me to cut the call. It took a few moments for the significance of her sign language to sink in. I stopped the conversation and put my head into my arms. After a few moments of silence, we both exploded with laughter. The spell was broken and I knew I could return to live in the cottage.

I left Paula in the kitchen and walked up the stairs into our bedroom. My Uncle Hank and his wife had stayed there the previous night, yet it was as I left it – there was no sign of any post-incident life. I went to the wardrobe to get a few more things to take back to the pub. The police photographer was coming to take some shots of the injuries, so I wanted to get some decent underwear – if my half-naked battle-scarred body was going to be peered at by judge, barristers, witnesses and jury I wanted to be clad in sporty rather than sexy attire. The fact my injured body was now public property was one of the many painful aspects of the aftermath I had to face.

I went through my clothes. There were bloodstains on many of them. I froze inside as I checked TC's. Bloody fingerprints and smudges. She'd been through our things. Another violation. I left the bedroom as quickly as I could and told Paula to drive me back to the pub, where Leo and Naomi were waiting for me like two anxious parents. Their care, generosity and love for me was incredible, partly rewarded with a definite increase in takings from my friends and family, not known for their abstemious ways.

Whilst staying at the pub I was still receiving flowers and cards. I also received a letter from Mum. It opened with the words, 'My darling girl'. She was unhappy about not being with me, but did not wish to upset my stepfather. The letter contained two foolscap sheets of Mum's big, bold handwriting. It was dated in the sixties. A red-topped knobpin held an extra scrap of paper in place with the words, 'I KNOW!' written in capital letters. I read it very slowly.

THE RETURN

Jenny's Vision

I've seen a place bathed in luminous light
So bright as to make this earth's brightest sun
Seem cold and old
I've seen roads paved in golden clouds
Meticulously etched – and yet
Billowing in their clouds of bright lit glory
I've stood in this glorious place
And discoursed
With beings draped in purest robes of golden white
I've felt a love so old of time
And so noble a feeling
That this very heart of mine
Did cry a cry
So strange, so old, so endless
They knew my name
And used it well
And I knew all of them so well
As to make my heart rejoice
To stay was my one intent
In that unifold embracement of perfect love
To leave
To wrench away this aching soul
From these – my counterparts
Of deepest Self
Not willingly
But with much reluctance
Did I depart
Leaving with them a part of me
Yet unknown to me
And yet
So endlessly known to them
And to me at that particular time
A consciousness so painful in its awareness
So naked in its beauty
Could find no home on this earthly plane
But it was there

In me
For that short while
And I was privileged the memory
To hold forever more
When I would once again
Return
To these my friends
Of old.

Carefully I folded the pages and put them into my briefcase.
Yes, she knew.

The convalescence raced away, day and night without edges.
The sound of laughter, debate and babble across the bar was
the best therapy I could have had – a reminder that life was
still living itself. I sang 'Danny Boy' as a duet with an old
drunk, allowed him to buy me a port, which I drank – all of
which I would have studiously avoided before the incident and
a definite sign I was experiencing some degree of breakdown.
Naomi gave me every job she could think of which used a knife,
intent on reminding me of the instrument's mundane function.
Whilst making incisions in the lamb joint for cloves of garlic,
suddenly, compelled by the desire to know the extent of the
force used against me, I lifted the knife and with all my might
thrust it into the cold flabby flesh. The blade did not go in as
far as I thought it would. As I looked at the knife sticking out of
the lump of meat I was reduced to a quivering mass and passed
out. Fortunately no harm was done, and no one noticed so I
did not have to explain my actions. Naomi catered for all the
friends, family and incident-related visitors with great generosity
and care and her gorgeous youngest son even agreed to tie my
shoelaces each morning with the proviso that after two weeks I
would be on my own.

The police came a-visiting and explained the legal procedure.
I was informed that it was a 'cut and dried case', which I felt
was yet another contender for the title in my banned words
competition. My assailant was obviously insane, her history was
that of a paranoid schizophrenic and after the committal at the
end of the month, when charges of attempted murder would

be brought by the crown, an insanity order would be requested and she would remain in custody until the trial. The trial, I was assured, would be a formality and she would in all probability be detained at Her Majesty's pleasure for the rest of her natural. The only question was whether she would be deemed mentally fit to plead and, in any event, it was very unlikely that I would be called as a witness. The detective inspector in charge of the case and his fellow officers were absolutely terrific, supportive and sensitive, and were keen to protect me from any unnecessary exposure – even of a celluloid nature.

I stood against the pub living-room wall, my jeans unzipped, my blouse undone and my bra lifted just enough to reveal the start of the chest wound as the camera man clicked away. Anyone listening outside the door could have been forgiven for thinking a very different type of photography session was in progress!

' . . . that's lovely, Julie . . . Now pull the zip down lower – yes, that's it – we've got it. Lift the bra – it's not a time to be shy – the people who will see these pictures know what they are looking for – that's better. Put your head back as far as you can – now . . . hold it against the ruler . . . let's show them how long it is . . . Put your mouth as close to it as you can . . . we've got to get the angle right to make it stand out. Well done! These will knock their socks off . . .'

The district nurse was a friend who gave me practical advice on how to deal with the injuries and recovery process. She removed the remaining stitches and clips from my body with great care and enough humour to detract from the pain. After the last clip had been squeezed out of my abdomen, I was allowed to take a bath. I lay in the warm scented water, initially frightened that the red angry line of scar tissue running down my middle would split open. With a nail brush and flannel, meticulously, inch by inch, I scrubbed away the scabs, old blood, nicotine-yellow antiseptic stains, sticky, dirty traces of plaster and matted flecks of lint and bandages. As I worked, I wondered what would be needed to eradicate the filth of memory.

If you would but stay in the moment . . . memory would have no hold, and therefore . . . no effect.

But how can I stop myself going back to the event and reliving it in my mind . . . over and over again?

Simple . . . replace the old script with something more pleasing.

TC had finished his course and the follow-up sessions and had returned to full-time life in the cottage. Wanting our lives to return to some sort of normality, he had channelled much of his energy into doing everything he could think of to make our home warm and welcoming for my return. Although almost everyone around us was angry with him, I was not. He was doing his very best. I knew he was shattered, shocked, exhausted and vulnerable. Even though it was unlikely we would remain together, the great love of our long-standing friendship could never turn me against him and I was longing for the two of us to be left alone in order to sort things out. I was in great need of some privacy.

Much against the wishes of my friends, I agreed to return to the cottage for an afternoon, to meet Cosmo Greene and his wife, who wanted to see me. I was by now curious about them. TC collected me, our first time alone together since the attack. Entering the cottage was much easier than the first time. With the help of some of his surgery staff and our wonderful home-help, TC had everywhere sparkling. All the lights were on, the fire was roaring away in the living room and beautiful music was playing throughout the house. Every room was warm, filled with the fragrance of fresh flowers, and Ben and Thomas were sleeping in their favourite spot draped across the top of the lounge radiator. TC took me into his arms and held me for a very long time. It was surprisingly good to be home. Together we walked into all the rooms of the house, as if to lay the ghost. On a stool outside the study door were two sweaters. They were hers. I picked them up and hurled them into the kitchen bin, my peace once again disturbed by this woman. Everyone must have assumed they were mine. In the study a message was flashing impatiently on the answerphone. TC played it back; a woman's weary voice with an Australian accent said she and Cosmo would be late and they were tired, very hungry and would like a meal when they arrived. It felt more like a command than a request.

Although we were not impressed by their lack of sensitivity, we raided the stock-cupboard and freezer and produced a meal of sorts. I was unable to bend, lift anything or use my right hand, so progress was very slow and by the time they arrived two hours later I was feeling very tired. He was a short stocky man with a ready laugh and strong personality, whilst she was dark-eyed, anxious and obviously older than him. Within moments of her arrival she was on the phone placating a daughter who evidently was not happy at being left alone. The atmosphere was tense, the conversation guarded. After we had eaten, Cosmo wanted to talk with me alone. We went into the lounge and sat by the fire, leaving his wife with TC in the kitchen. We chatted about the accident in a very general detached way, like two boxers skirting around the edge of the ring weighing up the opponent. I found his friendliness, charm and constant questioning left no room for me to express how pissed off I was with him and his course and I quickly fell into my usual polite persona. I found myself telling him how I had experienced more than just a physical attack and I intimated I knew what was beyond the body. I hoped he would be able to explain what was happening to me, given his career of leading people on a voyage of self-discovery.

He asked if I felt OK about reliving part of the experience. I did and closed my eyes as instructed. He took me back to a point where I could look into her eyes. Once again I was on the stairs. He wanted to know if I had seen those eyes before. I knew I had.

'Oh dear God . . .!' I screamed. 'Please – not again!'

Once again an ancient memory arose in my mind and I knew it was not the first time I had been wished dead in God's name. 'NO!' I cried, feeling myself starting to float into another reality. Far away I could hear the voice of Cosmo asking me where I was and what was happening.

I was standing on a grassy meadow encircled by a misty mountainous landscape . . . the haze was lifting . . . I could see flowers.

Sunshine. Caves. A castle high above me.

The evocative smell of wild herbs.
Heat. Blood. A circle of people.
White tunics. Red crosses. Swords.
Me.
Voices. Chanting.
'In the name of God!'
Me – silent. The voices screaming.
'Heretic!'
Me – guilty.
Voices sneering 'In the name of God'.
Cosmo Greene calling me, wanting to know where I was.
France. France. I was in France.
An enormous sword hacked through my neck.
Me – a dead body lying on a French hillside.
'In the name of God.'
Me – something watching it all.
I called out into infinity . . .
'How many more times have I got to die for you?!'
'I WANT TO LIVE FOR YOU! . . .
I WANT TO LIVE . . .
DEAR GOD . . .
LET ME LIVE . . .!
NO! NO! NO! NO! NO! NO! NOO! NOOO! NOOOO . . .!'
The echoes of my cries reverberated from the surrounding
mountains, and chased me back down a swirling vortex of clouds,
finally bouncing off the walls of the Hampshire stairway staring
into the eyes of my assailant.

Cosmo was talking to me. He wanted me to pretend I had a
weapon in my hand and to simulate defending myself by killing
my attacker. He told me to put as much energy into it as my
injuries would permit – somewhat ironic I thought secretly. I
went through the motions but knew I was still unable to inflict
harm. During the 'process' his wife came into the room and
reminded him they needed to be leaving because of a promise
to their daughter. He seemed irritated and the focus was very
much back in the lounge. I could not think why she had come
at all – it would have been better if she had stayed at home.

Cosmo then asked me if I knew anything about the 'Cathars'. I had no idea what he was talking about, so he explained a little about the southern French peoples of the twelfth and thirteenth centuries who were deemed heretics by the Catholic Church and systematically annihilated in a series of crusades that resulted in one of the least documented but worst cases of genocide in European history.

He asked me to consider doing the course and told me there was one coming up at a local venue in May. Some of the fascination that had been fired at the introductory evening was rekindled. He implied my doing the course would lead to deeper understanding about victimhood. He also intimated that past-lives would be explored. I told him I would think about it. We were interrupted again.

After their fraught departure TC and I sat in front of the fire. When I told him what had happened he looked very shocked. He told me that during the first course, most of the group had experienced a mass regression relating back to an incident at the time of the Cathars. I was not sure what to make of it all – even though I had no doubt we experience many lives on the earth plane. I did not feel comfortable about delving – if the memory of a past life naturally arises in our consciousness I felt it was only because something still needed to be learnt. If I had been part of a group of people who died because of their religious beliefs it would explain why, in my childhood, I had been so frightened to talk openly about my love of God. In fact, looking back I realised I had gone to great lengths to conceal my understanding, and was full of self-doubt and the accompanying cynicism that feeds on such a cover-up. TC went to clear up the kitchen, before taking me back to my public-house recuperation ward. I stared into the golden embers of the fire, talking to The Voice.

What do you make of this past-life business then?
We all choose many different overcoats in order to experience the truth of who we really are.
But I know of at least three Napoleons, several Cleopatras, not to mention the ones who keep thinking that they are Jesus.

**When there is a strong empathy with an historical char-
acter or event, then it does not necessarily mean you
were that person, or you were there. Most probably it
means you identify with certain beliefs that are reflected
in that scenario. There are times when the human
classroom needs events written across the heavens in
order for the maximum learning – in truth, there is not
one event or character that you are not connected with
– you would do well to contemplate this.**

So it is possible that I believe in persecution for my beliefs
and understanding.

Yes.

Then my life will keep throwing this at me . . . speaking my
truth equals punishment, derision, torture and even death?

Yes.

I can see how that is a major part of my life, but I cannot see
the way out.

But, my friend, do you speak out?

No – because I am frightened I stay quiet.

**Can you see that it is the silence which is causing the
problems?**

When Max used to beat my mother, the next day he would
pretend that he had not touched her, and I would go along
with it because I thought it would keep the peace. If I had
said something could he have changed?

Yes, in the words of truth everything can change.

I can see that – but what now?

**Write a book – tell the story which will unfold around
this awakening – without fear – tell your truth.**

NEVER! M'mm – the thought fills me with terror. I couldn't
do it. Never! Never! Never!

**You will, my friend – and you could even enjoy it.
Especially when you understand who is writing it.**

TC drove me back to a smoke-filled lounge where Naomi and
JR interrogated me. True to form, on the subject of my inner
thoughts I stayed silent.

THE RECOVERY

I sat on the stairs looking at the newly painted wall. Three weeks and one day ago in this very spot I would not have given good odds on my survival. Twenty-one pounds and over four hundred stitches less in body, light years wiser in mind and experiencing a strange freedom of spirit, I could never be the same person again. Perhaps a part of me had died on the stairs. The part which only identified with being a body. I was sitting in the very spot where I had passed through the door marked death into the realms beyond the human world. I had always believed in such a place, but now I'd had the experience. Nothing could ever be the same, especially with Veritas The Voice for company.

The police informed me that today was the day Helen was appearing in front of magistrates on a charge of attempted murder. She had been brought before them a week earlier but was not called as a witness and had been remanded in custody whilst police made further enquiries. Through her desire to kill me our lives were inextricably linked and yet her fate was now far removed from its entanglement with mine. How strange is the law which recognises a body, a home, a career, a family and a life that has been desecrated and yet the perpetrator's future has nothing whatsoever to do with the victim.

They also had told me about the young man who rescued me. He was a builder working on a nearby site – because he started work very early he had been on his way to a pub for his lunch. As he crossed the high-sided railway bridge just beyond our drive he thought he heard a scream. He had stopped and listened but heard nothing. In that moment he realised he had left his wallet in a jacket on the work site. He retraced his steps and of course, as soon as he left the bridge he saw me lying in the drive entrance with Helen trying to hack my head off. He had disarmed her. Whilst he went into the house to find the phone, she had gone too and found a second knife. By the time he got outside she was attacking me again. The police said he was a very brave and very shy young man who had rescued people before from life-threatening circumstances.

The Scene of the Crime
Three Weeks On

Dear Brave Young Man,
YOU SAVED MY LIFE.

I do remember the calm way you gently told her to put the knife down. There was not a glimmer of fear or anger in your voice. Suddenly a cocoon of safety wrapped itself around me, and the black shadow of that foaming hissing creature trying to saw my head off with a blunt knife vanished.

I remember telling you where the portable phone had probably fallen. I realise how brave you were to go back into the house to find it.

When she attacked me again with the second knife and you disarmed her once more, I wondered if you were real.

You were magnificent.

I will never forget your courage.
The Woman Whose Life You Saved.

My first night home I snuggled down into the delicious warm familiarity of my own bed with Thomas and Ben wasting no time to claim their positions, curling themselves at our feet. TC lay at my side, in silence we held hands, wide-eyed, watching the darkness. In less than three weeks so much had happened it was not possible to know what to say. I did not remember falling asleep but suddenly I was standing in intense white light. Before me was a marble-covered pyramid. It was the smallest of several, and balanced on its pinnacle was a large transparent globe. A shaven-headed priest in orange robes led me to a doorway carved into the stone.

We entered and slowly walked down the cold steps. The warmth and vibrant sandscape colours were replaced by mellow hues and dark shadows cast by burning torches. He led the way as we travelled into the very heart of the structure. My feet were bare and I too wore orange robes. We climbed down a narrow shaft into a small chamber. The walls were covered with strange symbols and incense was burning in each corner of the stone room. There were several other priests waiting for us and they bowed low as we entered. There was nothing in the room other than a small platform draped with silken fabric and strewn with small white highly scented flowers. The priests began calling to each other in a strange language, a haunting incantation which revolved around me. They stopped abruptly and, laughing, filed out of the chamber. I was left with the first older priest.

'This is the final part of the initiation – may the light of truth illuminate the way for you.' He dipped his long fingers into a small earthenware pot. The reddish oil glistened on his middle finger which anointed the space between my eyebrows. I placed my hands together and bowed to him – a farewell that I knew could mark the end of my life. He left taking all light with him as a great stone was rolled into the doorway. The quest was to find the way out. I wasted no time, feeling the smoothness of each stone, my fingers working across each square inch searching for some clue – a lever perhaps revealing a secret passageway, something. Time passed and my calmness became anxiety. I was trapped in darkness, once again buried alive. Even though some part of me knew it was only a dream I began to panic. It was a test and there had to be a way out. I could find nothing, and eventually, exhausted, I crawled onto the flower-covered bed, my heart pounding. The walls began to vibrate, echoing the sounds of the priests' chant. I lay very still and listened. The weird sounds became intelligible . . . the walls were speaking to me.

'The way out is beyond the physical. Use the mind . . . go to the place of stillness within . . . you are not the physical . . . go beyond the body . . . go beyond the mind . . . inside is the way out.'

And so it went on and on and on. I lay trembling in the darkness of the tomb for a long time listening to the sounds, when suddenly I realised what I had to do. I became very still and closed my eyes. My breathing was short uncontrollable panting which stopped abruptly. I concentrated on the silence. It was thundering all around me as I floated straight out of the body and looked down on a young male priest lying on the bed below. For a few moments I hovered and bumped around the ceiling. With every part of my awareness I concentrated on the other side of the wall and the beautiful kohl-lined eyes of the teaching priest. I immediately zoomed straight through the walls and was rocketing towards a very familiar-looking lake. The priest was sitting cross-legged on the ground, holding a burning torch.

'I knew you would come,' he said without moving. 'What have you learnt?'

'I have learnt that I am not my body,' I replied. 'Where is this place – this lake? I've been here before.'

'This is the starting point of your journey home.'

I puzzled, knowing I had heard that somewhere before. There was the sound of the stone rolling away from the tomb entrance. The priest and the lake were gone. With a thump I landed on the stone plinth bed back in the chamber to find myself surrounded by happy faces of fellow priests. Drums were banging and they were singing and whirling around me in a state of ecstasy. I had passed the test. I moved to get off the bed longing to join them but began to fall. There was no floor and I was hurtling at an unbelievable speed down a swirling black hole, unable to stop, crying out 'I AM NOT MY BODY' as I fell into the void. I came to a halt with a tremendous bang and judder. My vocal chords reconnected, I cried out in pain and shock. Much to my relief I was in my bedroom. I reached out to put on the bedside lamp. My hand went straight through the wall.

The dream within the dream within the dream WAKE UP!
I'm trying to wake up, for God's sake. What the hell is going on?
Indeed. What is hell? Believing the dream to be real. Hell indeed, WAKE UP!
I AM awake!
Are you?

It must be all the drugs in my system. I'm hallucinating.
Logic will never be your alarm clock.
What?
Go back to sleep.

The lamp came on. TC was fast asleep and Ben and Thomas were sitting upright on the bed, staring at me. I lay awake for the rest of the night.

TC left for the surgery and I was on my own in the cottage for the first time. I was very jumpy and tired after my strange dream. The walls of my life had fallen apart and nothing seemed real or solid. My cigarettes and Dunhill lighter were on the end of the kitchen table exactly as I had left them. I had not smoked for over three weeks, in fact I had been repelled by the fumes of others puffing away and I thought the memory of my full wheezing lungs had put me off for ever. I was wrong. Suddenly I was longing to smoke. I reasoned that only one would not hurt and foolishly justified the longing as a sign I was getting better. I took the cigarette from its packet and lit it. It was absolutely revolting. I smoked a second one which was marginally better and by the time JR arrived later that morning, I was once again a smoker.

I went through the March business schedule with JR. We had several magazines with imminent closing copy dates and not enough business. I did not feel able to phone clients and negotiate anything, so I had to leave it to her. We were under considerable pressure. She gave me a letter from our main contractor. It informed me that the several thousands of pounds in tax and insurance that I was deemed to owe the Inland Revenue was to be deducted from future commission cheques until the amount was recovered in full. Although it was easier than having to find a lump sum, it meant that I would have no income for at least the next three months. My other business transactions were longer term and would see no remuneration for months. I thanked God I had the small amount of money from the flat sale in the bank.

I waded through a mass of paperwork, finding it very difficult to concentrate on all the small print. In the pile of things to deal with was my filled out insurance policy dated the morning of the accident. Had I got that in the post three weeks earlier I would not be worrying about my cash-flow – I could have retired. I figured this must be what it is like to have the winning line on a pools coupon and to discover the entry hadn't been sent. It was a dreadful feeling. Even though the Inland Revenue declared me employed, I discovered I was not covered by my old company's policy. I then checked the household policy. It did not make provision for attack in my own home. It had a reversed liability clause which meant I could take the time and money to sue my assailant, but if I lost the case they MIGHT pay the costs. It did not tempt me. I felt overwhelmed by all the jargon and was in no condition to handle all I was supposed to do. Even though my stepfather could have helped me I decided to hire an independent solicitor. Under the circumstances it seemed the sensible thing to do.

The police came to inform me about the committal. They were able to fill in some of the missing parts in the jigsaw of my mind. I asked them what had happened before Helen got to the cottage. They said that very early on the morning of the incident a neighbour of Helen's had been woken by her screaming and shouting 'I want to give my lover my energy', or words to that effect. Some time later the neighbour saw her leaving the apartment block. She apparently boarded a London-bound train around 5 a.m. and was seen pacing up and down the aisles. Shortly afterwards she walked down the train totally naked and locked herself in the loo. She was noticed by an off-duty policeman who alerted the British Rail staff when the train stopped at Guildford. The police were called and she was taken to Guildford police station where she was not very co-operative. She gave a wrong identity, and was observed in an interview room, wearing only a sweater and tights, dancing about like a ballet dancer singing 'I would like to teach the world to sing'. A pity they hadn't mentioned that bit to TC when they phoned.

After considerable persuasion Helen had said that she wanted to speak to a Cosmo Greene who lived in London. No telephone number could be traced for the address she gave. Eventually she asked to speak to TC who was called. We knew the rest. I asked if they had any idea why she had been handcuffed when brought to the surgery. They said people in police custody were usually only put in handcuffs if there was a likelihood of some danger either to themselves or the police, or both – they did not mention the general public. Finally they told me about the young driver who apparently broke the rules taking me to hospital in his police car. He risked a great deal.

The Cottage
Three Weeks On . . .

Dear Young Police Driver,

Whatever it was that convinced you to break the rules and take me to hospital in your incredibly fast Volvo, that decision helped to save my life. I understand you had just passed your advanced driving test – you must have got distinction. I have only been driven at such high speeds before by the man who trained me to be a racing driver – he taught me to drive as if there was an egg on the passenger seat which, no matter how fast I drove, must not break. So you see, as one severely cracked human ready to be scrambled, I really appreciated the smooth drive. I hope that your superiors will be big enough to praise your initiative, and not punish you for it.

It was remarkable luck that you had just come from Guildford, and knew the motorway tailback was horrendous, because we certainly would have headed for there in the logical belief that it was the nearest hospital with an emergency department. It would never have occurred to us to drive to Cosham, so many miles further away.

Another life-saving factor in your decision to take me was that if I had gone in an ambulance, they would never have allowed TC to wrap himself around me, and without his bodily warmth and constant reassurances I know I could not have returned into my body.

You drove with such confidence. I will always remember the incredible speed with which you managed to deliver me into the hands of the waiting surgeons – every specialist I needed on duty that morning. What a miracle it all was.

You were bloody wonderful.

She Who Was Unable To Thank You At The Time.

My physical condition was still very weak. I could only walk very slowly and had no strength whatsoever. My right hand was virtually useless, still curled in a tight foetal position, making any lifting or carrying very painful. Fortunately I was able to use my left hand, so I managed to write in a fashion. The hospital had not given me any advice on how best to regain my physical condition. Instinctively I knew it was no good asking TC – he still could not discuss or face any of the physical aspects of the attack. Any attempt to talk about it broke down into tears or silence. He was a man still in deep shock. I did not know how much I should push myself, so decided to use the pool and sauna in our local hotel and golf club. It was exclusive and therefore expensive but worth it. I couldn't risk the public baths packed full of enthusiastic kids with each of their flailing little arms and legs a possible instrument of torture for my fragile frame. On my first visit I could not manage more than three strokes but it was the only way I could think of to build up my stamina and fitness. I watched the brightly clad golfers teeing off in front of the leisure centre and wondered if I would ever hold a golf club again. I'd always loved sport; squash and golf were amongst my favourites, although I played most racquet games. The impact of my injuries was really coming home to me – without the full use of my right hand a whole chunk of my life was wiped out.

I persevered almost daily, the combination of warmth, move-ment and water began to work wonders on my sagging and shattered muscle system. I closed my eyes and pretended I was swimming in the turquoise waters off a Greek island. I longed for a holiday. I experienced a very great sense of loneliness splashing around in that pool and once again began to drown in self-pity. Here I was, scarred and sore, no aftercare, no family, no income, no loving partner and no prospects for the future. I thanked God for my close friends, who supported me in so many ways, including chauffeuring me around. I couldn't figure what

I had done that was so terrible that I would be left in this way. An acquaintance who was a New Age therapist invited herself to see me for an informal chat, during which she told me I had probably done something very bad in a past life and this was my karma paying me back. I was not exactly uplifted by her theories. I reviewed my life as I swam but could not find anything in it that deserved this.

Perhaps you have done nothing wrong. Consider that. On certain pathways to truth your plight would be considered full of God's Grace.

Nice thought – but how could that be?

To lose everything of the material world in one swoop of the cosmic hand is to test your faith. God only offers these tests when you are ready for them. Instead of considering what you have lost, contemplate what you have gained ...

Well, for starters I have acquired you, whoever you are. I have travelled out of this body and experienced everything merging into One glorious light.

There are those who spend their entire lives searching for that experience. Could you not have just a teeny portion of gratitude?

Yes, you know, Veritas, when I remember that moment it all makes a sort of sense. You are right – I should be thankful. I'll try harder to drop the self-pity and perhaps I'll get myself out of the habit of expecting the people around me to provide me with love. If what I have been shown is true – that the answer to life's mystery lies hidden inside me – I guess that is where I should be directing my attention.

Yes indeed, it is the only place to look.

After only a week I was managing almost a length, which built my hopes for a complete recovery – and joy of joys, my hand was very slowly uncurling. Whatever the test, I was beginning to realise I was the only person who could lift me out of the depression and self-pity and, knowing this, I began to feel much stronger.

My first solo foray into the big wide world was to walk around the corner to the local supermarket. Normally it would have taken me less than five minutes. It took twenty. I wandered up and down the fluorescent-lit aisles. The food displays repelled me, so much was over-packaged and artificial. Since leaving hospital I found the world very garish and noisy. I longed for all things natural. I only wanted fresh fruit and vegetables and found I could only stomach home-cooked food and lots of water. Anything else was heavy, indigestible and unappetising. The smell from the meat and fish counter was so disgusting I reeled and nearly fell. I made for the check-out with a tired-looking bunch of watercress and a brown loaf. It was all I could carry. As I waited in the small queue I could not fail to hear my name and TC's being bandied about. The person on the check-out professed to have intimate knowledge of our lives and the incident, even though she didn't know who I was from Adam. Her mannerisms were perfect pantomime dame, the back of the right hand adjusting the ample bosom to punctuate the end of each slanderous sentence. As she rang up the prices of my things she was still describing the fight in the doctor's drive to an elderly customer. I put my face close to hers and whispered, 'I don't remember you being there.'

She looked puzzled.

'Pardon?' she said.

'When I was being stabbed by that paranoid schizophrenic – I don't remember you being there.'

She was dumb-struck and threw my money into her till as if it were on fire. A hot flush of colour raced up her neck.

'I'm sorry,' she whispered.

'Yes, so am I.'

I was strong enough to endure the hour and a half drive to my London dentist. I lay in the back seat as TC drove me into the West End. We arrived early but I was ushered straight in. After a couple of X-rays it was confirmed that my first lower left molar was irreparably fractured. I was given a local anaesthetic and watched woozily as each fragment was carefully removed. This was more than just a tooth I was losing – it was part of a fifteen-month investment down the tubes. As an adult I had undergone orthodontic treatment and had worn upper and lower braces – every tooth looped in metal for the sake of a straight smile. I had been mocked and teased, I had not enjoyed eating, I had been unable to smile without terrifying small children and any amour attempting to kiss me would have been safer placing his tongue in a mincer. All this I had endured because my dentist felt it would be better than capping my unusually strong teeth, which had no fillings. The day the taut wires and bands were due to be removed I went into an instant photograph booth in London Euston station. I put my money in and sat pulling my mouth as wide open as I could in order to display the full extent of the metal grin. I wanted a souvenir of the horror. I pulled four of the worst faces imaginable and waited for the passport-sized prints to exit the machine on a rush of warm air. I guarded the exit-shute closely, not wishing anyone else to see. Several bystanders sensed my desire to hide the photographic results and assured me everyone comes out looking like Dracula's latest victim. I waited.

The machine dispatched three sets of prints. I waited. Two people who had gone in after me got their photos. I waited. Half an hour later I was beside myself. Nothing had come down that bloody shute for me. There was a number to call out a technician if you had a problem. The thought of some cheeky cockney turning up and telling me 'It's not bleedin' surprisin' that the bloody machine jammed wiv a boat-race like yours, darlin'' was more than I could bear, so I walked away praying that the machine had failed to capture my metallic smile.

As I lay with pads of cotton-wool mopping up the blood-filled newly exposed gap I knew that if I ever became famous I would find out very quickly if those photographs existed.

The police visited regularly. I appreciated their company and concern for my well-being. They were astounded by the speed of my mental and physical recovery. They explained about a government award scheme for victims of violence, and brought me a pamphlet about how to claim compensation. I would, they felt, definitely be eligible for a substantial award.

They told me a conditional bail had been granted and my assailant had been moved to the psychiatric wing of a hospital not that far away from me, in order to be treated by her own psychiatrist. The conditions of her bail were that she would not leave the grounds, not contact us, not visit her home town and comply with her treatment. We saw a transcript of the proceedings. We did not agree with some of what it said and asked what we should do. By this time I had been visited by several course participants. They had told me things they had witnessed and discussed on the course regarding my assailant but were so terrified by what had happened they said they would not give evidence publicly. The police were convinced that it was not worth complicating matters, so we decided it was best to leave things as they were and let justice take its course. It seemed obvious that anyone inflicting that degree of injury on another human being would be deemed to be insane. The police were however concerned for my safety and peace of mind. A security officer came to the house and advised us how best to ensure the cottage was intruder-proof. Then the main rooms were wired with alarms linked directly to the police-station.

In the following weeks the alarm was inadvertently triggered by TC's youngest son who was staying with us. He had arrived with a card for me which he'd drawn himself and a gift of the piano music for the theme tune from *Chariots of Fire*. It was a lovely sensitive gesture which meant a lot to me. He had pushed the button out of curiosity only to find minutes later the house surrounded by police. It was rather a nasty shock and embarrassing for him but he handled it with his inimitable style – fortunately the police showed great humour, understanding and patience, especially needed when the cats also managed to trip the system a few weeks later.

TC bought me a rounders bat for self-defence which I kept under the bed. Part of me was amused by all these precautions, a little late, but they did offer me a modicum of comfort along with the hope that lightning never strikes twice. In the very early hours of the morning when TC was out on an emergency visit I had heard footsteps on the gravel drive. I was frozen with terror. I reached for the bat, and naked, crept down the stairs in order to peep through the study window. I was trembling from head to foot with terror and cold. There was definitely something out there. The moon cast enough light for me to see clearly from behind the curtains. Bat raised above my head, I had no idea what I planned to do if there was anyone out there, but I could not see anything. The drive was empty. Then the sound started again and, my heart pounding with terror, I flung the curtain back. Four hedgehogs scurried away. I laughed aloud with relief and went back to bed.

My mother phoned almost daily. My stepfather had apparently obtained details of the committal. He had written to my mother with his view of the case. It would never occur to me to write a letter to someone I shared my home and life with – a solicitorial habit perhaps. As he had not spoken with me about any aspect of what had happened, nor had he enquired as to my progress, I was not surprised to hear how judgemental and inaccurate his view was. My mother explained how he had forbidden her ever to set foot in my house again because he blamed TC for what had happened. She begged me to agree to meet her on neutral territory and told me she could stay in a nearby hotel, he would collect me from the car-park in the centre of the village and drive me to her. I could spend two hours with her whilst he played golf. It was a military operation and unless I agreed to his terms, I would not be able to see my mother. Hating myself for my weakness I agreed.

TC dropped me off. I was not really well enough to be hanging around in a wet, windy car-park, but I was longing to see my mother. A tight-lipped Herbert met me and drove me in silence to the hotel where Mum was pacing up and down outside. As he roared away to his golf we both shoved two fingers up and pulled our tongues out making a dreadful noise. It was inappropriate behaviour for the forecourt of a five-star hotel but made us feel a lot better. Arm in arm we walked into the hotel and spent two wonderful hours eating, talking, crying and laughing. She didn't blame TC any more and was just overwhelmed with gratitude to find me up and about. She kept taking my hand as if to check I was still there. We agreed it was best that I did not consult my stepfather professionally or personally on any aspect of my case as he was still hell-bent on destroying TC. I wondered why he had such a fixed and seemingly biased view of the affair.

On reflection, I wondered if he felt a need to discredit anyone loved by me, or my mother. Mart, she told me, was longing to see me on the assurance that he 'wouldn't catch anything' – as always beautifully straightforward about his fears. I wanted to see him too and arranged to visit as soon as I could drive again, preferably when a certain person was out at work. Apparently my Nan had only just been told of my condition – the family having protected her from the shock by playing down the seriousness of my situation and giving her the good news that I was well on the mend. My Nan is a very psychic person and I realised she would know things were being kept from her. I would give her a call to put her mind at rest.

Our peace was interrupted all too soon and I was returned to the rendezvous. TC came to collect me. It was so cruel to exclude him at the very time we both needed friendship, love and support. When we arrived home, from my neck to my navel was a bright red and angry rash, my frustration and exasperation manifesting in my body. I itched and scratched all night; even drenching myself in calamine lotion did not soothe the fires of intense irritation.

The front room became the place to receive my many visitors. Some of the people were strangers, others old friends. During this time a member of a neighbourhood Christian group had asked to see me. She was distressed and told me the group had been praying for something to happen to us, as TC and I were not married and his interest in acupuncture and alternative therapies was, in their opinion, the work of the devil. However, now they were shocked by the incident and felt guilty as they had not envisaged anything so violent happening to us. I was left speechless, and shocked that 'civilised' people could even think such things.

A priest in the area also asked if I would see him. When I was able to walk unaided for more than a few yards, I went to his house. He appeared to know my assailant and her family and wished to convince me of her gentle nature, the emphasis being on my forgiving her. I had no trouble seeing that part of her was timid and gentle, that is how I remembered her at the party. Then my mind flipped back to the cottage with the screaming, foaming-at-the-mouth form of Helen, holding the blood-drenched knife over my head. I was perhaps the only person to have witnessed the persona beneath the controlling drugs, a persona it seemed no one else wanted to acknowledge existed.

The priest cross-examined me regarding TC, the self-awareness course and other matters, none of which I felt at all inclined to discuss with him. He wanted to know what I knew about a process on the course where participants take an imaginary weapon into their hands and attack the problem people in their lives. I did not think it would help matters to tell him I had been taken through such a process only days earlier. A few facts taken out of context were building an inaccurate picture in this man's mind. I could not help wondering whether the fact certain people felt TC was doing devil's work had more bearing on Helen's desire to save the world in the name of Jesus than any course process. It was apparent the priest was looking for something or someone to blame, and with a fervour that I found unhealthy. He mentioned in conspiratorial tones that the elders of the church had been approached, with a view to performing an exorcism, something I thought existed only in the pages of pulp-horror books. Changing the subject, I gave him the medallion of Christ and told him how it had appeared on my chain, interested in his thoughts on the matter. He handed it straight back to me without comment, clearly very uncomfortable. I could not wait to leave his house. I am sure he meant well, but I found no solace from my visit.

JR drove slowly as I observed the passing landscape. Compared to the distorted view I'd had lying in the back of a racing police car, everything was so ordinary. We got to the hospital with time to spare and waited in the busy main foyer. This impersonal, over-lit, over-heated, sterile monument to modern architecture was the place where my life had been saved. The scene of my rebirth. We were called into the consultant's waiting room. It was packed with darkly clad, pallid-looking people, the atmosphere heavy with suppressed coughing and sneezing, whinging children and misery. I tried to guess what everyone else had wrong with them. Other than the fact that they had been forbidden to smile, I drew no conclusions as to which bits had been removed, sealed or reinforced, but it helped pass the time. We waited and waited. One and a half hours after our appointment time I was called in. Circumstance stood up as I came in. He was efficiently charming and brisk as he looked over my injuries and declared all was well. I told him all was not well, and asked him to recheck my puffy, still unusable right hand. He did, and then confirmed things were 'pretty bad'. I asked if there was any physiotherapy which would help. My tenacity paid off and he said he would write to my doctor and arrange it. I left his consulting rooms still no wiser about how I should be treating myself.

Twice a week I was to attend a physiotherapy session for my right hand in a nearby town. I arranged taxis and friends to take me – it was a real pain not being confident enough to drive. Ironically it was the first time since I'd passed my test that I had been without wheels. Just before the accident my lovely little Renault had been traded in for TC to get a BMW, and I was awaiting the money from this transaction. Sitting in the cold clinic having my fingers stretched and pulled I was overcome with indulgent impulses. If I was to look to myself for love and care, then I would have to be the one to treat myself to something wonderful. Some gift to delight me. Something I would never have done before. Something wild, extravagant and impractical. Something to celebrate my rebirth. I would buy myself a sports car, and if I had anything left I would take myself, TC and JR to a Greek island and I really would swim in that turquoise velvet sea. I felt an incredible thrill as I realised I might never be sensible about money again. The home-spun philosophy, have a good time because tomorrow you could be dead, took on a whole new meaning. Yes, bugger it . . . I was all set to have myself a really good time – for the rest of my life.

A knock at the front door heralded yet another visitor. It was my piano teacher. He stood with his music case under his arm and a determined expression on his face. He asked if I was ready for my lesson. Looking at the clock I realised it was the time of my weekly session with him. A music session I'd delighted in, thrilled to be playing again and learning from a teacher who was great fun and inspirational. As I made us both a cup of tea, with heavy heart I explained how I could never face the piano again. I fought back the tears. He took his tea and, as was his custom, he carried it into the front room and sat at the piano. He opened his case.

'I heard about your hand. I've written you a piece for your left hand and one finger of the right hand. Any idiot could play it. It will do you more good than all that bloody physiotherapy.'

He hid his emotion behind his bluntness as he waited for me to join him. Against all odds I struggled at the keyboard for over an hour.

Business matters went from bad to worse. It took just five weeks from the accident to lose everything I had worked for. It came in the form of a letter in which my longest-standing friend, now main client, advised that because my recovery was an unknown factor she had no option but to take back all her business with me. She was sure I would understand, etc etc, and wished me well. All my work in building up clients and contacts appeared to be worth fuck all. I knew in her position I would have had to do the same, but I minded very much that she had not given me any acknowledgement for all I had given to her and her company. It hurt that she had not made the time to come and see me, after all the hours I had spent being supportive around her tempestuous love-life, times when I took the brunt of her boyfriend's verbal abuse.

Why does it hurt so, Dear One?
Because I love her . . . I miss her. She's one of the few people I've ever met who I could really laugh with.
What else?
. . . and maybe it hurts because it's too much of a parallel with my mother's situation. I feel I have lost her friendship because of yet another partner who dislikes me. Why do I attract this? I feel as if I've spent my entire life watching the varying degrees of screaming histrionics from grown people, who all, with monotonous regularity, pretend they didn't do

it, deny the violence and even imply it was all MY fault. I'm
so pissed off with it all. It is getting ridiculous.

**If one looks into a clear mirror and does not like what is
reflected there is always a tendency to smash the mirror.**
But it's not the mirror's fault.

Precisely.

Mmm. So how does the mirror protect itself?

It reflects upon the light behind all reflections.

Do you mean it looks in – not out?

Yes ... and one other important point.

What's that?

The mirror NEVER takes anything personally.

AHHA! I like that.

**As for the love between you and your friend and you
and your mother – I can assure you nothing is lost –
for love is love and it is eternal. No one can ever take
it away from you.**

Veritas ... I'd love to believe you but, are you sure about this?

I made myself sit down and work out my finances. I was not
taking sick pay because I was doing a little work and couldn't
bring myself to lie, although many of my contemporaries thought
I was mad. Neither could I pretend I had no capital to the
unemployment office who told me to come back when I had
nothing left. I did have enough in future commissions to cover
the tax bill. I also had enough in the bank to spend on therapy,
which in my book included a new car and holiday.

Hank called me to tell me his company had landed a job
working on a film to be shot in Rhodes. He was flying out on
May 3rd and suggested I joined him. It was a perfect plan and
within hours of his call I had secured flights and accommodation.
It gave me a great thrill to call JR and tell her we had a very
important business meeting. She got her diary and I told her to
blank out May 14th to May 28th.

'JC! What sort of meeting is this supposed to be?' she
exclaimed.

'It is a very awkward client who needs a lot of time.'

'Two weeks! JC ... what are you up to?'

'Up to lots of good.'

'OK, so where is this meeting.'

'Lindos, on the Greek island of Rhodes.'

'JULES! I can't afford . . .'

I cut her off mid-sentence and told her she had been paid for. She went very quiet.

'We have an appointment with some sunshine, some sand and the sea. Put a do not disturb sign on your office door and start packing.'

'Oh wow!'

'JR . . . I don't know how else I can ever thank you for all you've done – we deserve this.'

I put the phone down on a very excited JR. I wished I had the money to take all the friends who had been so wonderful. I told TC when he came in from surgery. He was worried about sorting his dates out, but began to smile at the prospect of Greek yoghurt, honey and ice-creams. It was the first time he had looked happy in weeks and the first night I slept through till the morning without weird dreams, cold-sweat nightmares or bumping around the bedroom ceiling locked out of my body.

I felt well enough to have a go at driving. My right hand was improving slowly thanks to the physiotherapy, piano-lessons and swimming. I was able to grip the steering wheel, and although manoeuvring the control pedals pulled my still sore abdomen, I felt I was able to control the car. TC sat in the passenger seat just in case I couldn't cope, and his eldest son sat bravely in the back. My hand was fine, but my neck was so stiff I realised I could hardly turn it, making the whole experience very painful. I drove a few miles into a picturesque market town, where we stopped at a little café and had tea. It was delightfully English. We browsed in a bookshop and strolled around the arty shops. Things felt almost back to normal until we went into the sports-shop. TC could never resist sports-shops. His son and I joked together about whether yet another cricket bat or golf club was about to be added to the already large collection. Ship's chandleries were also a firm favourite, things for the yacht he shared but hardly ever sailed. He settled for some golf balls. The man behind the counter recognised him.

'Heard your wife and bird were 'aving a bit of a scrap over you then.' He winked at TC several times, with a smug 'I know all the details' expression on his face. We all froze, speechless in the face of such crass ignorance. As we left the shop TC whispered in my ear, 'You've got to laugh, Jules . . . I am probably one of the last men on earth my wife would want to scrap over.'

I sat in my silver two-seater sports-car waiting for TC. I was thrilled with my new, second-hand purchase, but not overly happy at the thought of a dinner with some of TC's colleagues from the first awareness course. It was my first social engagement, and I even wore a frock to mark the occasion. TC had reassured me about what a nice group of people they were and particularly wanted me to meet a chartered accountant called Richard. He really liked him because of his sense of fun and interest in sailing, and felt he was a possible third partner for his yacht. I had to face new people at some point, so braced myself, trying not to remember the last time I attended a course-related social engagement, which I suspected had in some way contributed towards my attempted murder.

It was a very strange evening and got off to a bad start as I was greeted by a rather large woman with a hug which was far too powerful for my still frail frame. The hosts had prepared for us an exquisite eastern meal which was, for me, the high spot of the evening. As we ate it transpired that the hosts' relationship had been examined under the course microscope, so much of the conversation revolved around what had been 'shared' during the course and how they were putting into practice some of the suggestions Cosmo Greene had made. Not understanding the jargon, much of it went over my head and the bits I understood seemed very bizarre. Course-speak prefaced most sentences with, 'I need you to know', or 'I'd like to share this with you all'. It was nauseating. I was feeling very distant. The outside world was still too bright, noisy and confusing for me to focus – especially as the chatter centred on things I had no experience of. The conversation was interspersed with cutting remarks aimed at TC's friend Richard, fired from the large woman who was his wife. He seemed strangely detached and made no attempt to reply to the allegations winging their way across the table. Richard, it would seem, was supposed to 'know' what he had done. The atmosphere was dreadful. TC cast desperate glances in my direction with a fixed grin and 'Let's-get-the-hell-out-of-here' expression on his face.

After the meal Richard's wife sat in an armchair weeping, with the hostess in attendance mouthing to the rest of us that she was halfway through a course and had a number of 'issues' to deal with. One of them was obviously Richard. I asked if I could smoke. It was frowned upon, but I was shown into a far corner of the room where it would be least offensive to everyone else. It was a great relief to be banished. Things settled down a bit as the tears subsided and quiet coffee and fireside chat began. I remained in the corner and was joined by Richard who understandably was in need of a cigarette. TC was right, he was a very charming and interesting man and I spent the rest of the evening talking with him, only interrupted when his wife had another outburst and announced to everyone what his salary was. In the embarrassing silence that ensued TC and I took our leave.

We fell into the night air, jumped into the car and drove away at great speed, both groaning to God. TC was the first to speak. 'Tabloid press headlines – chartered accountant's wife found with hatchet in back of head . . . husband charged. Friends of the accused shocked . . . he was always such a gentleman.' We both groaned again with relief. It never ceased to amaze me how one bad mood could pollute a room full of happy people.

'TC,' I whispered as we turned out the bedside light.

'Mmm.'

'We'll have to find him a new wife if he's going to share the boat.'

'Mmm . . . good idea. Got anyone in mind?'

'I'll think of someone.'

DELAYED SHOCK

I should have realised I was still in shock and therefore in no fit state to understand what was going on. TC, my family, friends and business colleagues were all so jangled by what had happened they resorted to the best-loved human answer to situations beyond comprehension – let's all pretend it didn't happen. The forbidden-words competition assumed on a far grander scale – for, with the exception of my close friends, it had became the forbidden-subject competition. I became a willing participant in the game. Even though much of the framework of my life had collapsed, I smiled sweetly at everyone and told them everything was 'just fine'. During that time the only thing in my life with consistent, if somewhat baffling advice, wrapped in abundant love, humour and compassion, was the mysterious Voice I'd nicknamed Veritas.

Two weeks of sunshine, swimming and many olive oil-drenched Greek salads improved the suppleness in my stiff and sore body. However, to begin with it was not the dream holiday I'd longed for. JR was ill and expected TC and me to minister to her needs. TC was distant, exhausted and didn't want to know about anyone's needs. Hank and his partners were working such long hours we did not see very much of them. For the first time in weeks I wanted to play, to sing, to dance and celebrate my new start to life, but I was the only one around in holiday mood. I had not the confidence to take myself out and give me a good time and so I made the best of what company was available. Veritas had told me that true love was freedom, yet never had I felt more trapped.

Each day as I swam in the velvet waters I promised myself I would find that freedom. I KNEW it existed. I dived down into the still waters of the natural harbour's lagoon and to my delight discovered a sea-bed strewn with ancient fragments from another civilisation. In the silent depths Veritas whispered to me that EVERYTHING we see on the outside of our life is a direct reflection of our inner state – his message clear – dive deep enough within myself and find the treasure. Words pounding in my brain – YOU SEE THE WORLD ACCORDING TO YOUR BELIEFS. As I surfaced with exploding lungs into the brilliance of the Greek sunshine suddenly I saw my life in a totally different way. EVERYTHING out there was a clue to my inner state. Everything. I caught sight of TC asleep on the beach and a snuffling JR nursing her cold and I laughed and laughed. My outer life was giving me huge clues and until that moment, I had been blind. It was rather apparent my inner state was a total bloody mess. The behaviour of my crotchety little friends lying under the parasol not-awaiting my return was most definitely showing me this. I was waiting for them to change when all along it was I who needed to make a few inner adjustments. Veritas told me repeatedly to change my mind but I hadn't put it into practice. As I swam to shore everything was beginning to click into place. What was it in me that believed it didn't deserve love, or fun? I stopped feeling irritable with them, realising for the first time it was all down to me. The implications were daunting, but for the rest of the holiday I had a ball – and interestingly enough, so did they. I returned to the UK stronger in all senses; my loneliness had served to deepen my yearning for a different life. A life where I could change my inner state and find the life of love I so longed for. I resolved to make this my quest; my first clue on the treasure map was the forthcoming Self-Awareness course.

It was the only place I could think of to start as the detective on my own case. I was so curious. Had anyone involved with the course known about Helen's past and mental condition? Did the self-enquiry contribute to her breakdown? And why had TC become hooked? Cosmo and his wife were charismatic and strong personalities. He was the only person I knew to have explanations of past lives, and I wanted to understand my own experiences, dreams and ancient memories. The introductory evening had whetted my appetite. Added to this, some of the course participants I'd met were professional and straightforward people who were very positive about the benefits they'd received. Although a part of me felt it was madness, I enrolled.

In early June I found myself lying on my back in a fast-food restaurant's darkened training centre. Thirty other supposedly sensible adults were alongside me as we waved our little legs in the air calling out for our mummies and daddies. I can only recall two thoughts. The first was the realisation that if this was the way to 'find' myself, being lost was preferable – the second was a fervent wish I had not eaten the brown rice and red-bean salad prior to the process.

I did not enjoy myself very much – especially as a woman participant experienced a psychotic breakdown, shedding most of her clothes and becoming very aggressive. I was terrified – it was too close to home for comfort. I made a breakthrough in my normal politeness and told Cosmo of my concern. He was reluctant to ask her to leave. After a number of hours of some very strange behaviour he had quite a confrontation with the hysterical woman, who was eventually carried out of the room across Cosmo's shoulders and taken away by her husband. It was true to say the behaviour of most participants was strange. Precision-aimed processes encouraged inhibitions to fall away, allowing a mass of repressed emotions to spew out in all directions. It was controlled mayhem. We had all made 'agreements' with Cosmo Greene before the course began, the crunch being we agreed not to discuss the course. Suffice it to say we put ourselves absolutely into his hands. I began to understand why TC had not been at my hospital bedside and why a woman with an unstable mental condition could have found it all too much.

There were some good things to come out of the experience. I befriended a lovely fun woman who was one of the helpers and a brilliant masseuse – during the following months her healing hands were to work wonders on my numb body. I was taught more about the mechanics of meditation which enabled me to delve further into my inner landscape, gaining insights about my life and a recall of long-since buried memories about childhood incidents which had shaped much of my adult life. I was introduced to some wonderful books. I did not, however, experience the euphoria I had heard about from TC and witnessed in some of my fellow participants. I felt myself to be under considerable pressure to continue with the follow-on courses. The implication was that the first course only scratches the surface and in order to be 'master' one needed to continue – not to mention the feeling of being a failure if one decided to leave. Mr Greene was a very persuasive man and leaving a course was seen as weakness. I was disappointed to find he was not the spiritual master I had hoped for, although he was most definitely a man with a great sense of fun and a gifted observer of human nature and behaviour. It was perhaps this which enabled him to hone in on TC's and my vulnerability, making us feel 'special and chosen' and part of an elite group – puffing up our egos whilst pandering to our fear of being failures if we did not continue with our inner journey, and therefore his courses. Whatever it was, it worked. Now we both were drawn right in.

It was mid-June when I found out what my injuries were. I admit it was underhand but curiosity got the better of me. One night I had dropped some documents into the surgery for TC. I had the keys and let myself into the empty building. I went straight into his consulting room and put the package on his desk. There sitting on the top of his filing tray were my notes. Paper-clipped to them was a hospital report. I felt like a criminal as I held the confidential folder, but in the yellow beam of his desk lamp I had to read it all:

'Emergency admission following multiple stab wounds with a long sharp knife. Almost exsanguinated. Taken to theatre immediately and abdomen was opened. The left lobe of the liver had been totally penetrated by the knife – all but severing it, resulting in a loss of virtually all the circulating blood – haemorrhaging stopped after suturing; injury in back reached deep down into the spinal processes; the neck muscles had been severed as had the upper lip – both sutured back together layer by layer using microsurgery. The right hand had sustained quite a degree of damage although extensor and flexor tendons appeared to be intact, however following check-up noted extensor mechanisms obviously damaged. Upper first and middle fingers cannot abduct or adduct. Physiotherapy arranged to try and get this one moving – should improve. Could take several years to regain feeling in palm. Chip of tooth removed in the Oral Surgery dept. Obvious damage to the buccal mucosa and tooth socket. Further dental treatment necessary. Made rapid recovery. No further hospital treatment necessary.'

I sat back in the silent surgery. It had taken three months to find out. The time span enabled me to distance myself from the person I was reading about, which cushioned the blow of a sliced-through liver. I thought how ridiculous it was not to have been told about what had been done to MY body and wondered if other people experienced the same lack of information on what to do after leaving hospital. No advice on eating/drinking/exercise/rest and yet such knowledge was essential to facilitate recovery. The biggest piece of information the notes gave me was the confirmation of just how much my outer world reflected my inner state at the time of the attack. With my victim mentality, I cannot have liked myself very much. Veritas's instruction to work on the fissures and wounds within my mind was becoming even clearer.

Do you remember what you have learnt?
Pardon?
Whose body?
My body.
Whose body?
MY BODY.
WHOSE BODY?
OK OK . . . The body I inhabit.
That's better. Treat this moment as if you are reading about crash repairs made to your car . . .
Oh. You mean let's hope they remembered to refill the oil and remove their tools BEFORE they screwed the engine back together.
If you wish. And, for good measure, let's hope the owner remembers not to drive too fast.

*　　*　　*

A posse of therapists, healers and soothsayers appeared out of the woodwork, all very keen to prove they could help me. An elder of my tribe had been an incredibly wise woman who had taught her family that offered help stinks. Until now I had never known what she had meant. After all I had experienced, still I was not listening to myself, still anxious not to offend and believing that everyone else knew me far better than I did.

In the name of recovery I'd been encouraged to cry, to shout and scream, to laugh, to fantasise, to pray, to meditate, to talk, to be silent, to role-play. My body had been pummelled, pressed, lasered, pierced, probed, steamed, sunned, hosed down, flushed-out, mud-wrapped, manhandled, scrubbed and stretched. I'd consumed copious quantities of fruit, vegetables, bitter herbs and pungent spices, pipette-dropped healing liquids, expensive homeopathic remedies, prescribed pills, potions, vitamins, mineral-supplements and French red wine. I played tinkly-bell New Age music which encouraged excessive bladder emptying rather than inner peace, I read all the 'right' books, I slept with strategically placed crystals and pyramid shapes dotted around the bed, I wore the carefully chosen healing textures and colours, and smoked one immensely enjoyable marijuana-stuffed cigarette. My mind, writing, aura, horoscope, hands and numerology were all analysed, each reading producing very different results. The cosmic smorgasbord I was feeding off reached its frenzied climax when an elderly spiritual healer took my head in his hands, looked deeply into my eyes, stroked my hair and said, 'Why did you do it, Helen?' The woman who had taken me to the healing service explained rather frantically that I was the 'other' one.

I knew all the help was well-intentioned but found many people who believed they had an exclusive on God's love and that their path was the only way to truth, peace and enlightenment. I was experiencing an altered state of awareness with increasing frequency – I would never be able to forget the incredible dance of human life I had seen as I had been flung out of my body during the attack, and because of this I knew that this thing we call God holds all of us in His arms, with no exceptions. It felt to me that every soul on the earth was on the path which was right for them – whatever it was. I could not as yet find anyone who could expand on, or explain this for me. I read about other people who'd had one-off out of body experiences, usually during surgery or accidents, but found no evidence to suggest they'd ever experienced it again. Yet I was spending night after night flying through heavens, hells and surrealistic landscapes, sometimes drawn towards a light so brilliant that it was impossible to stand the exploding feeling of love that radiated from it. I would scream into a silent void, sometimes crash-landing back into my body, other times bumping and banging around the bedroom ceiling, locked out of my human form and terrified. I had no control over what was happening. I had a consultation with Cosmo Greene to see if he could explain what was going on. He believed it was related to all my repressed squiggles which were seeping out of my subconscious and affecting my conscious mind. His answers were logical but I knew something more was going on and left the consultation still baffled.

Somewhere there had to be someone who knew what I was experiencing. I was riding a magnificent and mysterious horse and I'd found a myriad of people and books that could discuss the subject at length but NO-ONE who had sat on the creature and experienced the ride. I found myself avoiding people who said they were doing God's work – it was beginning to be a bad sign.

As with the rescue and the time in hospital, the real help came quietly. The ones who scrubbed and cleaned away the blood. The practical assistance in keeping the cottage running. The steady friendship without opinions. Those who reawakened the laughter in our lives. The loving cards. The encouraging letters. The thoughtful gifts. The private prayers for my well-being from so many I would never even know. The authors of great philosophical works. The gratitude I felt for them all would be written in my heart for eternity.

I arranged to see my mother and brother. I was to go for several hours on a day Herbert was not due home for lunch. The sun shone and I enjoyed three hours of hood-down, zippy driving, in high spirits, looking forward to chats, hugs and laughs.

As I pulled into the drive Martin was standing waiting for me. His beautiful little face lit up, and he was hugging me before I could get out of the car. Mum ran out to meet me, her arms open. She muttered that 'Sir' had suspected she was up to something and had come home unexpectedly. My stepfather hovered awkwardly in the background. She had prepared a wonderful lunch and we all sat around the outside table on the flower-fringed terrace. It could have been idyllic but the atmosphere was dreadful. My mother, wanting to include Herbert, talked non-stop about him in a voice that was too bright and too high. The underlying message was not to mention the incident, TC, or anything related to the subject – so I didn't. After the meal, when she was out of earshot, Martin was ordered to go to his room and I was told in no uncertain manner how tired my mother was and how it was time for me to leave. He had not shown one shred of concern for me – a very strange man. On the pretext of clearing the table I went inside and found Mum. She was crying. My very presence was putting her under great strain – we couldn't talk about anything other than superficial topics, Herbert sitting between us as if on guard, determined that Mum would not get emotional, and therefore I supposed, out of his control. As I announced my departure he was grinning, flushed with the pleasure of a self-righteous belief that 'it was all for our own good'. I drove away in low spirits but full of gratitude that I had not gone to them to convalesce.

On the journey home I called in unannounced on my grandmother. She was so thrilled to see me, flinging her arms around my neck and kissing me. We spent a delightful couple of hours talking – I spared her the gory details, telling her some of the funnier incidents. She told me she would have crawled to the hospital to help me if she had been told the full story. I explained we had kept her away because we loved her, and we knew her dear husband was a very sick man who needed all of her love and care. Always the go-between, I gave her news of Mum and Martin – we agreed it was ridiculous that she was not allowed to visit or telephone her daughter or grandson. It was a source of great hurt for her, and something she didn't deserve or really understand, although she respected their wishes for privacy and stayed away.

The solicitor I'd been recommended gave me some advice about how to complete my claim forms for the Criminal Injuries Compensation scheme. It was not as straightforward as I would have hoped, largely because my loss of earnings was so difficult to quantify and my injuries had not fully healed. He gave me an indication of what I could expect to receive, based on a calculation of so much per centimetre of scarring, so much for shock/trauma and so much for tangible material loss and out of pocket expenses. It was quite a lot of money. I would need further paid-for medicals, psychiatric reports, official photographs and audited accounts, plus anything else I could think of to substantiate my claim. It all felt very unfair. I was, because of someone else's actions, once again accountable and it was going to cost me time, money and a lot of work to prove my case. I didn't know where to begin. I asked him how much this was likely to cost me, and, waving his hands across his desk, he told me not to give a thought to his fees – they would be 'nominal'.

We then discussed any other options available to me. He suggested there was a possibility I could sue TC, although he felt it would be a long shot as he'd had a long conversation with the Medical Defence Union, the insurers for claims against doctors. The experts felt there was no case whatsoever for TC to answer to, as I was not his patient but his partner. Even if their advice had been to go for him, I knew I could never agree to it – what happened was certainly not his fault. On the other hand, the prospect of suing my assailant was no more appealing. She was almost certainly going to be found insane and therefore not responsible for her actions – making any claim against her tricky and long-winded. I asked myself if I really did want to spend the next five years of my life preparing a case in order to face her in battle again, with all the legalistic jargon the courtroom has to offer. No thank you.

To satisfy my own curiosity I had done a lot of detective work about my assailant's life, tracing much of her recent past including some details of her marriage and time in a sanatorium in Europe. It was a strange and sad story. Her mother had brought her back to live in the UK. Most of what I learnt came unsought, mainly from course participants and the police. I was told a number of alarming things about Helen. Apparently she had stood up in front of the entire first course and told them she was feeling so good she wanted to stop taking her drugs. The opinion was that it was not made clear what these drugs were, and that there was no mention of schizophrenia. It was assumed that Mr Greene knew what he was doing in supporting her decision to take responsibility for herself. This was the core of the teaching: to look to oneself for permission to make changes in one's life. Helen was living and working in the community, so it was natural to assume she was a normal adult with discriminatory faculties. It was also stated by some of the people I spoke with that so much was going on during the course for each individual, it was almost impossible to keep tabs on what anyone else might be experiencing. I had to agree, for that was my own experience. TC told me he had spent so much time taking notes, he remembers very little of what others were going through, and he had no memory of Helen standing up in front of the course.

I was told by two people that my assailant had confessed to them about a time she had been violent. After her attack on me, these informers were so frightened they made it clear that they would not be prepared to speak publicly. I understood. I was advised that the evidence I had of her life in Europe was therefore insubstantial, being based on hearsay from witnesses who were all scared to death, so my easiest option was to leave the prosecution in the hands of the Crown – in any event I did not want to have anything to do with Helen or her family. The solicitor agreed with my decision to pursue the government claim, and to let justice take its course. When I left his office he offered me one further piece of advice – not to look so well, as he felt it could reduce the amount of compensation. I wondered what sort of a society we were building for the future, where it pays to stay weak, sick and screwed-up. I drove away wishing I could be paid for how quickly I had recovered and how much

I had saved the system by getting out of hospital in seven days instead of six weeks.

We had started to receive hang-up phone-box calls. They were always at the same time, but not every day. After three weeks of it they were driving us crazy, so I reported it to the police. I felt sure they were from Helen. The police told me she was in the psychiatric wing of an ordinary hospital where there were public phones, but that she was under hourly surveillance. Sensing my distress, they agreed to speak to the psychiatrist in charge of her. We never had another hang-up call. I told this to the boys in blue. They took note and also informed us that the trial was set for October 23rd and that TC and I would be served with requests to be in court as possible witnesses. They assured me this was just a formality and, although we had to attend, they had no intention of putting us in the witness-box.

By the end of the summer I had wound down most of my business responsibilities and JR was looking for a job. I'd cleared my tax debt, helped by the fruition of several outstanding business deals resulting in healthy commission cheques. I still did not know what I was going to do for a living, so I cashed in a life policy and planned to lie low until my award was paid.

TC was heavily involved with the third-level Awareness course and both of us were learning more about the organisation behind it. The cottage was always bursting at the seams as we provided free accommodation and meals for participants, helpers and their friends. We were all as bad as each other, convinced we were on a special mission with an evangelical desire to save the world. Veritas whispered to me that the world did not need saving and if I really wanted to help I should concentrate on saving myself. At the time I did not understand such a statement so I ignored it.

We were invited to London to meet the man behind the whole set-up. He had flown in from the other side of the world to check on his UK operation. We sat with a few other specially selected guests in the garden of a fashionable Chelsea café. The big well-groomed guy and his second wife held court, speaking non-stop about their vision for a better world and what we had to do to take the teachings to a wider audience. The forming of a management committee was suggested and we realised we had each been selected to give free consultation in our specialist field of work – mine was marketing, advertising and public relations. The lecture went on for a very long time. Cosmo's wife was taking lots of pictures which when developed would tell an interesting tale. The body language of the Awareness disciples spoke volumes – we looked as if we'd been dropped from a great height and crashed at the feet of the master. Our facial expressions were reflecting utter boredom – lights on and definitely no one in. After the final tedious hour of instructions eventually a date was agreed for the first management meeting and I had a schedule of what needed to be discussed and done to make the Awareness organisation more efficient, business-like and successful. I left thinking it needed a miracle, but hooked by the challenge and flattered by their faith in my ability to 'make it happen'.

September was a busy month. I spent much of the time collating information for my compensation claim. My twice-weekly physiotherapy sessions came to an end, my right hand slightly more mobile, but still far from perfect. I was told it was the best I could hope for and I would have to learn to live with it. It marked the end of my competitive sporting life and, in spite of valiant efforts on my part and my teacher's, a dead-end for my piano playing. No one around me realised how devastated I was. I couldn't even hold a pen and write a letter without considerable difficulty.

Another photographic session, this time in a professional studio. I stood under the arc-lights and umbrellas, partially clothed and showing my scars to their worst possible advantage. When I raced saloon cars in the seventies I had spent a lot of time being photographed – I'd upset a trendy photographer then by refusing to take my bra off, painfully shy. Now, ten years on, I was wrestling with the problem of how to show the point of knife entry between the breasts without exposing any unnecessary flesh. Other than the charming and sensitive photographer, nothing much had changed.

I returned to hospital for a private medical examination in order to obtain an official report. This time it was Pomp. As I entered the room he was seated at his desk reading and did not look up. He told me to remove my top clothes and get on the bed. It was cold and I shivered as I awaited his company. With a brisk sigh he closed the folder in front of him and came to my side. He took my left hand and inspected it thoroughly asking me to wiggle my fingers. He pronounced it was very good indeed as he began writing something in his notebook. He then began to prod my middle. I asked him if he wanted to see my right hand, which was not very good indeed, as after all, it was the one that had been injured and was still causing me the most distress. He coughed and gave it a cursory glance. After the early episode with the bandages, I wondered what he'd got against it. After several more prods, questions and sighs it became obvious he was in a hurry. He asked me to sit on his scales, told me I was overweight and suggested I should consider marrying the man involved. He must have thought I'd had something other than a knife inserted without permission into my body. I left his office feeling lower than a snake's belly. At this point the large charitable donation he was due to receive from my mother, towards his chosen good causes, got cancelled.

CRISP WHITE COAT

SCARLET TIE

HOW MANY TIMES

EACH DAY

DO THOSE CRISP WHITE TEETH

MAKE WAY

FOR JUDGEMENTAL SIGHS?

AS YOU PONTIFICATE

ABOVE THE HEADS

OF THOSE

YOU HEAL

YET SO DESPISE.

I was so tired of misunderstandings at my expense I burst into tears and left the hospital sobbing in JR's arms. She was magnificent and in order to distract me told me we were going to do something we had never done before, with which she took me to a funfair on the local pier and made me play bingo. Much to the annoyance of the regulars, the two well-heeled business women scooped up more than their share of acrylic fluffy toys and factory-rejected china ornaments. It worked – I was distracted.

I attended the first SA management meeting to discover that only one of the other seven members had turned up. It was TC's friend Richard, who was the financial man in the team. We took ourselves to an Italian restaurant and spent several hours crunching our way through the agenda and crudités. Thankfully he had a great sense of humour, which made it one of my more memorable and enjoyable business lunches – even if I was unpaid.

The trial was due in October. TC and I were all set to go when we received a call the day before informing us it had been taken out of the list for hearing because of serious doubts as to Helen's fitness to plead. The spokesman from the DPP's office was of the opinion she would not be deemed sane enough but the issue of her sanity would be tried before a jury in early December. If they decided she was able to understand the charges and differentiate between guilty and not guilty, there would then be a full trial with a different jury. It all sounded very long-winded to me. I just wanted the matter over with. The case was bizarre and the police warned us that the tabloid press were likely to latch onto the story. We planned to go away for a few days immediately after the trial. I spoke to my solicitor asking him if I needed to attend the new hearing. He said he would confirm with the DPP and let me know. I felt it was a good idea in case there was a full trial – it seemed sensible to know what was being said. Several days later I received an attendance affirmative via the DPP's office, on the basis that I 'wouldn't view it as an opportunity to stand up and hurl abuse'. The totally unbiased, unopinionated voice of the law had spoken.

My life was gathering pace in spite of me. After considerable pressure from TC, Cosmo, Richard and other committee members and trustees, I found myself agreeing to manage the London offices of the Awareness organisation. It was a mistake.

The hours were impossibly long, the pay virtually non-existent and the direction was from a committee that could never agree on anything. This was not the way to ease myself back into the routine of a working life. Cosmo and Felicia were rarely in accord on policy matters and the staff were nearly all ex-course volunteers, an ever-changing unpaid group of mixed ability and willingness. My often reluctant helpers wafted around in varying states of I'm-being-very-spiritual-doing-this-for-nothing. I was forever in trouble with Felicia for playing loud rock music throughout the offices in order to speed them all up a bit. Not only was I expected to run the offices, update and do the mailings, coordinate and supervise the volunteers whilst managing reception and telephone enquiries, but I also had to do the cleaning, counsel the distraught, court the media and juggle the bank accounts and payments in order to keep the creditors at bay. In between this, it was essential I took all the courses. Naturally it was madness. Veritas had totally gone from my life, I hardly saw TC and my step-grandfather died.

However, whilst sorting the filing systems out I did stumble across Helen Black's application form for the courses. She had listed the drugs she was on and some background information about psychiatric care. There was no mention of schizophrenia, her psychiatrist or TC. I could not see how a lay person would know the significance of the drugs and wondered if anyone in the organisation had picked up the fact they were to control schizophrenia. When I went back to the file a week later, it was not there. That same day I was asked by Felicia to increase the insurance thresholds against the likelihood of course participants suing the organisation.

Without consulting me, Felicia made an appointment for me to see a healer. She insisted he was the best, so although I didn't think I needed one, I went along resenting the fact I was about to spend thirty pounds for something I didn't want. I spent one hour in a hotel bedroom with closed eyes and a strange man telling me to find the light in my heart. I didn't think I had experienced much but that same night I was awoken with the sound of Veritas calling my name.

*　　*　　*

J-U-L-I-E . . . Wake up!
Veritas . . . I don't believe it . . . you're back.
No my friend . . . it is you who has returned.

The Trial

It was the first of December and the day of the trial. For some reason my solicitor did not turn up at the cottage, so we left without him. TC, JR and I arrived outside the courtrooms in plenty of time. The superb thirteenth-century Great Hall of Winchester stood majestically, an historically famous court presided over by the kings of England. Alongside was a twentieth-century atrocity housing the modern halls of justice, presided over by a security officer checking our bags for hidden bombs. We were met by the police, who were as considerate as ever for my feelings. Anxious to ensure I did not have to face the woman who had so wanted to deprive me of life, they ushered us straight into a lift situated in the over-heated reception area. We exited on a wide mezzanine floor just above the entrance foyer. They offered to buy us all a coffee, and taking my arm led me to a small canteen area where drinks and snacks were available. I sat down at a formica-topped table whilst TC and the police went to the counter to buy the drinks. Even though I was assured I would not be called as a witness, I felt all the sickness of fear I used to experience when I peeped through the back-stage curtains and watched Max perform. In those days my immediate future peace of mind had rested on whether the audience would be receptive or hostile to a man in a wig. On reflection, there were many similarities in my current situation.

I looked up to see a familiar face. Sitting at an adjacent table was Helen, flanked by two uniformed officers. I was so surprised to see her at such close range I gasped loudly and protectively held my middle. Thankfully she did not look in my direction. It was hard to believe this languid-looking woman had inflicted such harm on me. I did not enjoy the coffee.

Before entering the visitor's gallery I went with JR to find the ladies. I was trembling from head to foot. One other woman was in the institutional-looking cloakroom. She was unaware of our presence as she preened herself before the mirror, pouting as she checked her hair and appearance. I felt sure I knew her and racked my brain trying to place her. She looked at me as she left but there was no glimmer of recognition in her eyes.

We entered the courtroom and sat by ourselves on the left-hand side in the front row. The right-side seating was already full of people, including the preening woman. I realised why she was familiar as TC told me it was the mother of Helen. It looked to me like a family outing, complete with sandwiches. I wished my mother could have been with me. The priest I had visited arrived with his wife in tow. On seeing us he came over, patted my back and muttered how hard it must be for us and went and sat with my assailant's family. I considered this very strange as in my naivety I thought men of God did not take sides.

Looking down into the press gallery directly below I could see it was full. All the memories of childhood flooded back and my mind raced with the fear of what these people could do to our lives. I remembered how Max had been told by a leading national newspaper's editor he was to be a target for the popular press, and if he'd got any sense he'd get out of the country. He was told in no uncertain terms his career, reputation and relationship with my mother would be destroyed. Within hours heavily distorted stories of the beauty queen and the comedian hit the headlines. He was made out to be a wicked, evil man who had left an ex-wife and children impoverished to be with this younger beautiful woman. Of course the fact he had been separated before he'd even met my mother was never mentioned, or that in 1955 he was paying out £2000 p.a., an enormous amount of alimony, based on his earnings at the height of a career which no longer existed. It was financially crucifying him. His ex-wife was more than willing to add petrol to the blaze. From then on two courageous people were pursued relentlessly by a hunt of pressmen screaming for blood. It took time and a steady campaign of vitriol, but in the end, the popular press got their victory. I was thinking about how little faith I had in the ability of journalists to tell a straight story when the strangest thing happened. Apart from a couple of very young-looking hacks, all the owners of sharpened pencils and grubby notepads hurriedly left the courtroom.

What's going on?
Have faith. All is well. It is time to release your fear about what is written. Rise above the criticisms, the flattery, the false accusations. Find out what else is going on. To the wise man, what he reads will often tell him more about the writer than it will ever tell about the subject ...

The court rose and the judge entered. I sat riveted to my seat as the trial opened, as keen as everyone else to discover why she did it, and how the legal boys would interpret the bizarre facts. I could see the jury, barristers and judge, but Helen and the police were out of sight somewhere beneath the over-hanging public gallery.

I watched the be-wigged be-frocked QC's dance, prance and prattle their respective sides of the case before another grown man sporting a stiff wig and large black gown. British justice is very theatrical. They looked remarkably silly. And so edited highlights of the story began to unfold. It was confirmed that on the morning of the incident she had been on her way to London on an early morning commuter train and having taken her clothes off wandered naked down the aisles to the toilet, because she needed to cleanse herself in pure water. A fleeting image of British Rail train toilets came into my mind – they would not have been my first choice for a cleanse. Taken from the train by the police she refused to put her trousers back on because they were the colour of the Devil. When it got to my part in the story, she said she didn't like the evil way I looked at her and knew I was a different God who had to be destroyed. That 'pram' look getting me into deep trouble once again. The learned view was that it could have been anybody, so it would seem that I drew the short straw. There was only a fleeting mention of the fact she had developed a crush on TC.

Only two witnesses were called. The first was her psychiatrist. Most of what was said I already knew. Apparently her schizophrenia had developed in the seventies when she lived abroad. She'd spent some time in a psychiatric hospital, her marriage ended in divorce and, eventually, her husband had custody of the children. Her mother brought her back to the UK, where she went straight into psychiatric care. Controlled by the medication she was able to return to Europe in order to be near her children but suffered from a form of blindness for eighteen months, in that she could not or would not open her eyes. She was brought back to the UK, and again received treatment. It was recommended by the man in the box that she be allowed to live a more independent life and she moved into her own flat. Six months later her sight returned. She was able to get some part-time work. Twice in the eighties she had relapses due to stopping her self-administered medication. It was stated that her past had no history of violence or offence and that her medication, when taken, controlled her very well. The second witness, a consultant psychologist, said she had told him she had been very well while maintained on the prescribed dosage, but was encouraged to reduce her medication by the self-help group.

The defence counsel then launched into a full-scale attack on the courses and TC, implying that the organisation gave her encouragement to reduce her medication and he felt they must have known her mental background. Furthermore her GP, who was on the same course, albeit by coincidence, should have known it was an unsatisfactory situation. The well-rehearsed speech was designed to lead the jury to the conclusion it was the fault of the course and TC. He was just beginning to suggest that TC had encouraged his client in believing her medication could be stopped when the judge intervened. In a raised voice tinged with measured patience he pointed out that any fair-minded person must see that there was no one from the course to answer allegations and that TC had denied what the lady had said. He then reminded the court that this was a VERY disturbed woman and he was not going to make ANY criticism of those who run the courses or TC and how it would be WRONG of the general public to take the attitude that they had in some way been wanting.

How wonderful it was to hear plain speaking and common

sense coming from the man who had in all probability far more information before him than was being squeaked out publicly. The mood in court changed gear and proceedings gathered momentum. The knife was displayed. The jury winced and our fellow observers in the gallery drew in sharp intakes of breath. I thought of the mountain of meat and vegetables it had sliced and chopped in its time. Descriptions of its length fluctuated by several inches depending on whether prosecution or defence was speaking. I was surprised to see my silver bangle held aloft – I'd forgotten I'd been wearing it. Large indentations in it were pointed out – I realised it had saved me more than a few stitches in the wrist. Then the police photographs were given to the jury. Me, an anonymous face in the crowd peering at twelve strangers peering at my semi-naked body. All very odd. I was relieved I couldn't see the detail of what they were looking at.

The judge then summed up. The evidence was all one way. The jury got the message and did not even retire to consider their verdict: Not guilty of attempted murder due to insanity.

The judge ordered the defendant to be detained at the discretion of the Secretary of Home Affairs. What an interesting job title.

It was over.

Winchester Crown Court
December

My Dear Head Shrinker,

Although we have never met, I have had to read and listen to a great deal about your opinions. If today I had been granted one wish, it would have been for permission to ask you a few little questions of my own.

You stated during my assailant's bail application that you were surprised by your client's reactions when off the drugs and that you would have expected more religion but not violence. Well, my little pumpkin popper, perhaps you'd like to explain to me how someone who thought she was the original Christ, that I represented an opposing God and had to be killed in order to save the world, and that her course teacher was a God, could have squeezed any more religion into our short and near fatal encounter? As for the violence . . . well, it is a matter of opinion. During that first hearing, she admitted the last time she came off her medication she had tried to commit suicide – in my book, taking a life, even your own, constitutes an act of violence. You see, the sages say, 'The world is as you see it.' Perhaps the morning she put on my sweater she projected everything she hated about herself onto me . . . in other words was she still trying to kill herself?

It was you, was it not, who decided that this woman needed more independence and deemed her mentally fit enough to cope with life in her own flat within the community? You confess you did not know she was on the Self-Awareness course and that had you known you would have stopped her and she also admits she knew she should not have stopped the drugs. Why didn't she consult you about this? You were the one prescribing them. Had you laid down any conditions for her day-to-day life or was she free to do her own thing and make her own decisions? Today you and your colleague admit there was no guarantee she would take her medication if she was released, and confirmed that twice before she had stopped her drugs. Incidentally, who did you all blame on those occasions?

It seems to me that your client has demonstrated a determination to experience life without drugs. She is not the first to do so and I doubt whether she will be the last. I have read that the side-effects of these pills can be severe, creating misery and depression in the recipient. Can't you experts come up with another way to help schizophrenics? Drug-induced sanity is not the same thing as being a normal member of the community. There should be a distinction, so I am relieved to know that the responsibility for administering the medication is now out of her hands. Forgive me for feeling a little bitter, but why oh why couldn't you have done that before?

You seem to want to play down the *idée fixe* she developed for TC. Why? Does her desperate desire to be loved not provide you with clues to her unbalance? I was told by several people who were on her course about how she fixed the lifts with TC in order to be on her own with him ... and she'd explained to a male participant that there were three men on the course she wanted, one of them in particular. She told the embarrassed listener how it was making her very sexually frustrated, and that she had received some telephone counselling about it. She'd followed the advice and had been enthusiastically engaged in an activity known to encourage blindness. She needed to talk about it even further but the listener curtailed the call as soon as he could.

I think the thing that surprises me the most is that you and your colleague both have taken her word that the course and her doctor told her to stop the drugs. Did you also take seriously the fact she thought that the president of France was speaking to her on her television and that the eye movements of her dog had special significance, not to mention the fact she believed she was the original Christ and thought Cosmo Greene was a god?

You were one of the early links in a chain of events which have caused major havoc in many people's lives. I wonder if you ever give it a thought? If you or your loved ones had been on the receiving end of all this, how would you be feeling now?

Without much regard,

The Woman you felt your Client had not chosen for Personal Reasons and therefore could have been ANYBODY.

A few days after the trial the police came to tea. I asked them if they knew why the journalists had fled the courtroom. They explained that, moments before the start of our case, an inquest on the death of a pilot in the next courtroom had revealed his plane crash was in fact a suicide, a story which had made the headlines and mercifully spared us a mention in the nationals. The local press, however, wrote our story, full of inaccuracies and sensation-grabbing headlines.

The officers I'd befriended over the months were about to

leave my life. They had one further duty before departure. They handed me a polythene bag in which were my very blood-stained knife, a battered silver bracelet and no longer white leather shoes. In silence I signed for their safe receipt, then handed back the knife asking them to dispose of it. They asked me if I ever had nightmares.

'Yes . . . sometimes,' I replied.

I should have realised I was still in shock . . .

The Nightmare

She was punching holes into the flesh of my chest
The wounds deep gushing blood
Red, steaming, streaming onto my white shirt
Yawning black holes entering the solar plexus
Leading to secret galaxies
Beyond illusory pain.
I remembered I remembered
The relentless force of the attack
Guttural screams
My blood flung
Towards her face
Blinding her
The relentless machine of ignorance
Slowly peeled off me by
Black metallic-clad policemen.

Operating theatre bright lights
White wellingtons
Green gowns
Watered-down blood and plasma ebbed and flowed
An oil-slick over sterile tiles
I was awake
I was watching myself awake
In the body feeling out of the body
Detached in out in out in out
I could feel
Feel the tightly stretched rubber-gloved hands
Entering my body
Probing swabbing testing repairing stitching cleansing

I could feel pain
Pain of stretched skin
Acidic lacerations collapsing organs
Imploding mind exploding heart
Sweet sweat of terror dripping from a smashed identity.

Long institutional corridors
Long lonely nights
Terror
She is in the room next to me
Light on seeping buttercup yellow under the door
Singing
The shrill voice of madness
'I'd like to teach the world to sing'
Laughter she knows I am next door
I can crawl
Crawl out of the curdled cell
Wounds ooze strawberry jam through grubby bandages
I can see
See her every move in the eye of Truth
Sitting naked singing
Sharpening every knife I have ever owned
Dribble falls onto his photograph
Flickering tongue licks his image clean
Pale happiness in her victory
The world believes her sane
Her false accusations paper the walls of her room
We showed kindness and compassion
For which we were found guilty!
Guilty by reason of insanity
You are to be punished for caring
Were you mad
The hawk-eyed judge
Spits his decision
Whilst contemplating lunch and his mistress
Barristers solicitors erecting
Gold-plated castles
Teetering on foundations built

With well-fingered notes
Stained with the fluids of other's misfortune
Extracted with dental precision
In the name
Of the Law
That only works
For lawyers.

I find a warden
I beg at her white-clad feet for protection
She orders me back to my cell
Unmoved
She tells me my fears are impossible
Impossible I am told
The woman is not here
She is safely locked away in the middle of society
In the community living her normal life
Her split mind cemented together
Controlled by drugs so very safe
I will be free too when I agree to the drugs
They will release me
I scream I beg I implore
We are all in terrible danger
The weight of the drugs only conceal
The weight forever having to be increased to keep
Out of sight the ugly mind
Tied with ribbons of cunning
Nothing has changed
Steel-grey shutters glaze her eyes
Her ears seal
The case is closed.

Silent stone men straitjacket me
Blood weeps through the padding
In tears of disbelief
She is out of her cell
Out gone
Open door empty room

Knives all gone
The over-glossed walls whisper
I am waiting for you
You you you you
You will all pay
Faces float and gloat on the ethers
Family judge lawyer priest
Psychiatrist
She is normal
Faces puce with insistence
Look! Look what she has done
I scream
I rip apart the jacket exposing a body
Sculpted with her knife
We see nothing she is normal
Tape of their programming plays
Over and over again
She is normal we see nothing
Their opaque eyes close
They cannot face me
They cannot face what she did
They pretend all is well
Energy of their joint delusion
Propping up the screen on which
Her feeble life flickers in black-and-white
Feeding from the cesspit
Of their combined
Ignorance
You have not helped her
I cry
She needs protecting
From herself
I know
She remembers
I know
She suffers
Pretending to be normal
Is not helping her

They fade into the over-glossed walls
Sulphuric steam hisses and spits
Euphoric glee her voice whispers
I am waiting
You will all pay.

I awaken
From the dream
Within a dream
Faint specks of blood lay in memoriam
On the white
Egyptian cotton sheets
Of my bed
I pray
Dear God
Wake me up!
Something within me
Knows
I am still sleeping.

THE ROMANCE

I found Richard another wife.

One starlit evening in the fairytale setting of Warwick Castle's state dining room, I raised my glass and toasted my husband. Twenty-four elegantly dressed guests rose to their feet and cheered – none louder than TC. It was a glorious celebration marking the culmination of three extraordinary years.

Richard and I had been thrown together more and more, initially due to our involvement with the Self-Awareness set-up. Management meetings and courses nearly always dragged on into the early hours of the morning and on these occasions I would sometimes give Richard a lift to his home, which was only a small detour from my return journey. We had become good friends, in and out of the course-room, but neither of us ever spoke about our respective relationships, nor the stabbing incident. I did manage to find him a secretary. Someone friendly, helpful, like-minded and in great need of a job. It was JR, who was to become another factor in bringing my path closer to his.

One very late, frosty January night, heading south in the light of a stunning full moon, I asked my gentle passenger why he had enrolled for the courses.

'I wanted to get close to my children,' he replied, lighting a cigarette.

'And have you?' I asked.

After some time he cleared his throat and answered, 'No.' It was apparent he didn't wish to expand on the theme, so I didn't pursue it.

'Jules, what are your dreams?'

'One day, Richard, I will just keep heading south – onto a ferry, into France, on and on and on. When I go, that will be it, I will never look back.'

He made no comment. In silence I drove him to the gates of his executive home. He got straight out of the car and stood on the pavement, deep in thought, looking up at his dark house. I whispered goodnight to him and drove away. In my mirrors I caught sight of his motionless form silhouetted with intense silver light. I arrived back at the cottage wide awake in spite of the lateness of the hour. TC was sleeping, the cats sprawled out across his chest and feet. None of them stirred as I slid into bed. I was shocked. I realised that, until now, no one had ever asked me about my dreams – my reply had been even more amazing.

The following week I had a lunch meeting with Richard to discuss his many duties as administrator of a February course. We met in a Chelsea restaurant at one o'clock – four hours later we were still there. We had covered every aspect he needed to know about the six-week build-up and three-week duration of the course. Walking out onto the cold Thames river embankment he asked me when I was going to come out of mourning. I didn't understand the significance of his question and looked at him quizzically.

'You nearly always wear black,' was all he added.

His question disconcerted me. He was right, I did wear a lot of black.

We met again the following week. We sat in a smoky booth of a packed Italian coffee bar. It was the night of the February course's introductory programme. We both had an hour to spare before it started, so we took the opportunity of grabbing a quick bite to eat.

'I've done everything I can think of,' he said, closing his eyes and rubbing his forehead.

'Yes, you have been wonderful – it should be a good evening.'

'No, actually I wasn't talking about tonight.'

I put my cup down and looked at him.

'I was talking about my marriage.'

'Hey, all relationships go through the blues. It will pass,' I said, trying to cheer him up.

'It has passed. I'm just a machine who gets up, goes out and earns money, which is never enough to meet the incessant demand. I spend my life chasing an ever-increasing debt. I am told my children are frightened of me but no one can tell me why. My wife spends most of the time huff-puffing about how bad I am but I don't know what it is I have done – and frankly, after this Christmas I no longer care. I've had enough.' He took one of my cigarettes and lit it. 'Jules, I decided I would do everything I could think of to make it a happy family time. I was, to the best of my ability, the dutiful, loving husband and father. Remember your New Year's Eve party?'

'Of course I do,' I said. I remembered he had been in a strange mood and in fact I'd hardly seen him all evening.

'I didn't drink and I deliberately avoided you. You may not realise that my friendship with you is a source of jealousy. I think my wife is a rather insecure woman.'

'I guessed something was amiss, and yes, it is apparent I am not liked. In fact, I may as well tell you, Felicia called me into her office and told me it was inappropriate behaviour for me to be having an affair with you.'

He looked shocked and then laughed. 'Oh Jules, how embarrassing.'

'Richard, don't worry, I told her that her information was inaccurate and intrusive and, in any event, what I choose to do with my life is no one's business except mine. I'm sorry that our friendship has caused so much misunderstanding. Anyway, did your good Christmas behaviour win approval?'

He leaned forward, his chin resting on his hands, and shook his head. 'I don't think they noticed. I'm just the "old man" who keeps them below the manner to which they want to be accustomed.'

I suggested ways he could coax his wife out of her angry, huff-puff, 'you know what you've done' silence. It was clear he had tried everything he could think of and was not interested in looking for any more solutions.

'Have you got love in your life, Jules?' he asked, suddenly turning the spotlight on me. Another disconcerting question. I thought of TC. He had just booked himself to go on a three-week holiday and cricket tour in Africa. I worded my answer carefully.

'TC is a great friend, and I love him for that, but no, he is not the love of my life.'

'Have you ever really loved someone?'

'I think so. Once. He was married. He told me he loved me. I believed him. There was an intense attraction between us. I don't really know how or why it happened but it was, for a while, amazing. Perhaps we'd been lovers in a past life, who knows what lights the fire in our hearts? He was a lovely man but it was an incredibly painful affair for all concerned. You are looking at a mistress who had to buy her own place, earn her own living and bale her lover out of several financial disasters. I didn't even get taken to Paris. I learnt a bitter lesson – about what love is not. What about you?'

He was smiling. 'Twice. I've been in love twice but I let it go. I didn't follow my heart. You see, Jules, I was a man of DUTY. When I was young, more than anything I wanted to join the RAF – or be a tea-planter in India. This was most definitely not approved of, so I opted for the parentally approved path and became a chartered turnip. Everything I did from then on was incredibly practical, sensible and conventional. I thought I had my emotions under control – stiff upper lip and all that. My wife thinks I'm going through a mid-life crisis. She's right. I am. I can't pretend any more – you see, I believed absolutely that tomorrow things would be better. Jules, I can at last admit that tomorrow is never going to come. In a way it's a relief. It is in no way a criticism of her – she is a nice woman, but her ideals, her dreams, interests and standards – even the way she wants to bring the children up . . . they're so far removed from my own that everything has become a compromise. That is not fair on any of us.' He stubbed his cigarette out and got up. 'We'd better be going,' was all he said.

Later that evening, before going our separate ways, he came up to me and took me in his arms, kissing me on both cheeks.

'Thank you for your friendship,' he whispered. 'It's the one thing I don't want to lose.'

He had gone before I could reply.

On Friday the 13th of February, a tall, black-leather-clad motorbike messenger came into my office. He did not remove his helmet, his muffled voice asked for Julie Chimes. I told him it was me and he handed me a small, brown-paper-wrapped box. I did not have to sign for it. My name was handwritten and the only thing on it. I shut the office door and full of curiosity I opened it. An exquisite orchid. Even though it was the day before Valentine's day, I couldn't imagine who would have sent me such a thing. TC was hitting cricket balls several thousand miles away, and never had sent me anything in the past – it was not his style. I took the small white card out. It too was handwritten in block capitals: 'HAVE FAITH. EVERYTHING WILL WORK OUT. ALL MY LOVE – RICHARD.'

I sat back in my chair, my heart pounding. What did he mean? We were good friends, but what was going to work out? And all his love – we communicated all the time regarding our work, he never signed letters in that way. This was getting out of hand. A few days earlier I had received a call from his wife. She sounded hysterical and told me she was coming to the office as there were a few things she 'needed me to know'. It left me feeling scared – another strange woman on the war-path stomping into my life. She arrived looking as black as thunder. We talked. She proceeded to tell me what a dreadful man Richard was, and I was left at the end of her whirlwind visit thinking that, if this man was really so awful, she and her children should be relieved that he was preparing to leave her. In her confused behaviour, I could see she had convinced herself he was having an affair with me, and this justified his wanting to depart from his marriage.

I looked at the orchid and wondered if she had sent it to me. She was due in later to help on the first night of the course . . . perhaps she wanted to catch me with it and cause a scene. I stopped my prattling thoughts and decided to phone Richard.

'Hello, Richard, it's Jules.'

'Hello, JC. All set for tonight?'

'Yeh, everything's organised. Um ... Richard, it was very nice of you, but, well, I don't know what to say.'

'Whatever's the matter?'

'The flower. The orchid. I don't know what to say to you.'

'Jules, WHAT are you talking about? What flower? Is it something for the course?' He sounded genuinely puzzled.

'The flower you sent me ... it was very nice of you, but ...'

'Julie. I haven't sent you a flower. Look, I'm about to go into a meeting, I'll catch up with you later.' He hung up.

I read the message again. I didn't know anyone else called Richard. It was a mystery. I hid it away, not wanting to explain its presence to my colleagues, and highly suspicious of its origin. Someone, somewhere was up to something. By the time Richard arrived several hours later, I was not in the best of moods. I felt embarrassed that I'd assumed it was from him. I felt I'd made myself look a fool, and so was deliberately cool when he walked into my office.

'I think we'd better talk,' he said, his face drawn and serious.

'Yes,' I agreed, 'that would be a good idea.'

We went for a walk around the block. I showed him the card.

'Julie, it has nothing to do with me,' he insisted. I knew he was telling the truth. 'Look,' he continued as we walked, 'this is all getting beyond a joke. Let's cool it for a while. You know, just put our friendship on hold.' He did not look at me.

'Yes, of course. Richard ... What is going on, for God's sake, we haven't bloody well done ANYTHING.'

He walked off without answering me. I felt bereft as I stood watching the river Thames. Tears. Disappointment. All because of an orchid – I didn't even like orchids. But I liked him. Was it only his friendship I didn't want to lose ... or was it more? Had I been so blind? So naive? It had always been there. The ease, the humour, the working together, the commitment to understand life – to know God. The love. Yes, that was it. The love. The bursting, burning, beautiful passion for a man, a man with a wife and three children. I had good reason to weep – this situation was not exactly top on my list of possible futures. I resolved to conceal the surge of divine feelings awakening in my heart. To be as bright, breezy and casual as was possible. I did not have any idea where the card had come from, but I would have faith, as it instructed. I walked back to the centre with a distinct feeling it was all out of my hands.

Richard's Tale

I turned, leaving my puzzled friend staring at the Thames, and walked away towards the centre. Suddenly my relatively calm life was topsy-turvyed by an orchid. What was going on, what was happening? An orchid, an orchid. I'd never send an orchid; freesias and daffodils, yes, but not an orchid, it was not one of my flowers. So who sent it, for what reason, and why now?

I forced my mind on to the coming evening's session of the course. It couldn't and wouldn't stay there. Was there another Richard, was there another Julie Chimes ... at that address? Why the mystery, and why was it bothering me? On top of that I'd just come out with the words 'Let's cool it for a while' ... Cool what, I wondered, where did those words come from? I felt odd and extremely jangled. A whirlpool of feelings undermined my normally steady state. Back inside the centre I found it hard to focus. Julie returned soon after. Conversation with her was brief and course-related.

That night I was exhausted but could not sleep. I was only able to think of the orchid and my friendship with Julie, and realised I wished I had been the Richard who'd sent her flowers. I felt as if I had a hole inside me that was just growing bigger and bigger. What was going on?

The next day, Saturday, was increasingly filled with an explosive feeling that I wanted to release yet felt compelled to suppress. A feeling that had been around and growing for some weeks. A feeling that I had dared not admit to, let alone put into words, and was therefore to be held down, set aside, avoided, and certainly on no account given any recognition. A feeling that drew me to be where Julie was, and yet also caused me to ignore her. Suddenly, at some time during that evening, I was unable to contain this feeling and the realisation erupted. I knew I was holding a time bomb with an unknown length of fuse already lit. The feeling was love. Yes, love was the bubbling, fizzing sensation that had pushed aside the fears, responsibilities, and other constraints that had attempted to hold it in check. It was my love for Julie. It had been there for a while, and I simply had not been able to allow it to surface; then the orchid blew the top off.

I recall little else of that day, not even driving to a friend's house for the few remaining hours of the night. I prayed for clarity and divine intervention to lift from me the weight of the possible consequences of the way that was opening to me. Where was my karma taking me?

Was the only option open to me to declare my love to Julie? A scary option. She might not accept it; that would be devastating. If she did some of the consequences had weighty implications. Was it a no-win situation? Yet to deny this love would cause such pain inside me. I was exposed to a bottomless sense of vulnerability, as if I was about to disintegrate. There was no escape, I knew I had to speak my truth to Julie. I felt an intensity of attraction to her that I had not experienced in my two previous 'true loves'. There was a sense of inner recognition, a level of subtle compatibility which was beyond the physical. It was as if I was renewing a friendship and love that I had known before. But I feared rejection. I was more than a few years older; would that matter? I was married with children and I would need to make appropriate arrangements, but that seemed to be already on the menu anyway. Julie might simply see us as friends and my declaration might blow a beautiful friendship. There were all sorts of other doubts and fears bobbing around. Yet the risk of rejection was much more tolerable than battening down these amazing feelings. I had to follow my heart, for me; it was time to love myself. How and when and where would I reveal my heart?

After some sleep I awoke to a bright dawn. A most beautiful morning spread across the sky, and I remember a sensation of expansion inside me as I watched the bright yellow sun light up the rooftops and leafless trees. I drove through a sunny quiet London Sunday morning with the glow of excitement replacing the overnight anxiety of heads I lose, tails I lose.

I arrived in plenty of time to prepare for the last full day. Julie breezed in, my heart pounded erratically, my throat went completely dry and I just about said hello. Somehow I managed to focus on the tasks in hand. As the day got under way I felt able to postpone any action for a while, thank goodness. Nothing like positive inaction to lull the mind into a numb state, coupled with a 'tomorrow things will have sorted themselves out' attitude.

Everything was fine until the first meditation. Cosmo gave the instructions and the soothing background music induced in me a relaxed state. I found myself getting up from behind my administrator's desk at the back of the room and going to sit for the meditation with the helpers on their row of chairs. Surprise, no surprise, there was an empty seat next to Julie. Eyes closed I meditated, my mind whirring with thoughts of love, helpless hopelessness, and great agitation at finding myself in a very hot spot in all senses. The music faded and with it a great calmness swept over me. I turned quietly to Julie, gently moved my lips close to her ear and whispered 'I love you' with all the intensity of truth a whisper allows, touched her hand and moved quickly and quietly back to my desk. I was astounded. I was out of control, I really was out of control, and the outcome was also out of my control. What had happened? The fuse of the bomb was burning very fast, the detonator had just been primed, would it explode into a cascade of glittering lights, go off with a horrible bang, or fizzle out?

The next session was under way. I looked fixedly at Cosmo up front, not daring to glance in any other direction. What inner turmoil again. Time stopped. I sensed movement at my side. A delicious fragrance enveloped me. A whisper in my ear, 'I love you, too'. A hand briefly on my arm. I turned; a brief smile of joyous knowing lit up Julie's face, and she was away back to her chair. The powder of love exploded into exquisite sensations which tingled every part of me. My heart thumped with joy. There was no time, no thing, no place, only love.

I had jumped into the void without a safety harness, thrust

by an energy that came from I knew not where, and I had soft
landed. Nothing mattered. The ecstasy in my heart, my lightness
of being were indescribable. Thank you, orchid, and thank you,
whoever sent you.

The Cottage

I prepared a delicious supper and filled the kitchen with flowers and candlelight. I wanted to break the news to TC with tenderness and love. I felt apprehensive. I couldn't bear the thought of hurting him and yet I knew it had to be done now, any delay would only make things worse. I closed my eyes and sat very still. I started to pray.

Dear Father, give me the strength to find the right words. Please let me speak Your truth ... help me leave his life with love between us and not hatred and resentments. Please give Richard the same guidance. My heart is aching for any hurt I am causing through my actions. Please guide me. The trouble is ... I feel so sorry for all of them ...

Implicit within such a comment is the belief that God exists more in one person than another. This is a very important moment for you to contemplate. Dear friend – how could it be That which is omniscient would not be equally and abundantly present within each particle of consciousness?

But why do I feel their pain?

You misinterpret what you feel. Your heart opens naturally towards those who cannot yet see that which they are. They are part of you – so yes, you feel them ... how could it be otherwise? These feelings are empathy. Compassion. Not sympathy. You can see their perspective when they cannot yet see anything other than their own. But this does not make them any the lesser – nor you any the greater. You are simply more awake. You all do a disservice to mankind when you feel sorry for someone. You see ... it only serves to keep them small.

Veritas . . . that all sounds very grand but how best to tell TC
I'm leaving him for one of his best friends?
**Focus your conversation on that between you which will
never be lost. Highest Truth is never contested.**

When TC arrived home all cylinders of my being were firing and
I delivered one of the most passionate speeches I had ever made
in my life. The words poured out of me. I knew we had a choice,
either to focus on all the negative reasons for going our different
ways, or to honour all the wonderful things about each other and
concentrate on all the reasons why we could remain friends. He
sat in silence listening. Tears rolled down his face. I felt more
love for him that night than I had ever done before, a direct
experience of the greatest love of all – love without conditions,
expectations or boundaries. He felt it too. True freedom. We
dined together in a state of mixed sadness, apprehension and
excitement, toasting each other's possible futures and promising
each other life-long friendship.

Three weeks later Richard and I moved into a rented London
flat together and the voyage of love took on another dimension.
He left twenty years of marriage with only a plastic supermarket
bag full of washing. I told my mother. She said if I had found
love she was with me all the way, and wished us both courage
and strength. She also asked if, when I related the story to
anyone, I would say that he arrived with all his worldly goods
in a Harrods bag – she felt it sounded better. Fire and brimstone
hissed and spat around the boundaries of our newly unfolding
life; rumours abounded amongst families and colleagues, some
of whom disowned us. We were ostracised and accused of many
things, but we remained unshakeable. Between us there were
no doubts. No regrets. No fears. No questions. In fact, it was
the start of the most pleasurable time of my life.

We did not remain involved with the Awareness organisation
for very long after joining forces. In December, independently
we had both enrolled on their six-month course. It was a
gruelling schedule involving a number of full weekends, weekly
evening sessions and even further commitment to support and

work within the organisation. The night we were all volunteering for the various jobs by show of hands, Richard sat on his, and then crawled under a desk in the back of the hall and fell asleep. He was accused of being full of resistance, which was true. The theme for that night was integrity. Realising integrity meant adequate rest and free time to rebuild his life; he was the first to opt out.

Working for the organisation made my departure a little more complicated, but three weeks later I followed in his footsteps and left the course. I received a late night phone call from Cosmo to persuade me otherwise. He told me I was at the 'last hurdle in the race' and was determined I should see what a tragic failure it would be to withdraw from the course. His arguments were persuasive, his attack on my decision relentless and at half-past eleven at night he was still on the phone. One and a half hours of battering, yet I had not found the words to express myself with clarity. Suddenly they came, a fountain of truth exploded from the depths of my being.

'The world is my classroom. Everyone I meet is my teacher. There is not one moment when I am not learning about the nature of God. You think I have left the track and am about to veer off course. I think I have just gone into pole position and the race is about to begin.'

He did not reply and another section of my journey was almost completed. As my head hit the pillow Veritas reminded me that words of truth always hit the target.

Richard and I attended our last management meeting in order formally to resign, stating before it began that we would be leaving at a specified time. Cosmo and Felicia reallocated all areas of responsibility. A definitely cool atmosphere. At the designated hour we took our leave. I looked at the newly elected elite, sitting around the meeting table, enthusiastic, eager to please and full of ideas on how to expand the potential market and make the organisation more efficient and successful. I saw my own early enthusiasm in every one of their faces. I looked at Cosmo and Felicia and felt gratitude for their part in my life's journey. Even difficult relationships have something to teach us. I walked out of their play smiling and entered into a new theatre, showing the next act of my life's drama. The set was wonderful, the opening scene two people very much in love, dining out in a bustling London restaurant.

I was invited to attend a two-day workshop, run by the healer I had been sent to by Felicia. I felt compelled to go – especially as this quietly spoken man had heralded the return of Veritas in my life. From the outset of the course I knew Thomas was extraordinary. I sat in a London basement flat watching workmen in the road above cordon-off an area, put up their little hut, place a kettle on a portable gas stove and install themselves for the day – directly outside the course-room window. On the dot of 9 a.m. as the course was about to start, the pneumatic drill began. It was deafening. Unperturbed, Thomas watched them, smiling. The fifteen or so people gathered in the room looked at each other, shrugging shoulders and pulling faces. I watched Thomas. He closed his eyes and, becoming totally still, he placed his hand over the area of his heart. Within less than a minute the drilling stopped. The workmen had a brief conversation, took the kettle off the stove and packed up. As they drove away Thomas opened his eyes. He was looking at me. I knew I'd found one who could ride the horse of truth and he knew I knew.

The following year travelled at a cracking pace. I found full-time work as a freelance marketing consultant and Richard worked flat-out in the city. We needed every penny we could raise as, in order to minimise the material disruption to his family, he was paying for everything in the same way as he'd always done, which involved three children at private school and quarterly telephone bills, reflecting all their hurt and anger, of over one thousand pounds. It was almost crippling, but between us we generated enough money to cover the huge demands, until the divorce proceedings were underway and Richard found a terrific solicitor to help us negotiate our way through the mine-strewn route to freedom.

My mother became very ill. She had been diagnosed as being a brittle diabetic – she needed twice-daily insulin injections to live, but had violent reactions to them which left her sick and weak. In a matter of weeks she went from being a bonny woman down to a skeletal frame weighing little more than five stones. She could hardly eat or keep anything down. I drove the two-hundred-mile round trip to her home twice a week and sat for hours at her bedside. She was often delirious, shouting and muttering, revealing the content of her troubled mind. Other times she was wonderfully lucid, speaking of the realms of Light part of her was experiencing. One thing was very clear – she did not want to live. She wanted to see her mother, my widowed Nan, who came immediately and tended to her every need with all the love and sensitivity a mother gives to her child. Between us we kept a vigil, as well as cooking, washing, ironing and dealing with Martin. My stepfather was beside himself – for all his controlling, his world was falling apart. He made great efforts to understand what was happening, but he was so cemented in tradition and convention he could only blame the doctors, not considering that something else might have been behind my mother's breakdown. My heart went out to him. For the first time in my life, I realised that if someone has made up their mind to die, even Herculean efforts on the part of everyone else cannot save them. Every time my phone rang I expected it to be the dreaded news of her death. I prayed and prayed for help.

Then Veritas had his say, telling me in no uncertain terms that I had to help my mother find reasons to live. '**She has lost her appetite for life**,' he told me. I had to guide her away from all the bitterness and resentment she was feeling. He explained I was like someone trying to shovel the darkness out of a room, when all I needed to do was turn on the light. Finally, he told me to massage her spine and feet. Immediately I put his words into practice, as well as giving my Nan the instructions. I explained things to my stepfather wrapped in the language of the mundane. He grasped the point of making everything more appetising for her and willingly took instruction on how to make her food, room and immediate environment more tempting. We filled the house with fresh flowers, and I played tapes of beautiful music in her bedroom. Nanny and I massaged her sparrow-like body till our arms were dropping. We talked only of positive things and happy memories. It was a miracle when she began to respond.

'My little Ju, always there to look after me in my hours of need,' she said the first time she had been fully conscious for over a month. 'When you were very tiny, sometimes I would come into your nursery if Max was having one of his brainstorms. You would tell me to get into your bed, where you promised Max would not hit me because you would protect me. You were right – it was the only haven I had in that madhouse. I've been a lousy mother – I hope you'll be able to forgive me one day.'

I held her in my arms and told her she had been the best mother in all the world and that I wouldn't have changed one precious particle of her. She smiled, but didn't believe me.

'What's the worst thing I ever did to you?' she asked.

'Not believe me,' I answered. She raised her eyebrows.

I reminded her of the time she and Herbert were courting. It was a lunch hour and they were dancing together in the living room of our rented apartment. I'd been home from school for lunch and was making myself scarce in the kitchen. On my way out I had taken the rubbish to place it in the cupboard in our private hallway. This small bin-sized space had another outer door opening onto the communal landing which the caretaker had access to, in order to remove the offending bags each day. All very civilised. I'd put on my blazer and hat, checked my satchel and shouted goodbye to the lovers waltzing around the front room. I threw the refuse sack into the cupboard and screamed as it was flung straight back at me. Curled in tight foetal position, covered with potato peelings, tea-leaves and eggshells, was Max. In sheer panic I slammed the door shut and bolted it. I ran into the kitchen and opened the serving hatch. The lovers were eyes-closed and kissing. It was hopeless. I flicked bits of bread at my mother, but got Herbert on the nose. A man of single-mindedness even in those days, he hardly flinched. Eventually I hit my target. She opened her eyes. I waved my arms frantically, mouthing and signalling for her to 'get him out of here'. She mouthed a popular phrase involving a homosexual act and a voyage. I mouthed back that it was an emergency. After what seemed like an interminably long time, the lounge door opened. They kissed, cuddled and declared lovey-dovey things all the way down the hall. I held my head in my hands waiting for the gunshot. It never came. After Herbert left, she came into the kitchen demanding to know what was going on. With a degree of smugness, I admit, I went into the hall and opened the refuse-cupboard door. She looked at Max. He looked at her. I looked at them. They looked at me. Then, as if finding her ex-husband in the rubbish bin was the most natural thing in the world, she asked him if he still took sugar in his tea. I hurried back to school to be greeted with a frosty geography teacher and a detention for being late.

Mum was laughing so hard her eyes filled with tears which rolled down her pale cheeks. She told me she dismissed me from my childhood duty of protecting her and promised in the future to look after herself. She was on the mend. I thanked God all the way home.

My own solicitor was making very slow progress with my much needed compensation. Over the months I had obtained all the documentation the Government body asked for. To speed things up and save on fees, I had sent as much of the information as I could directly to the Board, bypassing my solicitor. I had still not altogether forgiven him for not turning up for the trial. He was frequently off sick and therefore hard to get hold of. To my surprise, Pomp's report had been very fair; he'd emphasised the fact that the scars would be with me for life, and that the damage to my right hand was creating serious problems for me. I discovered that quantifying pain is almost impossible. I was rarely without physical discomfort and my food and liquid intake had to be carefully monitored – any excess left me in agony as my cobbled-together torso stretched to accommodate it. In any event, helped by Richard's love and support, I was learning how to manage my inner and outer injuries. The Criminal Injuries Board informed me they had a backlog of claims running into the thousands, and I would have to be patient.

We got to know Thomas. It was inevitable. He held the key to the next stage of our spiritual journey. Over the months he taught us how to recognise and interpret the outer world as a reflection of our inner world. More importantly, he knew how to transmute ignorance into love. He had great faith in Veritas, and encouraged me to listen to him more. Veritas had great faith in him and told me that the right teaching will always be made available to those who ask with a deep yearning. Thomas did not have an organisation.

He had no interest in bums on seats. He never advertised. If one person came or one hundred arrived on his course he gave his time and love. His price remained constant and excellent value. He taught us so much about the nature of love.

After one year, he invited us and a small group which included TC and JR to spend two days with him. He told us it was his final teaching. It was a bank holiday weekend when we assembled in a West London house. He guided us through a series of intense meditations and contemplations. Then he told us he would meet us in a café situated in London airport's busiest terminal. Our instructions were not to speak to anyone unless spoken to, to make a mental note of our observations and to sit only in groups of two or three when we got to the café.

We had no idea what to expect or what we were supposed to experience. The airport had been packed – it was one of the busiest weekends in the tourist aviation calendar. But it was strange. It was totally calm. Children were quiet and well behaved, people were smiling, the queues were orderly, an abundance of luggage trolleys was available and the flight boards indicated that everything was running on time. By the time we found the designated café, we were bemused. Thomas was waiting for us, as always smiling. As his students filtered through, all the other people in the café began to leave. He joined Richard and me and asked us what we'd noticed the most. We both agreed the peace and calm, and the way the café had emptied of its customers in direct proportion to the arrival of our colleagues.

He nodded, and said 'Well done'. Drawing his chair close to the table and leaning across the table he whispered, 'I have brought you to the busiest place I could think of, in order to demonstrate what effect your inner calm will have on the world. Remember this day.' He cast his eyes around the café before adding, 'And remember that fear often cannot sit next to love. It has to leave the room. When you leave here today, I do not care what you do. I do not care where you go. I do not care who you are with. I do not care if I never see you again . . . because?' We looked into his eyes. There were tears. His voice almost inaudible, 'Because I Love you.'

*   *   *

It took eighteen months after our union to follow my dream. We sat breakfasting on the cross-channel ferry heading for France. Everything we owned had been either sold, stored or was now packed neatly in our new four-by-four truck and trailer, parked in the car-deck hold somewhere below us. Between the croissants and coffee, maps were spread out as we pored over our possible routes down through France and into the region of northern Spain called Catalonia. We had rented a recently modernised, luxury farmhouse for a year.

We left our affairs in good order. Richard had agreement on the settlement for his divorce. He was advised to make a lump sum payment, which almost drained him financially, but gave us a clean start to build our new life together. I gave my solicitor power of attorney to receive the award on my behalf, as being in a part of the world with unreliable post and a house with no telephone complicated matters unnecessarily. I gave him all the original claim documents in my possession, for safe keeping. Richard was with me when I asked him what his bill was. Once again he told me not to worry about such a minor detail, but when pushed he said it would not be more than five hundred pounds, and that he would deduct it from the award when it was made, if that was OK by me. It was fine. I left his office understanding there was nothing more to be done except to wait.

Our UK departure was blessed with a party, for all of our friends. It was a magical evening, marred only by a phonecall from my stepfather calling me a 'murdering bastard' for, as he saw it, deserting my family, and the threat that if I told my mother what he'd said, he would kill me and the 'lazy idle bastard of a man' I was going with. He had a way with words. After he had slammed the phone down, I felt a wave of enormous relief. I was getting away from the barrage of his emotional blackmail, rudeness and relentless disapproval. And there was sadness. What was it in me that couldn't have two loving parents to wave me off on my great adventure? I didn't tell my mother. I knew she was as thrilled and excited by our new life as we were, and wanted to get strong enough to be able to visit us.

After two days of leisurely driving we arrived at our destination in the full blaze of an august Spanish sun, all set to have ourselves a good time. The farmhouse was, in fact, still being modernised, and luxury, we realised, is a matter of opinion. The swimming pool we'd been told about was available for us to use, if we finished building it. The small job of blasting the old beams clean, fumigating them and hand-painting the ceilings had been arranged to happen under our supervision. On the day the English owners left us to it, a bulldozer which was piling all the builders' rubble into a rockery of sorts ripped out the power lines. Then we had storms the like of which I had not seen. We soon discovered how many pots and pans we had, as we placed them under the rainwater pouring through the roof. We had paid a year's rent in advance for the house, as well as a sizeable deposit. We were in love and on an adventure. The sun shone almost every day, the sunsets took our breath away, the hillsides were covered in wild lavender, thyme and rosemary, the Mediterranean was crystal clear, the coves enchanting, the people welcoming and my beloved geraniums – everywhere. In spite of the house, everything was wonderful.

In late September, with great excitement, I received a notification that within the next fortnight the Criminal Injuries Board were considering giving me an interim award, to go towards all the expenses I'd incurred. By December I'd heard nothing, so sent a fax to the solicitors with the fax number of our French neighbours to use for any reply. It took three weeks for an answer, telling me an interim award had been made on the basis that more photographs, medical and psychiatric reports were required. I was asked to sign an agreement and was surprised to see the award had been made over six weeks previously, on the 3rd of November – I thought it odd the solicitor had delayed the good news.

Early February, yet the money had still not arrived in my bank account. I spent over fifteen pounds trying to get hold of my solicitor, his receptionist putting me on hold three times, only to inform me in the end that once again he was off sick. I sent a stroppy fax, waited a couple of hours and went into town to phone again. I asked to speak to one of the partners, who was able to confirm the money was in their bank account waiting to be allocated. Although I had given all instructions in writing, I gave them again. The following day I received a fax with a statement of the amount paid into my bank account. Over eighteen hundred pounds had been deducted for fees and disbursements. More than three times what I'd been told. I was not happy and wrote back by return asking to see an itemised bill. Nothing.

In early April I wrote again. I received my answer, wrapped in profuse apologies, at the end of the month. I was promised an itemised bill and assured that it looked like money was 'in the bank on account' for future work. Other than me sending another medical report to the board, which was at my expense, I didn't see what more work had to be done. I wrote and expressed my discontent once again.

I went for my medical report to a highly reputable private clinic in Barcelona. The doctor we were seeing was one of Spain's leading lights for trauma-related injury. Although we could both speak some Spanish, we were assured the examination and the subsequent report would all be in English. Richard and I sat in the luxuriously appointed waiting room. The walls were lined with heavily framed certificates. It seemed our man was a member of the Active Knee Society. Very encouraging. We had to fill out copious forms, all written in the local Catalan dialect and very difficult to understand. Then we paid the equivalent of over one hundred pounds to the red-nailed receptionist. After a long wait, something I was getting very used to in medical-related matters, I was called into an examination room. The white-coated man who ushered us in explained in Spanish that he was not the chief honcho, but one of the lackeys. He would do the pre-examination. Once again, because of the actions of Helen Black, I was removing my clothes in front of another man with cold hands. With great seriousness, every square centimetre of scar was examined, accompanied by much note-taking. After over an hour of examination and not much conversation, I dressed and was dispatched to the X-ray department. More forms were filled out by an incredibly patient Richard. Over eighty pounds was forked out for the X-rated pictures. I undressed and exposed my bones to the camera. I dressed. At last we were ushered into the top man's waiting room. We waited. After another long hour we were both well versed in who was doing what in Spanish society – no magazine was left unturned. Then we went in.

One of the longest desks I have ever seen almost hid the slight, dark-haired Daliesque man behind it. He was flanked by stiff white-coated assistants and trainees. He extended a thin hand. As we approached, Richard told him not to get up, and in good music-hall manner that Max would have loved, we both realised at the same moment that he was already standing. A great start. He took a cigarette from one of the four packets stacked on his desk, and placed it between his lips. Three lighters appeared in unison, fighting for the right to ignite it. Richard raised an eyebrow. I bit my lip. I was cross-examined – in Spanish. I asked if he spoke English, at which he and his keepers all laughed. Very funny. I undressed, and three men and one woman had a poke, as they say. I dressed. More questions.

Perhaps it was the fact that I couldn't stop grinning, or maybe it was an insidious way of making extra money, but we were informed that it was IMPOSSIBLE for him to make a full assessment without a psychiatric report. It could be arranged this very day. Fingers snapped. The team jumped. Phone calls were made. We asked for assurance the interview would be conducted in English. 'Por supuesto,' he spat at us, with all the might of continental contempt for the pink-and-white blobs from northern Europe. Of course it would be in English.

We walked over a mile to the shrink department. We paid out another seventy-five pounds and were told we had to wait for two hours. We decided to find something to eat, as we were both starving. It was a residential area, and there were no restaurants or bars to be seen. We started walking into the centre and found a Chinese restaurant. We ordered from the interesting English translation menu. I had wedge tables with hot child sauce, whilst Richard partook of chick-hen with spicy fried Moors. When it arrived it turned out to be a black rice, the literal Spanish translation was slang for the invading Moors. All things considered it was very tasty.

We arrived back for our appointment full, breathless but with several minutes to spare. We waited another hour and a half before being welcomed by an attractive woman of about my own age. The best news was that I did not have to remove my clothes, the worst, she spoke not one word of English. It had taken a whole day, but it had eventually got to me. I was seriously pissed off and it showed. I discovered more about her than she me. I filled out a tick-the-right-box-style questionnaire, which was in English, and about as interesting as a 'How would you cope if . . .' quiz in a down-market women's magazine. I came out with Spanish words and phrases that amazed me, whilst greatly impressing Richard and my interrogator. We left strict instructions on how to forward the final reports, in English, *si, si, si*, directly to the Criminal Injuries Board, *si, si, si*, and a copy to us in Spain, *si, si, si*.

In early June I got notification that my full award had been made. It was only one third of what my solicitor and counsel had advised I could expect, and they were shocked. So was I. I felt bitterly disappointed. It did not even cover my loss of earnings. There was still no explanation about the excessive bill. I telephoned my solicitor. He was not there. With reluctance I faxed my acceptance of the award and enquired what were the chances of an appeal. After hearing no more, I made a telephone appointment with him. Ten pounds worth of pesetas later, I secured a meeting with him for late July, when we would be back in England, and could sort out the matter of the bill, and discuss the possibilities of an appeal against the award. The next solicitor's fax which arrived had us whooping around our farmhouse kitchen with delight. Richard's Decree Absolute had arrived. He was a free man.

We flew back to England to arrange our marriage. After the announcement of our engagement we received a tape recording from my stepfather and also a letter laying out the terms and conditions for the celebration of our nuptials. I played the tape in the car and Richard and I listened in silence as the monotone voice went through a list of guests we were not allowed to invite, with the reasons why. Then there was the question of where we could hold the celebration – or, more to the point, where we could not. Finally, and most importantly, it was a question of cost. We were narrowed down to several guests and a sandwich in a pub at least fifty miles away from his home, and it would be better for 'everyone' if we stayed in Spain and got married there – not that he thought it would be allowed.

I considered it miraculous that, after hearing his stepfather-in-law to be, Richard still wanted to marry me. In fact, he laughed for the rest of the day and told me how lucky we were that we could now feel free to arrange and finance our own party. With light hearts we set off for the land of our birth.

Our meeting with my solicitor was a fiasco. We waited in the dingy reception area to be told after one hour that he wasn't there. He hadn't turned up. We demanded to see anyone else who could help us and were eventually ushered into the office of an articled clerk. He was flushed with fear. Richard told him we wanted the file back. There was a lot of huffing and shuffling but he found it for us. I asked where the detailed bill was. There wasn't one, obviously five months was not long enough for them to have worked it out. Before he gave me the file, he said he knew it was a bad moment, but would I mind very much paying the £34.03 that was 'outstanding'. With surprising restraint I told him that I minded very much indeed, took the folders from his shaking hands, and left the office.

Systematically we went through the file. It was in a terrible mess. No sign of the original documents I'd entrusted the solicitor with, no photographs, and letters with requests and queries from the Criminal Injuries Board which I had never been informed about. There were also copies of police statements I'd never seen. It took hours, but we read through every document and put the papers into some semblance of order. We decided the best thing to do was to go directly to the Board, whose offices were located in central London. There, we encountered one of the kindest and friendliest of people, who went out of his way to explain about making an appeal against an award, which they felt was more than justified. We filled out the necessary paperwork which would release the claim file back to us. He explained that as we had appointed a solicitor, the rules were that they could only deal with him and any communications which had come to them directly from me had in all probability been sent back to him. This was news to me.

The wedding plans worked themselves out with ease. We booked the marriage in Warwick registry office for a number of reasons, mainly because of its central location for my mother, who was still not well enough to travel, my stepfather who had only recently regained mobility after suffering a stroke, and my Nan who lived nearby. It also meant my sweet brother could attend. Having sorted out the ceremony, we walked into the July sunshine.

Neither of us could bear the thought of a traditional reception in a stuffy hotel or banqueting suite and were standing in the middle of the street contemplating where to go next, when I caught sight of the towers of the medieval castle, flags flying, its history permeating the entire atmosphere of the old market town. I took Richard's arm, leading him in the direction of the main gate. He was laughing and wondering what I was up to. I explained to him how earlier on the trip Veritas had reminded me that, if you do not ask for what you want, it is very unlikely that you will ever get it. Furthermore, it was pointed out that most people do not know what they want and drift through life thinking it is not fair, oblivious to the fact that they spend their entire life thinking about what they don't want. This little piece of profound wisdom helped me to realise how much I wanted to do something wonderful to celebrate not only our love, but the miracle of my survival and new life. The bringing together of those we loved to join in our happiness in a magnificent castle felt like a great way of doing it.

The gate was manned by local pensioners, the entry queues enormous. We went to the head of the queue of sweating tourists, and asked if it was possible to hold a private function in the castle. The gatekeeper wasn't sure but said he would phone through to the catering manager. With us in his little office he made the call; his rheumatoid hand over the receiver he asked us what exactly we had in mind. We told him we wanted a dinner for a maximum of twenty-six guests, to celebrate our marriage. He grinned and gave us a thumbs up, and before we knew it we were ushered straight into the castle to visit the catering department. Our official guide took us there, giving us both a big hug as he left us in the restaurant. He told us he loved weddings and wished us luck. Whilst we were waiting for the manager Richard comforted me with the thought that if nothing else, we had found a way of queue-jumping and free entry into famous tourist attractions.

The manager arrived. No, they had never done a wedding. They only catered for corporate functions of a 100-person minimum in the medieval banqueting hall. He asked us how many guests we had in mind. We told him twenty-six. He looked at us both for a long time before smiling and asking us to follow him. It was true, he explained, that they had not thought of private functions before, but there was one thing which might interest us. He ushered us into the state dining room. The furnishings, tapestries and paintings had witnessed generations of royalty and aristocracy dining in splendour. It seated twenty-six people. We looked at the magnificent room, each other and then the manager. Yes. Yes, yes, yes, yes, yes. Everything was agreed in less than one hour. We went to see my mother to tell her the news. She jumped up and down with excitement. We told my stepfather about the arrangements we had made and that Richard was paying for it all. He did not share our delight, but said that if he could afford it he would make a contribution. We were far too happy to care.

We were back in Spain when the documentation to support my claim came into my possession. We opened the package, an innocuous-looking envelope which contained all the gory details of an event I did not enjoy thinking about. We sat down and pieced the jigsaw together. We could not believe it. There were no photographs, and the entire award hinged on a report which my solicitor had written at his first meeting with me, where he had jotted down rough estimates of my costs and losses. The updated documentation relating to my business, income and loss was missing. None of the last year's medical reports were included, and the medical report I'd obtained in Spain had been written in Spanish. The Board had asked for a translation, but I was not told. I now understood why the award was so low. I wrote to the solicitor asking him to explain what was going on, confirmed I did not wish him to do any further work for me, demanded an itemised bill and pointed out that it is polite to tell clients if you don't intend to turn up for meetings. I never received a reply.

I appointed another solicitor, having prepared a case out of the wreckage. I then wrote to the Solicitors' Complaints Bureau, to see what recourse, if any, I had against what I considered to be gross incompetence. I was approaching the most precious day of my life, my wedding, and yet I was still haunted by Helen. I had been told by friends that she was now a free woman, with not a mark on her, and here was I, two and a half years on, still trying to recoup some of my losses incurred because of her insane behaviour. Even with the wisdom of Veritas, I could not understand why everything was so unfair. He told me, in his inimitable way, that one day I would understand and that all would be well. I didn't believe him.

In time, I got the answers to most of my questions. The new solicitor had taken my case to a specialist for advice as to whether it was worth appealing. The award was low, but there was too much documentation missing to support a new claim and taking further costs into consideration, the learned view was that it was not worth the risk, time and stress. I paid out another five hundred pounds in fees and accepted the award. The Solicitors' Complaints Bureau could not make any comment about the bill or performance until they had been through the file and made their own assessment. As most of the file was missing, never to be traced again, there seemed little point in pursuing that avenue. The answer to my query about my original solicitor arrived. Rumour had it that he had a chronic alcohol problem. How did I pick them?

One glorious evening in Warwick Castle's candle-lit state dining room, my husband raised his glass and gave a toast to me, the woman he adored. I watched a light of brilliant blue as it danced and leapt around the head of each cheering guest. It came towards me. Richard took my face in his hands and kissed me. I closed my eyes. There was one more message for me to hear. Veritas.

When two hearts open in the name of love all of consciousness rejoices. Blessings, my Dearest One. Welcome to Paradise.

POSTSCRIPTS . . .

O n the afternoon of the last day anyone could be legally blamed for the events of March 11th, a well-timed writ arrived for TC. Helen Black was suing him for a six-figure sum of money for alleged medical negligence, backed by the advice of a law firm specialising in claims against doctors. He thought they were just 'trying it on' and therefore he did not take it seriously. They did.

In May two years later I flew from my home in Spain specifically to give evidence on behalf of TC at a meeting in the London offices of the Medical Defence Union, an organisation that insures doctors for claims against them. The MDU and their legal advisers were to decide whether my attacker's substantial claim for damages against TC was defensible. I considered the whole thing to be an outrage. I felt for her sad mental condition, and thanks to the wonderful guidance and support I'd received from so many bright souls, I had come to a peaceful understanding about what had been done to me. But for her to be demanding money was unbelievable ... and that her claim was even considered I found to be an absolute mockery of all I thought justice stood for.

I had given TC all the support and information I could during the build-up of legal wrangling. From what I could make out, the seeds of blame sown by Helen's defence counsel during the trial were growing once again, in spite of being cut down by the judge. In fact, in the hot-house environment of the legal world, they were being fertilised, watered and positively flourishing. The MDU felt TC was vulnerable in certain areas but it seemed to me to be a case of his word against hers compounded by several assumptions.

She said it was TC who told her she could come off her drugs.

He said that he had a brief conversation with her about her medication, but both in his police statement and subsequently he swears he did not give her permission or encouragement to stop taking her drugs. He pointed out that she had longer discussions with the other doctor on the course, Cosmo Greene and various course-participants than she did with him.

The family assumed she was safe on the course because Helen had told them her GP was on it.

He made it clear that he had nothing whatsoever to do with her being on the course and that he had never been consulted officially or unofficially by Helen or her family as to its suitability.

The MDU said, weighing the facts, the claimant may point out that he should have realised that the course was unsuitable.

He was doing the course in the first place to discover what it was about in order to answer the questions of patients who were interested in these things. He said how could he be held responsible for what patients choose to do in their free time? When he is off duty, should he, for example, stop a golfer from teeing off, or ban a player from the squash court just because they are his patients but are being treated for a heart condition by a specialist? Should he rush back to the surgery and check-up on the notes, or is he supposed to memorise the medical history of all the five thousand patients on his list? Her mental condition was not handled by him. Where should he draw the line?

Cosmo Greene said he assumed she was on the course with TC's permission.

TC said he phoned the organisation before the course began to confirm that if any of his patients were on the course, he would not have to do group work with them. He had been assured that he was there in his own right and not as a doctor. This was confirmed again during the second course when Cosmo had a discussion with him regarding Helen.

The MDU felt there was a real prospect of a court finding that he should never have allowed her to go to the cottage.

He pointed out that three senior rail personnel, six experienced police officers, a practice nurse and the head receptionist all saw her that morning, and nobody said to him she was psychotic. She was depressed, lonely and tearful and did not wish to stay in the surgery, or to be with her family. She asked to be with me. He did what he believed was in her best interests, and had it been any other patient or course participant his actions would have been considered generous, respectful, caring and above the call of duty. In the aftermath of the attack, all who knew Helen were only too keen to point out how gentle she was and that violence was the last thing they would have expected from her. So how was he supposed to predict her behaviour?

They said he was naive.

He said that was an easy label to pin on him with hindsight but perhaps one day in the future, with hindsight, it could be they who are considered naive.

They said although they would financially cover all preliminary costs and any settlements if he wanted to take it to court it would be at his own expense.

He said he couldn't afford to even think about that option.

Their reply is unknown.

His word or the word of a woman who had been found 'not guilty' of attempted murder due to her insanity at the time of the attack? Her 'disturbed-at-the-time' mind was suddenly able to 'remember' enough about that time to bring a case, yet she could not be held responsible for her actions. The law working for her, but rendering her almost untouchable by anyone else, including myself. Further, were the claims and allegations entirely hers or were they the work of specialist lawyers skilled in extracting compensation from doctors through their insurers? I felt I HAD to speak to these people.

The legal, medical and insurance 'experts' assembled in the London offices were totally thrown by my presence. As TC introduced me, they clucked and spluttered with embarrassment, a youngish woman dug her fingers into my arm and with vice-like grip ushered me out of the room before I had a chance of saying 'good afternoon', muttering that they realised no one had suffered as much as me in all this, but patient confidentiality meant they were not interested in my statement, and that I was not permitted to remain in the room. As I was pushed into the lift I was assured they would fetch me if they needed me. They never came.

Waiting in the gloomy reception area I began to realise that what was taking place was more than a matter of justice, and more than a debate about how to avoid damaging publicity at minimum cost. I saw how the systems we have can encourage lying and manipulation, and I saw the outdated rules that lurk beneath the veneer of what I once considered to be a largely honest and morally upright society. Speaking out is not encouraged and, in my case, not permitted. A great deal of attention to the interests of my assailant, but what about those of the recipient of the violence? Who cared for my rights? The nightmare was coming true. I put my head in my hands and wept. Was there nothing to have faith in any more? I was trapped by the belief that I should always remain silent and pretend nothing was wrong, trapped by my fear of punishment and reprisals if I dared to break the mould. It was my lowest point. I was so overwhelmed with the feeling of helplessness that I considered flinging myself under the nearest juggernaut. Then, I thought of my love for Richard. It saved me. I thought of the wisdom in Veritas. It guided me. I thought of the bravery of my mother. It gave me courage. I thought of my longing for a different world. It inspired me. I opened my briefcase and wrote on the back of my unwanted evidence: 'This is a true story. Well, as true as my understanding can be within this moment of infinity.' I paused. My pen began to race across the page.

Veritas – please help me. I know I am feeling a victim but I want to stop this. Please. Help me see how to be strong in the middle of all this.
I am here. I am always here for those who ask. It is a time for clarity, Dear One. Time to end the 'poor little me' routine.

Yes. I know.

Let us begin by asking a question . . . What is it in you that motivates you to be here today?

Friendship . . . support . . . care . . . justice . . . love . . .

And what do you believe motivates those connected with what you perceive as the opposition?

Care . . . friendship . . . love . . . well, all the same things, I suppose.

Yes. You have a lot in common! Do you begrudge these things?

For her? No, of course not.

Then let all thoughts of her go. Right now. Begin to consider your own role within this moment, and what you can learn from it. Others will reap the fruit of their actions.

Well, I'm surrounded by people angry with me although I have not done anything wrong . . . they are frightened I might speak out. I think it is yet another scenario about life not being fair . . .

Now you have seen this, we can move on. Why do you believe there is imbalance? Is it really there, or is it dirt on the lens of your spectacles?

Well, a lot of the time I am told I am lucky, so I feel guilty about what I have – do you know, Veritas, I even feel guilty that I survived this attack, that I got well so soon, that I had some money in the bank . . . I must always give to others, but I cannot receive, so situations such as this hurt like hell. It feels as if I am being punished.

Have you felt this in your life often?

Yes . . . the false accusations, having to pretend all was well in my childhood when often it was a nightmare, being teased and punished for having famous parents, oh God, the list goes on and on . . .

Let us wipe away some of the dirt from your view. Tell me what you have gained and learnt since this event in your life.

Gained? Oh! Well, I'd never really considered gain. Richard . . . my beautiful Rich. Feelings of love, friendship, support.

283

My dreams of travel, life abroad, someone to share it with, sunshine, like-minded people, teachers of truth, wonderful literature, poetry, places and adventures. And of course, you, whoever you are. I've never stopped learning. I KNOW whatever I am, it is so much more than this body . . .

Rather a lot, wouldn't you say?

Are you showing me that everything is in perfect balance? I have received so much, but because it wasn't money I didn't recognise it?

Good. You are beginning to expand your vision. Now, tell your truth. The book . . . it is time for you to speak.

I was paid compensation four years after the incident. After deducting expenses it came to a net amount of approx £13,000, but that does not allow for many hours of my time. It has occurred to me that I forgot to claim for the knife – worth over £50 . . .

The award for the best use of forbidden words goes to one of my many hospital visitors, with the unforgettable description of a mutual colleague:

'That sex-starved harridan – she'd stab you in the back before you could say knife.'

Seven years after stabbing me mercilessly, Helen Black was awarded a substantial out of court settlement.

TC was told he had been let off lightly as the allegations would have certainly got worse. He did not have to pay the damages, nor was he disciplined, but the outcome of the case left him feeling very disillusioned. After years of being asked to justify and defend his actions, the onus on him to prove his innocence had taken its toll. This, coupled with many other frustrating aspects of his work, led to a change of direction, and in 1994 General Practice lost another dedicated doctor.

In the spring of 1994 my beloved mother, Jenny, passed from the physical world into the realms of spirit. At a small family dinner the night of her funeral, my stepfather asked for Richard's and my forgiveness for the cruel and spiteful way he had treated us over the years. His campaign to discredit those my mother loved had carried on from TC to Richard, and finally openly against me. The apology was, of course, accepted. Later that night, in middle England, a small earthquake shook the village.

In 1990 Max Wall, famous comedian, actor, songwriter and show-biz personality, died in London, collapsing as he left one of his favourite restaurants.

The autumn of 1994 saw the solicitor I'd appointed to help me check out of life in what were described as 'sad circumstances'.

THE SCAPEGOAT

In the Mosaic ritual for the day of Atonement (Leviticus 16) two goats were brought to the altar of the Tabernacle and the high priest cast lots, one for the Lord and the other for the rebel angel's leader. The Lord's goat was sacrificed. The other was the scapegoat; the high priest having by confession transferred his own sins and the sins of the people onto it, it was taken into the wilderness and allowed to escape.

In the twentieth-century ritual of someone-must-pay-for-all-that-is-wrong-in-society, two people with beliefs and lifestyles different from the thronging multitudes were chosen. She would be sacrificed by multiple stabbing followed by throat-cutting just to make sure, and he, in a ceremony which would last seven years, would have all the blame transferred upon him, and be cast into the social and professional wilderness.

And it came to pass that the multitudes were shocked and stunned for in seven days she uncovered her wounds, picked up her bed and walked, not surprisingly a long way away from the village. After the seven years had passed he escaped. They met frequently, bonded by mutual experience. They found new friends.

One fine day, in a far-off land, they all sat together in a marbled courtyard filled with fragrant blossoms and exquisite flowers. Before them was a Great Being. A Master. And one by one, in the fire of sacred knowledge, their scars, guilt, wrong understandings, fears and burdens began to be polished away, and they were seen to smile a lot more.

THE PRAYER

I pray that we, as human consciousness, can wake up enough
to see the loving purpose of each moment.
I pray that we can feel big enough to expand beyond the
frightened little 'i' of our egos.
I pray that we can remember with all our passion the greatest
dreams we ever dreamt.
I pray that we will find the strength to ride the tidal wave of
loving energy that is flowing through our universe.
I pray that we will be brave enough to voice our totality from
moment to moment.
I pray that we can open our hearts and arms and let everything
move within and without.
I pray that we can look into the eyes of man without judgement,
and equally hold our own gaze with loving compassion.
I pray to All-That-Is that we will be open enough to absorb the
message of infinite love.
I pray we will shine with the knowledge of who we are.

THE JOKE

Dear God,

Have You heard the great story of the wise old man reading his paper on a rush-hour London Underground train? He is sitting amidst the crush when a young man asks him for the time.

'Fuck Off!' replies the old chap, with surprising strength.

The young man is astounded.

'How rude, sir, I only asked for the time. I am astonished that a man of your years would treat me in this manner.'

'Young man, Fuck Off!' came the reply with even more vigour.

'What could I possibly have done to upset you so?' said the affronted young man.

The old man sighed wearily and put down his paper.

'So, I give you the time, we both realise we are Jewish, we chat, I discover you are travelling in my direction, I invite you to my home for a drink, you accept, I have a beautiful daughter, you are a handsome young man, you both chat, you fall in love, you date, you want to get married, you come to ask my permission . . . So, don't waste my precious time . . . Fuck Off! I will never let my daughter marry a man who cannot afford a watch.'

This story has really taught me something.

THANK YOU.

One Of Your Sparks Who Has Just Got Brighter.

THE REVELATION

Veritas.
Yes?
How's this sound? We are on the train of life. We each sit in our different carriages, according to our beliefs. Sometimes we defend our part of the train, sometimes we cannot wait to leave it. Other times we are so guilty about how lovely our carriage is, we can never relax in it or enjoy it. Something in everyone knows there are other compartments, but the passageway is often blocked. The enemies of our own hearts stand guard, and we must defeat them in order to have access to the next section of the train. So, in my case, I was born into the 'life's not fair carriage'. It was packed . . . and where better than whinging, uptight England to experience the journey. I found the way out very early on, but my great enemy guilt kept on pushing me back again. It manifested in an interesting way. Those I left behind screamed blue murder . . . how dare I have a good time and enjoy myself when they and others were suffering. I would say, but look, here is the way out, come and join me. They would tell me to get back in line, and pull me back into the grey carriage. How am I doing?
Just fine.
But I could never rest and kept exploring in spite of the opposition. The more I experienced of the train the freer I became to move around in it and the more I began to enjoy the ride. A paradox began to reveal itself: as the train became smaller the journey became bigger. I had to learn to discriminate between those who wished to expand my awareness and those who wished to keep me trapped. Yet in each section I found a guide to signal the way out. It

came in different forms – I had to be awake to spot it. Maybe literature of truth, or a clue to my next move reflected to me in the behaviour of those around me, and of course voices, dreams, premonitions and teachers willing to help guide me through into the next carriage. As I conquered the enemies who wished to halt my progress, each barrier being my fear personified, I began to understand the nature of the journey . . . and then the nature of the One who guides us. One who had been where I was and knew where I was going next. We can pace up and down impatiently, we can carry all sorts of baggage and burdens, we can relax and enjoy the journey . . . we're all heading in the same direction even if we appear to be walking towards the darkest, dankest carriages. Veritas, no matter where we are on the train, no matter how lowly or how grand, no matter how many appear to help us or hinder us, there is only One who watches all. One who is the station of departure and yet is also the destination. The train and the lands through which it will travel are all part of That. That which peers through the eyes of all on board. That which is the journey. That which is so vast. When I first began to access this, in my ignorance – I thought I was special. Chosen. I believed only a few had this line of communication, this understanding. In itself this forms yet another carriage on the journey, and until we pass the enemy of pride we remain trapped. Then you came into my life. The shepherd looking out for the lost ones in His flock. You kept reminding me that You were me. I didn't understand. You promised me I would. And now I think I am beginning to. You are the part of me who remembers. The part who is not sleeping. The part of me who is all seeing. The part of me who knows only love. The part of me who could take me beyond my physical and mental limitations. The part of me who would teach me how to sustain the knowledge and encourage me never to stop again on my journey into infinite love. Slowly the state of awareness awakening within me realises it is the destiny of every particle of consciousness to reveal the One within. And with this . . . comes gratitude. The knowledge that I am ordinary, the heart of me the same as everyone else.

And with that knowledge a vision of where the path leads. I must bow before You and offer You all that I thought was mine alone. And as my individual life burns in the flame of Your love, another of the lambs of God will be returning to the fold. Please take me home.

NO WEAPON CAN PIERCE THE SOUL;
NO FIRE CAN BURN IT;
NO WATER CAN MOISTEN IT;
NOR CAN ANY WIND WITHER IT . . .
THE SOUL IS IMMUTABLE
ALL PERMEATING
EVER CALM
AND IMMOVABLE –
ETERNALLY THE SAME.
THE SOUL IS SAID TO BE
IMPONDERABLE, UNMANIFESTABLE
AND UNCHANGEABLE.
THEREFORE, KNOWING IT TO BE SUCH
THOU SHOULD NOT LAMENT.

BHAGAVAD GITA II 23–25

THE REFLECTION

She was punching holes into the flesh of my chest
My mind froze as it watched
Watched futile attempt of earthly ignorance
Believing it could destroy
That which is indestructible
I remembered I remembered
The place where we agreed to meet
The space between the thoughts
The limited distorted thoughts
Of the one who is sleeping
The place beyond illusory pain
The place where you and I
Cease to exist
The place where
$2 + 2 = $ ONE

Oh my heart
My dearest heart
That could lead me so deeply within
To that point
Of exploding love
Love which is burning
Burning with an intensity
An intensity
Burnishing the dirt of ignorance
From the sullied glass
Through which human consciousness peers
And squints

Its view distorted
Its vision impaired

Oh love
Love beyond all that is earthly
Love ever constant
Always there
Love that manifests as the
Light of a million suns
A brightness no human eye
Can tolerate
A brightness in which
Grovelling unworthiness
Shrivels
To nothing
And in that nothing
Exists something
In the vast space there is
Something
In the nothing
Exists everything
I witness
Witness it all
The world
The lives of its teeming inhabitants
A collective dream
So real
And yet ...
Totally unreal
I witness the dying
As they exit stage left
And move into realms
Unseen to all but a few
A few who are awake
In the room where
All are sleeping
Only those awake
Know who is awake

THE REFLECTION

The Masters
Know
They are here
They never leave
The children of createdness
They shine
As beacons in a dark world
They know
They give their light
Unceasing
Without need of reward or acknowledgement
Without question
They give
For such is their nature
They wait
For infinite is their patience
They wait for us
To ask
Ask them in
Into our hearts
They lead us
Out of the illusion
Into the remembering
The devotion
The love
The true nature of man
They are here
We must
Must find them
It is the quest
Of us all
To seek the One who knows
There is no other job
No other point
No other reason

I feel the lightness
Of myself

A STRANGER IN PARADISE

Myself without physical form
Me who can fly
Fly through the heavens
At speeds of light
Exhilarating energising explosive speeds
Wondrous out-of-control movement
Accompanied with equally out-of-control laughter
Laughter
The Divine Joke

At last
I understand
The Comedian of the Universe
I laugh
I laugh and laugh and laugh
For one moment
Within infinity
I know
I know
I was
A Stranger
In
Paradise